THE KINGFISHER

Illustrated Thesaurus

THE KINGFISHER

Illustrated Thesaurus

GEORGE BEAL

Kingfisher
NEW YORK

KINGFISHER
Larousse Kingfisher Chambers Inc.
95 Madison Avenue
New York, New York 10016

First American edition 1994

10 9 8 7 6 5 4 3 2 1

LIBRARY OF CONGRESS CATALOGING-IN-PUBLICATION DATA
Beal, George.
The Kingfisher illustrated thesaurus/by George Beal:
Illustrated by Gary Rees.—1st American ed.
p. cm.
1. English language—Synonyms and antonyms—Juvenile literature.
[1. English language—Synonyms and antonyms.] I. Rees, Gary, ill.
II. Title.
PE1591.B385 1994
423'.1—dc20 93-50709 CIP AC

ISBN 1-85697-520-7

Editor: John Grisewood

Illustrations: Gary Rees

Designer: Robert Wheeler

Printed in Great Britain

Introduction

THIS book is called a thesaurus, which is a Latin word of Greek origin, meaning "a treasury or storehouse of information," particularly when it deals with words and collections of words. If you examine what this book contains you will see that is exactly what it is: a collection of words. It is a kind of dictionary, with a list of words in alphabetical order.

Instead of simply giving the *meaning* of a word, it tells you of other words that have a *similar* meaning. Suppose you began a letter to a friend with the sentence *I hope you have a nice time on your vacation*. The word *nice* sounds dull in this case. If you look up the word *nice* in this thesaurus, you will find that it gives you a short list of words that you could use instead: *pleasant, agreeable, amiable, charming, delightful*. Such words are known as **synonyms**. The word *nice* also has another meaning, which is quite different: *precise, accurate, fine, subtle*.

To go back to our letter, you could now write *I hope you have a* ***pleasant*** *time on your vacation*. Your friends could write back to you and tell you that *we are having a* ***delightful*** *time on our vacation*! As you can see, the thesaurus helps you to write in a better style, and to use words other than the very ordinary, perhaps even boring ones.

In addition to giving these alternative words, this thesaurus also shows you *opposite* words. In the case of *nice*, you will find the opposite word *nasty*. These opposite words are called **antonyms**. In many cases, there are cross-references to other words of similar meaning which are to be found elsewhere in the book. Below is a key to show you how to find the various words and their meaning.

Parts of speech: *adj.* = adjective; *adv.* = adverb; *conj.* = conjunction; *n.* = noun; *prep.* = preposition; *v.* = verb.

Opposite words: These are shown with an asterisk (*) and in ***bold type**.

Cross-reference to other meanings: If a word is shown with an arrow ▷ and in *italics*, it means that you can look up that word to find further, similar, meanings. For example, if you look up the word *ruffian* you find, at the end of the list, the word ▷*rascal*. So, if you look under *rascal* you will find other, similar, words.

A **homonym** is a word that sounds the same as another, but means something quite different. Such words are shown in small capitals, like this: GAMBOL.

If a word has a number of quite different meanings, each different meaning is shown by a bold figure in a square: **[1]**, **[2]**, **[3]**.

George Beal

A a

abandon *v.* forsake, give up, leave in the lurch, surrender, sacrifice, ▷*leave, quit*

abate *v.* lessen, slacken, dwindle, fade

abbey *n.* monastery, priory, cloister, church

abbreviate *v.* shorten, cut, contract, reduce, ▷*abridge* ★**expand**

abdicate *v.* resign, retire, renounce, ▷*quit*

ability *n.* aptitude, knack, flair, talent, gift, skill ★**inability**

able *adj.* skillful, competent, talented, strong, ▷*clever,* ★**incapable**

abnormal *adj.* unusual, exceptional, erratic ★**normal**

abode *n.* home, residence, haunt, dwelling, lodging

abolish *v.* destroy, cancel, do away with, exterminate ★**restore**

abominable *adj.* detestable, foul, hateful, horrible, loathsome, atrocious, ▷*awful* ★**desirable**

about *prep.* & *adv.* near, nearly, touching, concerning, around

above *prep.* & *adv.* over, beyond, exceeding, on high, aloft ★**below**

abridge *v.* condense, compact, ▷*abbreviate*

abroad *adv.* overseas, far, away, apart, adrift ★**home**

abrupt [1] *adj.* sudden, curt, blunt, brusque [2] steep, hilly ★**smooth**

absent *adj.* not present, away, elsewhere, missing ★**present**

absent-minded *adj.* distracted, heedless, forgetful ★**attentive**

absolute *adj.* perfect, complete, certain, positive, ▷*utter* ★**imperfect**

absorb *v.* take in, soak up, assimilate, devour, pull in, swallow, consume ★**emit**

absorbed *adj.* intent, rapt, engrossed, preoccupied

abstain *adj.* refuse, refrain, give up, keep from, avoid, forbear ★**indulge**

abstract [1] *adj.* theoretical, intangible [2] *v.* withdraw, steal, remove, take away

absurd *adj.* preposterous, nonsensical, foolish, ▷*silly* ★**sensible**

abundant *adj.* ample, profuse, rich, plentiful, overflowing ★**scarce**

abuse *v.* damage, injure, spoil, maltreat, misuse ★**protect**, *n.* mistreatment, attack

accelerate *v.* speed up, hasten, quicken, urge, ▷*hurry* ★**delay**

accent [1] *n.* stress, beat, rhythm, emphasis [2] brogue *Eileen speaks with an Irish brogue,* drawl, pronunciation

accept *v.* receive, take, admit, adopt, take on ★**refuse**

accident *n.* chance, casualty, disaster, calamity, mishap ★**purpose**

acclaim *v.* applaud, praise, approve ★**denounce**

accommodate *v.* oblige, lodge, receive, admit, adapt ★**deprive**

accompany *v.* be with, go with, escort, attend, convey ★**abandon**

accomplice *n.* ally, confederate, helper, partner

accomplish *v.* perform, fulfill, finish, complete, ▷*achieve* ★**fail**

accord *v.* agree, consent, harmonize, allow ★**differ**, *n.* agreement, harmony

account [1] *n.* bill, invoice, record, score [2] tale, story *Mary told us the story of her trip to Australia*, narrative, history

accumulate *v.* collect, grow, gather, hoard, increase, amass ★**scatter**

accurate *adj.* careful, exact, faithful, precise, ▷*correct* ★**defective**

accuse *v.* charge, incriminate, taunt, denounce ★**defend**

accustom *v.* acclimatize, get used to, familiarize ★**estrange**

ache *n.* pain, twinge *v.* hurt, pain, sting, smart

achieve *v.* fulfill, accomplish, reach, ▷*attain* ★**fail**

achievement *n.* accomplishment, attainment, exploit, deed, completion, ▷*feat*

acid *adj.* sharp, vinegarish, acrid, sour, tart ★**sweet, mellow**

acknowledge *v.* admit, avow, recognize, own, accept, yield ★**disclaim**

acquaint *v.* inform, tell, teach, notify, advise ⋆**deceive**

acquaintance [1] *n.* friend, pal, associate [2] knowledge *You will need some knowledge of Spanish if you visit South America*, familiarity, experience

acquainted *adj.* aware, familiar, informed

acquire *v.* gain, earn, obtain, get, capture ⋆**forfeit, lose**

acquit *v.* discharge, release, exonerate, dismiss, liberate ⋆**accuse**

acrid *adj.* bitter, harsh, sour, ▷*acid* ⋆**mellow**

across *adv.* & *prep.* crosswise, athwart, slantingly, over against ⋆**along**

act *n.* deed, performance, action, step, presentation, *v.* operate, work, function, perform *Our society is to perform a play by Ibsen*

action *n.* operation, movement, feat, deed, exercise ⋆**rest**

actual *adj.* correct, true, positive, certain ⋆**possible**

acute *adj.* sharp, pointed, keen, penetrating, severe, distressing ⋆**blunt**

adapt *v.* fit, adjust, accommodate, suit, conform

adaptable *adj.* flexible, usable, adjustable

add [1] *v.* total, add up, tot up ⋆**subtract** [2] affix, annex, connect ⋆**detach**

address [1] *n.* residence, place, home, domicile [2] *v.* talk to, speak to, accost, call

adept *adj.* expert, adroit, handy, skillful, ▷*clever* ⋆**clumsy**

adequate [1] *adj.* sufficient, ample, plenty [2] equal, able, qualified *After three years at sea, she was well qualified as a sailor*

adjacent *adj.* near, neighboring, next, bordering, touching ⋆**separate**

adjoin *v.* border, touch, verge, annex

adjust [1] *v.* regulate, rectify, correct, amend, revise [2] get used to *Our puppy quickly got used to her new home*

administer [1] *v.* execute, perform, carry out, conduct, direct, manage [2] dole *The nurse doled out the pills each morning*, give

admirable *adj.* praiseworthy, commendable, excellent ⋆**despicable**

admiration *n.* adoration, affection, approval, delight, respect ⋆**contempt**

admire *v.* approve, esteem, appreciate, ▷*respect* ⋆**despise**

admit [1] *v.* pass, permit, grant, concede, allow, let in, acknowledge [2] confess, own up ⋆**deny**

ado *n.* hubbub, commotion, fuss *Let's get on with the meeting without any fuss*, excitement

adopt *v.* assume, select, choose, employ, apply, take over

adore *v.* worship, idolize, admire, revere, venerate ⋆**despise**

adorn *v.* beautify, decorate, embellish, deck, garnish ⋆**deface**

adrift *adv.* loose, afloat, floating, distracted

adroit *adj.* handy, skillful, dexterous, expert ▷*adept* ⋆**awkward**

adult *adj.* grown-up, mature, full-grown ⋆**immature**

Adjust

Our puppy quickly got used to her new home.

advance [1] *v.* progress, increase, further, go, go on, proceed **★retreat** [2] lend *Helen said she will lend me the money,* loan
advanced *adj.* beforehand, ahead, modern
advantage *n.* benefit, upper hand, opportunity, assistance, boon **★hindrance**
adventure *n.* experience, escapade, venture, undertaking
adversary *n.* foe, opponent, antagonist, rival, ▷*enemy* **★ally**
adverse *adj.* unfavorable, hard, hostile, unfortunate, ▷*unlucky* **★fortunate**
advice *n.* counsel, suggestion, guidance
advise *v.* urge, suggest, prompt, inform, persuade **★deter**
afar *adv.* far, far off, away, abroad **★near**
affable *adj.* courteous, gracious, easy, frank, open **★haughty**
affair *n.* matter, business, concern, romance, liaison
affect [1] *v.* assume, adopt, feign, sham, put on airs [2] sicken, upset *We were all upset to hear that Jo was ill,* afflict
affection *n.* desire, fondness, feeling, kindness, liking, ▷*love* **★indifference**
affectionate *adj.* warmhearted, fond, loving, ▷*tender* **★indifferent**
affirm *v.* assert, state, declare, endorse, maintain **★deny**
affix *v.* attach, fasten, unite, append **★detach**
afflict *v.* trouble, ail, distress, upset
afford [1] *v.* be wealthy, be rich [2] produce, provide *The stream provided good, clean water,* yield, bear **★deny**
afraid *adj.* timid, cautious, frightened, alarmed, ▷*fearful* **★fearless**
after *prep.* behind, later, following, succeeding **★before**
again [1] *adv.* frequently, repeatedly, anew, afresh [2] furthermore, moreover
against *prep.* opposite, over, opposing, resisting **★for**
age [1] *n.* period, date, time [2] old age, senility **★youth** [3] *v.* grow old, mature
aged *adj.* ancient, antiquated, ▷*old* **★youthful**

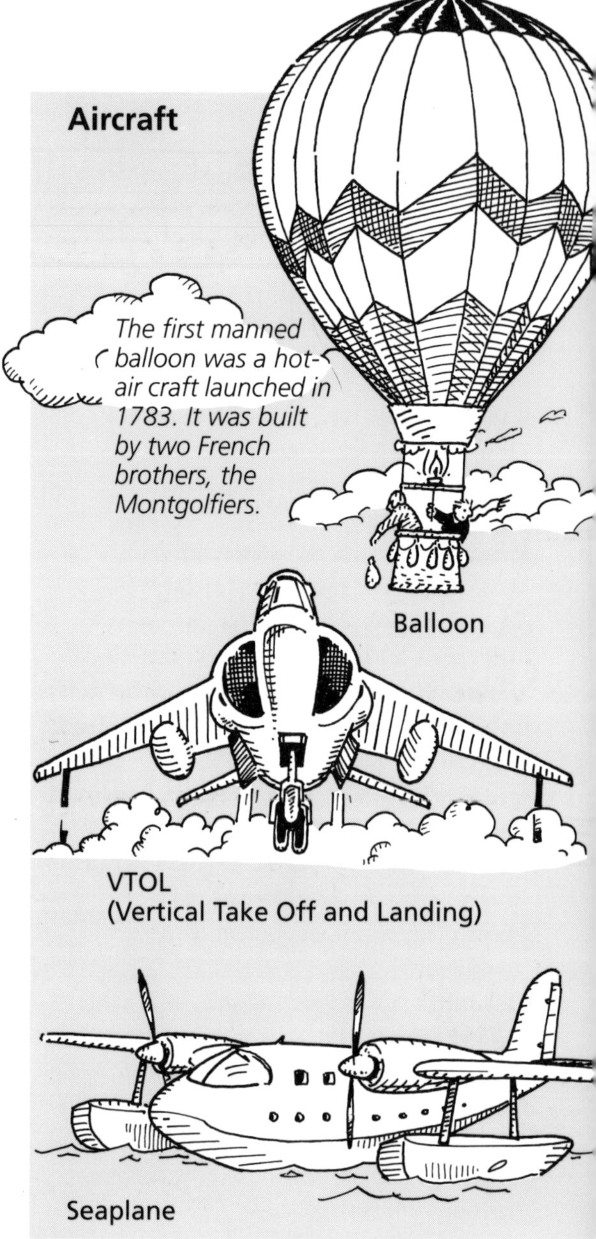

agent *n.* doer, actor, performer, operator, worker, representative
aggravate *v.* increase, make worse, worsen, **★mitigate** [2] irritate, annoy
aggressive *adj.* offensive, warlike, military, pushing **★peaceful**
aghast *adj.* astonished, dumbfounded, bewildered **★calm**
agile *adj.* nimble, active, fleet, brisk, alert, ▷*lithe* **★clumsy**
agitate *v.* disturb, trouble, excite, stir, fluster **★smooth**
ago *adv.* past, gone, since **★hence**

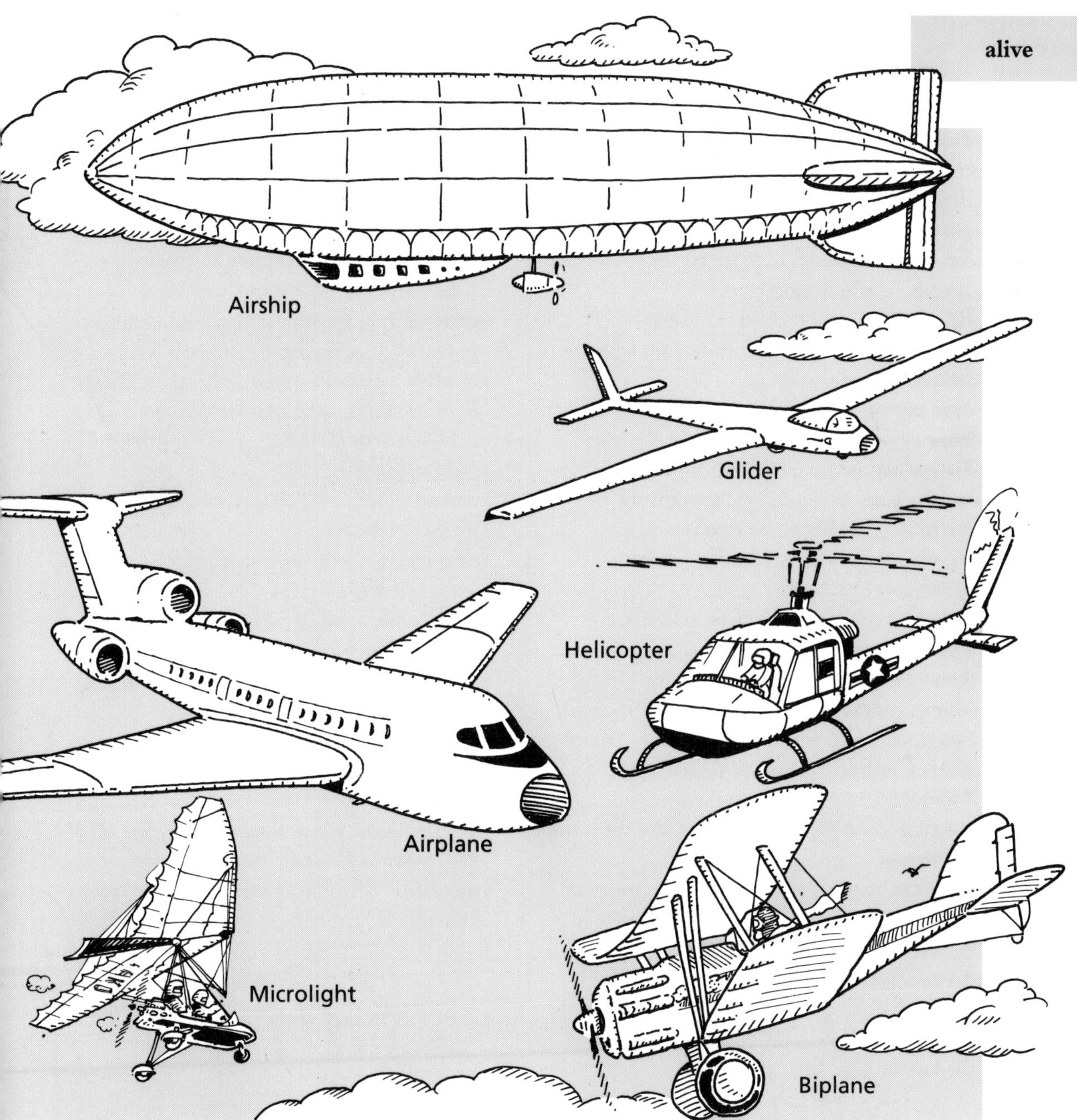

agony *n.* torture, torment, distress, pangs, ▷*pain* ★**comfort**

agree *v.* accord, fit, harmonize, combine, tally, suit ★**differ**

agreeable *adj.* obliging, welcome, acceptable, grateful, ▷*pleasant* ★**disagreeable**

agreement *n.* contract, undertaking, obligation ★**difference**

ahead [1] *adv.* forward, onward [2] before, in advance ★**behind**

aid *v.* assist, support, encourage, serve, ▷*help* ★**hinder**

aim *n.* object, goal, purpose, end, intention

aisle *n.* path, corridor, passage, way ISLE

akin *adj.* related, similar, allied, like ★**dissimilar**

alarm *v.* fear, frighten, terrify, startle, ▷*scare* ★**compose**

alert *adj.* active, ready, wakeful, watchful, ▷*agile* ★**drowsy**

alien *adj.* foreign, strange, remote ★**akin** *n.* foreigner, stranger

alike *adj.* similar, resembling, allied, like ★**unlike**

alive *adj.* living, breathing, warm, alert, brisk ★**dead**

all *adj.* whole, entire, complete, total ★**some**

allot *v.* apportion, give, deal, dispense, grant ★**retain**

allow *v.* grant, permit, concede, owe, tolerate, entitle ★**deny**

ally *n.* friend, companion, supporter, accomplice, colleague ★**foe**

almost *adj.* nearly, about, approximately, well-nigh

alone *adj.* lone, lonely, lonesome, forlorn ★**together**

aloud *adv.* loudly, noisily, clamorously, audibly ★**softly** ALLOWED

already *adv.* at this time, now, just now, previously

alter *v.* modify, vary, convert, transform, ▷*change* ★**retain** ALTAR

altogether *adv.* completely, wholly, outright, totally ★**partially**

always *adv.* ever, forever, eternally ★**never**

amass *v.* collect, accumulate, heap, pile ★**scatter**

amaze *v.* astound, surprise, stun, dumbfound, ▷*astonish*

ambition *n.* aspiration, desire, longing, zeal, aim, ▷*goal*

amend *v.* revise, mend, correct, repair, improve, ▷*alter* ★**deteriorate**

amiable *adj.* affable, kindly, pleasant, amicable, ▷*agreeable* ★**churlish**

amount *n.* figure, volume, sum, number, total

ample *adj.* bountiful, liberal, sufficient, plentiful, ▷*abundant* ★**scanty**

amplify *v.* increase, raise, enlarge, elaborate *Our teacher explained the problem and went on to elaborate on the details*, make louder ★**abbreviate**

amuse *v.* entertain, charm, beguile, please ★**bore**

ancestor *n.* forebear, parent, forefather, antecedent, predecessor

ancient *adj.* aged, antique, primeval, time-honored, ▷*old* ★**modern**

anger *n.* wrath, ire, resentment, indignation, fury, ▷*rage* ★**patience**

angry *adj.* wrathful, irate, resentful, furious, infuriated, indignant ★**good-tempered**

angle [1] *n.* corner, bend, fork, branch [2] aspect, phase, point of view *We quarreled at first, but then I saw my friend's point of view*

anguish *n.* torment, torture, pain, ▷*agony* ★**ease**

announce *v.* broadcast, declare, propound, reveal, herald, ▷*proclaim* ★**conceal**
annoy *v.* tease, vex, irritate, disturb, harass, ▷*upset* ★**soothe**
answer *n.* reply, response, solution *It was a difficult puzzle, but Emma came up with the solution* ★**question**
anticipate *v.* expect, prepare, hope for, foresee, predict
anxious *adj.* fearful, afraid, apprehensive, worried ★**careless**
apart *adv.* away, separately, asunder, loosely ★**together**
aperture *n.* slit, hole, orifice, opening, cleft
apologize *v.* express regret, excuse, explain, plead, atone ★**insult**
apparel *n.* clothes, robes, vestments, raiment, trappings, attire
apparent *adj.* plain, conspicuous, unmistakable, clear, ▷*obvious* ★**dubious**
appeal *v.* address, request, urge, entreat, invite, ask ★**disclaim**
appear *v.* emerge, become visible, seem, look, come into view ★**disappear**
appearance *n.* aspect, look, shape, form, impression, likeness
appease *v.* pacify, moderate, satisfy, stay, soften ★**provoke**
appetite *n.* hunger, palate, relish, liking
applaud *v.* clap, cheer, praise, approve, encourage ★**denounce**
apply [1] *v.* use, appropriate, employ [2] devote, direct, dedicate *Sue was a real worker, dedicated to her job*
appoint *v.* name, assign, nominate, engage
appreciate *v.* esteem, recognize, respect, value, enjoy ★**misjudge**
appropriate [1] *v.* use, employ, adopt [2] *adj.* fitting, proper *If you do this job, you must use the proper tools*, timely
approve *v.* acclaim, admire, appreciate, favor, agree ★**disapprove**
approximate *adj.* near, close, rough
apt [1] *adj.* fit, clever, liable, likely ★**unfitted** [2] liable, prone, inclined *Jack and Meg are both inclined to be late, so we'll wait a while*

ardent *adj.* passionate, warm, eager, fervent ★**indifferent**
arduous *adj.* hard, laborious, tough, strenuous, ▷*difficult* ★**easy**
area *n.* district, region, place, expanse, tract
argue [1] *v.* discuss, debate, talk over [2] quibble, quarrel, disagree
arid *adj.* parched, sterile, ▷*dry* ★**moist**
arise [1] *v.* awaken, get up [2] begin, come into existence, originate, crop up, take place
army *n.* troops, legion, force, soldiery
around *adv.* about, encircling, on every side ★**within**
arouse *v.* awaken, excite, disturb, alarm ★**pacify**
arrange *v.* sort, order, dispose, deal, classify ★**confuse**
arrest *v.* seize, take prisoner, hold, detain, stop ★**release**
arrive *v.* reach, attain, land, get to, appear ★**depart**
arrogant *adj.* supercilious, proud, haughty ★**modest**

art *n.* skill, artistry, cleverness, talent
artful *adj.* cunning, knowing, crafty, wily, sly ★**innocent**
article [1] *n.* thing, object, substance [2] essay, treatise, typescript
artificial *adj.* invented, fictitious, fabricated, synthetic ★**real**
ascend *v.* climb, rise, go up, get up, move up, scale, mount ★**descend**
ashamed *adj.* shamefaced, abashed, confused ★**proud**
ask *v.* demand, query, inquire, appeal, ▷*request* ★**answer**
aspect *n.* front, face, side, appearance, presentation, look, expression
aspire *v.* wish, long, desire, aim, hope, crave
ass [1] *n.* donkey, mule [2] fool, dunce, idiot, booby, dolt
assault *v.* attack, assail, set upon, charge, invade ★**defend**
assemble *v.* meet, gather, convene, come together, muster, collect ★**disperse**
assent *v.* agree, comply, accept, consent ★**dissent**
assert *v.* pronounce, maintain, state, aver, ▷*declare* ★**deny**
assess *v.* estimate, evaluate, appraise
assign *v.* appoint, name, apportion, entrust
assist *v.* aid, support, protect, maintain, sustain, ▷*help* ★**obstruct**
association *n.* union, connection, companionship, society, company, club
assortment *n.* variety, kind, sort, batch, parcel, collection
assume [1] *v.* believe, accept, suppose, admit [2] confiscate, take, possess oneself of
assure *v.* promise, guarantee, warrant, encourage ★**deter**
astonish *v.* startle, surprise, confound, alarm, scare, ▷*amaze*
astound *v.* stagger, stupefy, ▷*astonish*
astray *adj.* lost, gone, vanished, missing, loose ★**safe**
astute *adj.* shrewd, brainy, knowing, sharp, acute, crafty ★**simple**
atrocious *adj.* monstrous, enormous, shameful, cruel, abominable, vile ★**noble**
attach *v.* fasten, append, unite, tie, ▷*connect* ★**unfasten**
attack *v.* assault, invade, set upon, pounce, descend upon ★**defend**
attain *v.* extend, master, obtain, acquire, grasp, ▷*reach* ★**fail**
attempt *v.* endeavor, strive, seek, tackle, ▷*try* ★**abandon**
attend [1] *v.* listen, heed, notice, observe, follow ★**disregard** [2] be present
attentive *adj.* mindful, particular, heedful, observant ★**careless**
attire *n.* costume, robes, clothes, garments, ▷*apparel*
attitude *n.* disposition, bearing, outlook, posture, position, aspect
attract [1] *v.* draw, influence, tempt, prompt, pull, drag [2] fascinate, enchant, captivate ★**repel**
attractive *adj.* agreeable, beautiful, handsome, pretty, tempting ★**repellent**
avail *v.* benefit, advantage, suffice, use, help, profit
available *adj.* convenient, handy, ready, attainable
avenge *v.* retaliate, revenge, pay back ★**pardon**
average *adj.* usual, medium, middling, ordinary ★**extreme**
avid *adj.* eager, greedy, grasping
avoid *v.* shun, desert, quit, keep clear of, evade, ▷*dodge* ★**seek**
awake *v.* rouse, arouse, awaken, stir ★**lull**
award *v.* reward, give, bestow, grant, donate ★**withdraw**
aware *adj.* conscious, sensible, informed, assured ★**ignorant**
away *adv.* absent, not present, afar, elsewhere ★**near**
awe *n.* fear, dread, shock, consternation, wonder
awful *adj.* fearful, terrible, alarming, dreadful ★**commonplace** OFFAL
awkward *adj.* ungainly, unwieldy, uncouth, clownish, gawky, ▷*clumsy* ★**dexterous**
awry *adj.* crooked, askew, twisted, wrong ★**straight**

B b

babble *v.* prattle, blab, cackle, chatter, gossip
baby *n.* babe, infant, child, toddler, bairn
back [1] *adj.* after, rear, hind, posterior ***front** [2] *v.* uphold, support *The party will support Tina Johnson at the next election*, endorse, be loyal to
backer *n.* supporter, ally, champion
backward *adj.* slow, shy, reluctant, unwilling, retarded, ▷*dull* ***forward**
bad [1] *adj.* imperfect, dreadful, unsound, awful, atrocious [2] naughty, wrong, wicked, ill-behaved [3] rotten *This barrel is full of rotten apples*, spoiled ***good**
badge *n.* emblem, hallmark, symbol, crest
badger *v.* bother, hector, nag, ▷*pester*
bad-mannered *adj.* impolite, boorish, uncivil, ▷*rude* ***polite**
baffle *v.* puzzle, perplex, frustrate, bewilder, mystify, ▷*puzzle*
bag *n.* net, sack, holdall, pouch, purse
bail *v.* scoop, ladle, dip
bait [1] *v.* tease, bother, rag, rib, needle, ▷*pester* [2] *n.* decoy, lure, snare BATE
bake *v.* cook, roast, harden
balance *v.* weigh, adjust, equalize, compare
bald *adj.* hairless, severe, stark, bare, unadorned
balk *v.* hinder, baffle, thwart, prevent, foil ***aid**
ball [1] *n.* dance, masquerade [2] globe, orb, sphere
ballad *n.* ditty, song, serenade
ballot *n.* vote, election, franchise, poll
ban *v.* prohibit, forbid, deny, stop
band [1] *n.* stripe, strip, zone, belt [2] orchestra, ensemble, group BANNED
bandit *n.* outlaw, robber, highwayman, thief, crook
bang *v.* crash, slam, smash, collide
banish *v.* expel, eject, exclude, exile, deport, cast out, ▷*dismiss* ***welcome**
bank [1] *n.* shore, ledge, terrace, coast, embankment [2] safe, vault, treasury
banner *n.* ensign, standard, streamer, ▷*flag*
banquet *n.* meal, feast, repast
banter *v.* chaff, tease, ridicule, joke
bar [1] *v.* obstruct, block, blockade, forbid, shut out [2] fasten, bolt, lock, latch
bare [1] *adj.* barren, empty, void [2] naked, unclothed [3] severe, blunt *We expected a polite reply, but got a blunt refusal*, bald BEAR
barely *adv.* hardly, scarcely *The barrel had run dry, and there was scarcely enough water for all of us*, just, simply
bargain *n.* pact, deal, *adj.* low-priced, cheap
bark [1] *n.* rind, husk, peel [2] yelp, growl, cry
barrel *n.* cask, keg, drum, tub, cylinder
barren *adj.* bare, unfertile, empty, ▷*arid* ***fertile** BARON
barrier *n.* obstruction, obstacle, block, fence, ▷*bar*
barter *v.* swap, exchange, trade
base [1] *adj.* low, sordid, cheap, corrupt [2] dishonorable, vile [3] humble, menial [4] *n.* bottom, foundation [5] *v.* found *Robinson Crusoe was founded on a true story* BASS
bashful *adj.* shy, timid, modest, coy ***bold**
basin *n.* bowl, pot, vessel, tub

Band

Banned

batch *n.* lot, amount, assortment, collection
batter *v.* beat, strike, shatter, break, smash
battle *v.* clash, combat, fight, struggle, wrestle
bawl *v.* shout, yell, roar, bellow ★**whisper**
bay [1] *n.* inlet, gulf, basin, bight [2] *v.* bark, yelp BEY
be *v.* exist, live, breathe
beach *n.* shore, sands, seaside, strand BEECH
beacon *n.* signal, lamp, light, guide
beak *n.* snout, bill, nose
beam [1] *n.* ray, light, streak [2] plank, joist, girder
bear [1] *v.* tolerate, put up with, endure, suffer ★**protest** [2] bring, fetch, carry BARE
bearing *n.* manner, behavior, appearance, attitude, posture *He was a tall man with a military bearing* BARING
bearings *n.* direction, whereabouts *In the storm we totally lost our whereabouts*, location
beat [1] v. strike, pound, thrash, ▷*batter* [2] throb, flutter, thump *My heart thumped when I heard the sound of shouting in the street* BEET
beautiful *adj.* handsome, lovely, graceful, delicate, gorgeous ▷*pretty* ★**ugly**
beauty *n.* elegance, charm, loveliness, grace ★**ugliness**
because [1] *conj.* for, owing to, by reason of, since *Since Tom and Jane are here, I will stay too*, as [2] *adv.* consequently
beckon *v.* signal, call, nod, summon
becoming *adj.* graceful, suitable, comely, fitting, attractive
before [1] *prep.* ahead, in front of, forward, preceding [2] *adv.* earlier *Here is a pie that I baked earlier*, previously ★**after**
beg *v.* ask, request, entreat, beseech, plead, pray ★**insist**
begin *v.* commence, initiate, found, launch, ▷*start* ★**end**
beginner *n.* novice, recruit, learner, pupil
beginning *n.* start, opening, origin, outset, foundation ★**end**
behavior *n.* conduct, demeanor, manners, ▷*bearing* ★**misbehavior**
behind [1] *prep.* after, following *Bill arrived to meet us, with his dog following* [2] *adv.* in the rear of, later, afterward ★**before**

Bells

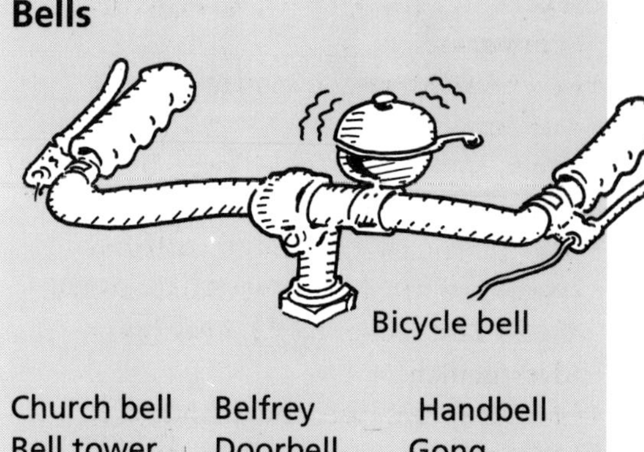

Church bell, Belfrey, Handbell, Bell tower, Doorbell, Gong

being *n.* creature, animal
belief *n.* faith, confidence, opinion, trust ★**disbelief**
believe *v.* trust, assent, have faith in, think, suspect ★**disbelieve**
bellow *v.* roar, shout, cry, ▷*bawl*
belong *v.* relate to, pertain, be owned by
below *adv.* under, beneath, underneath ★**above**
belt *n.* strap, sash, girdle, strip
bend *v.* curve, incline, turn, yield, relax ★**stiffen**
benefit *n.* boon, advantage, profit, favor, aid, blessing ★**disadvantage**
beside *adv.* alongside, side by side, next to, abreast, together ★**apart**
besides *adv.* in addition, furthermore, also, moreover
best *adj.* choice, prime, unequaled, finest ★**worst**
bestow *v.* award, donate, confer, present ★**deprive**
betray *v.* deceive, dupe, expose, unmask, inform on ★**protect**
better *adj.* superior, finer, preferable *I think it would be preferable to visit the museum this afternoon instead of this morning* ★**inferior**
between *prep.* amid, among, betwixt
beware *v.* be careful, refrain from, heed, avoid, mind ★**overlook**
bewilder *v.* confound, dazzle, mystify, confuse, ▷*astonish* ★**enlighten**
beyond *adv.* over, farther, past, more, after ★**near**

bicker *v.* quarrel, dispute, wrangle, argue ★**converse**

bid *v.* proffer, present, tender, request, propose

big *adj.* large, great, wide, huge, bulky, fat, important ★**small**

bill [1] *n.* statement *This is a statement of your investments with us*, account, invoice, check, chit, reckoning [2] beak [3] poster, advertisement

bin *n.* box, can, case, chest, crate, tub

bind *v.* tie, fasten, secure, lace, swathe ★**untie**

birth *n.* origin, beginning, source, creation ★**death** BERTH

bit *n.* morsel, piece, fragment, part, crumb ★**whole**

bite *v.* gnaw, chew, rend, champ BIGHT

bitter [1] *adj.* harsh, sour, tart, ▷*acid* [2] severe, stern, ▷*sarcastic* ★**mellow**

blame *v.* chide, rebuke, reproach, criticize, accuse, condemn ★**praise**

bland *adj.* soft, mild, gentle, soothing ★**harsh**

blank *adj.* empty, bare, void, bleak ★**full**

blare *v.* blast, boom, clang, roar, sound

blast *v.* explode, split, discharge, burst

blaze *v.* burn, flare, glare, flicker

bleak *adj.* bare, open, exposed, dismal, stormy, chilly, raw, desolate *The farm was a cold and desolate place in winter* ★**sheltered**

blemish *n.* spot, stain, mark, speck, flaw, blotch

blend *v.* mix, unite, harmonize, merge, fuse, combine ★**separate**

bless *v.* hallow, praise, exalt, endow, enrich, consecrate ★**curse**

blessing *n.* advantage, boon, approval, godsend ★**curse**

blight *n.* pest, plague, disease

blind [1] *adj.* eyeless, sightless *These salamanders live in underground caves and are sightless*, unsighted, unseeing [2] ignorant, uninformed

blink *v.* wink, twinkle, glitter, gleam

bliss *n.* joy, ecstasy, rapture, blessedness, happiness ★**misery**

block [1] *n.* lump, mass, chunk [2] *v.* obstruct, bar, arrest BLOC

bloom [1] *n.* flower, blossom, bud [2] *v.* blossom, flourish, flower, thrive ★**decay**

blot *n.* stain, blotch, ▷*blemish*

blow [1] *v.* puff, gust, blast [2] *n.* shock, stroke, impact, bang

blue *adj.* azure, turquoise, indigo, navy, ultramarine, cobalt BLEW

bluff [1] *adj.* frank, brusque, abrupt, plain-spoken *Freda Jones will never be elected mayor; she's too plain-spoken* [2] *v.* deceive, pretend *The lion closed its eyes, pretending it had not seen the antelope*, conceal

blunder [1] *n.* mistake, error, slip, fault *It was my fault that the plates were broken*, oversight [2] *v.* slip, err, bungle ★**correct**

blunt [1] *adj.* plain, abrupt, curt, ▷*bluff* [2] dull, not sharp

blush *v.* redden, color, crimson, flush

board [1] *n.* plank, table [2] committee, council [3] *v.* lodge *The new teacher is going to lodge at our house,* accommodate BORED

boast *v.* swagger, swell, bluster, ▷*brag*

boat *n.* ship, vessel, craft, bark, barge

body [1] *n.* corpse, trunk, carcass [2] corporation, company, society

The Body

bog *n.* swamp, morass, marsh
bogus *adj.* fake, false, spurious, sham, counterfeit ★**genuine**
boil *v.* cook, steam, poach, seethe, foam
boisterous *adj.* tempestuous, stormy, uncontrolled, loud, noisy ★**serene**
bold *adj.* fearless, courageous, adventurous, valiant, daring, ▷*brave* ★**fearful** BOWLED
bolt [1] *v.* run away, take flight, flee *After the revolution, the queen had to flee the country* [2] devour, gorge, eat, ▷*gulp* [3] *n.* lock, latch, fastening
bond *n.* tie, link, joint, band, fastening
bonny *adj.* fair, handsome, healthy, shapely, buxom, ▷*pretty* ★**plain**
bonus *n.* premium, benefit, award, prize
booby *n.* blockhead, sap, oaf, chump, nincompoop, dunce, fool, numbskull ★**oracle**
boom [1] *n.* thunder, roar, rumble [2] prosperity *After the recession came years of prosperity*
boon *n.* blessing, windfall, advantage ▷*benefit* ★**drawback**
boorish *adj.* unrefined, loutish, bad-mannered, rude, clumsy ★**refined**
boost *v.* strengthen, upraise, heighten
border *n.* fringe, edge, margin, frontier
bore [1] *v.* tire, weary, annoy, vex *Mother is quite vexed if the cat sleeps on her bed* [2] drill, punch, perforate BOAR
bored *adj.* uninterested, tired, jaded, fed-up BOARD
borrow *v.* take, imitate, adopt, assume, raise money ★**lend**
boss [1] *n.* stud, knob [2] chief, manager *Helen is manager of the new beauty salon*, employer
bossy *adj.* domineering, tyrannical, ▷*arrogant* ★**modest**
bother *v.* alarm, annoy, concern, distress, ▷*disturb* ★**calm**
bottom *adj.* undermost, deepest part, floor, ▷*base* ★**top**
bough *n.* branch, limb, shoot
boulder *n.* rock, slab, stone
bounce *v.* leap, spring, bound, bump, jump
bound *v.* rebound, prance, ▷*bounce*
boundary *n.* bounds, limits, border, frontier, ▷*barrier*
bounty *n.* donation, gift, grant, ▷*bonus*
bow *v.* bend, bob, nod, stoop, kneel, yield, submit BOUGH
bowl *n.* plate, basin, dish, vessel, casserole BOLL
box [1] *n.* carton, case, chest, coffer *The town's coffers were empty, so they had to raise taxes*, pack [2] *v.* fight, spar, punch
boy *n.* lad, youth, fellow, youngster BUOY
brag *v.* crow, swagger, vaunt, ▷*boast*
braid *v.* entwine, weave, plait BRAYED
branch [1] *n.* shoot, limb, twig, ▷*bough* [2] department, office, division
brand [1] *n.* trademark, emblem, label *This label shows that the cloth is of high quality* [2] blot, stigma, stain
brandish *v.* flourish, parade, shake, swing, wave
brash *adj.* brazen, foolhardy, hasty, impetuous, impudent, ▷*rash*
brave [1] *adj.* audacious, fearless, daring, dauntless, gallant, heroic, ▷*bold* ★**cowardly** [2] *v.* dare, defy, endure
break *v.* batter, burst, crack, snap, fracture, shatter BRAKE
breathe *v.* draw in, gasp, inhale, sniff, gulp, wheeze, emit
breed *v.* reproduce, produce, cause, bear, rear
bribe *v.* corrupt, buy, grease the palm, fix
brief *adj.* short, little, concise, terse, crisp, curt ★**lengthy**
bright [1] *adj.* clear, cloudless, fair, airy [2] cheerful, genial *We were pleased to find so many genial members in the club* [3] clever, ingenious, acute ★**dull**
brilliant [1] *adj.* lustrous, shining, radiant, dazzling, luminous [2] clever, intelligent ★**dull**
brim *n.* edge, brink, rim, fringe
bring *v.* bear, fetch, deliver, carry, convey
bring about *v.* bring off, accomplish, achieve, cause, make happen
bring up *v.* breed, develop, raise, educate, foster
brink *n.* margin, border, boundary, limit

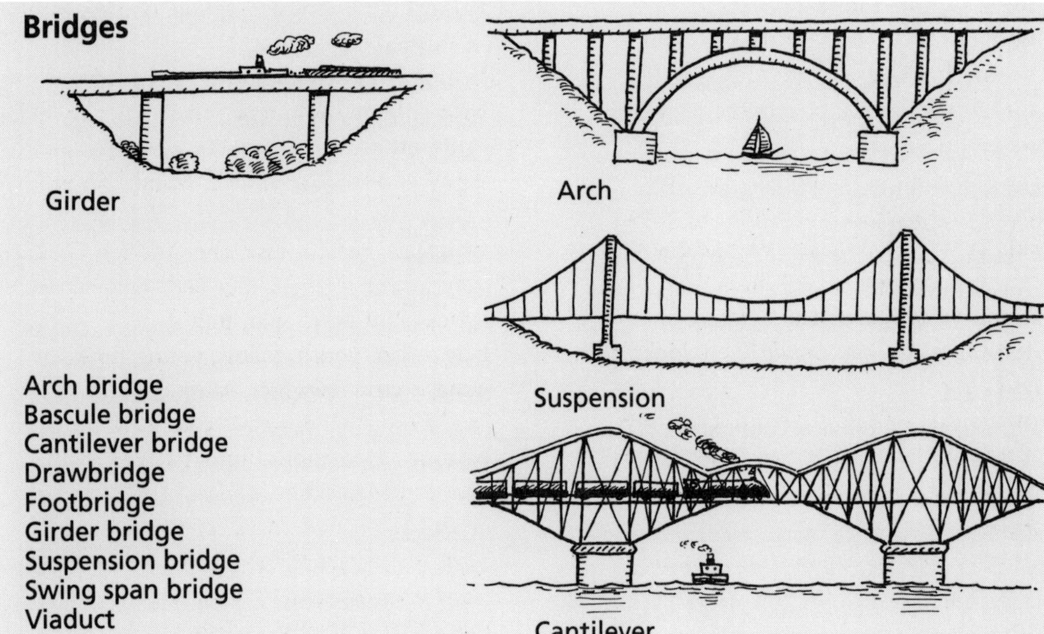

brisk *adj.* agile, alert, busy, energetic, active, nimble, invigorating ★**sluggish**

brittle *adj.* breakable, fragile, delicate, ▷*frail*

broad *adj.* wide, expansive, roomy, open, vast, large ★**narrow**

brood *v.* sigh, agonize, dwell upon *You must try to forget your disappointment, and not dwell upon it,* languish BREWED

brook *n.* stream, beck, rivulet, watercourse,

brow *n.* forehead, face, front, brink, edge, summit

bruise *v.* damage, discolor, blemish, injure, wound BREWS

brusque *adj.* abrupt, discourteous, gruff, ▷*blunt* ★**polite**

brutal *adj.* cruel, inhuman, savage, barbarous, bloodthirsty ★**humane**

bubble *n.* drop, droplet, blob, bead

buckle *n.* catch, clasp, clip, fastening

bud *n.* sprout, germ, shoot

budge *v.* propel, push, roll, shift, slide

build *v.* make, form, assemble, construct, erect, put up ★**demolish** BILLED

bulge *n.* bump, swelling, lump, billow

bulky *adj.* big, huge, unwieldy, massive, cumbersome *I never liked that chair; it's so big and cumbersome*

bully [1] *n.* ruffian, hector, bruiser, tyrant, browbeater [2] *v.* domineer, oppress, terrorize

bump *v.* collide, hit, knock, strike, jab, jolt

bunch *n.* batch, bundle, cluster, collection, lot

bundle *n.* group, mass, heap, pack, parcel

bungle *v.* botch, blunder, mess up, ruin, fumble ★**succeed**

burden [1] *n.* load, weight [2] strain, hardship *We suffered great hardship during the war*

burly *adj.* beefy, big, hefty, brawny, muscular ★**frail**

burn *v.* blaze, flare, glow, singe, scorch, char, incinerate

burst *v.* break open, crack, explode, shatter, erupt

bury *v.* inter, conceal, cover up, hide, lay to rest BERRY

business [1] *n.* occupation, career, profession, [2] company, enterprise, firm [3] problem, duty, affair

busy *adj.* active, brisk, industrious, active, bustling ★**lazy**

buy *v.* acquire, get, purchase, procure *If I can procure a computer, I'll do the job for you* ★**sell** BY, BYE

C c

cab *n.* taxi, taxicab, hackney carriage
cabin [1] *n.* hut, chalet, cottage, shack [2] berth, compartment
cabinet [1] *n.* cupboard, closet [2] council, committee
cackle *v.* chuckle, giggle, snicker
café *n.* restaurant, coffee shop, snack bar, tearoom
cage *v.* shut up, confine, imprison ★**free**
calamity *n.* catastrophe, disaster, misadventure, ▷*mishap* ★**blessing**
calculate *v.* reckon, figure, estimate, ▷*count*
call [1] *v.* cry out, shout, hail [2] name, designate [3] summon, telephone [4] visit *We will visit you when we reach your town*, drop in
calling *n.* occupation, job, profession
callous *adj.* unfeeling, harsh, hard-bitten ★**sympathetic**
calm [1] *v.* soothe, ease, pacify, comfort [2] *adj.* easy, composed, mild, ▷*peaceful* ★**excited**
can *n.* tin, container, canister
cancel *v.* abolish, erase, put off, obliterate ★**confirm**
candid *adj.* fair, honest, open, sincere, truthful, ▷*frank* ★**devious**
capable *adj.* talented, able, competent, ▷*clever* ★**incompetent**
capacity [1] *n.* space, volume, extent [2] ability, aptitude *Jenny has an aptitude for learning languages*, intelligence
caper [1] *v.* dance, gambol, frolic [2] *n.* jape, jest, lark
capital [1] *n.* cash, assets, funds, finance [2] *adj.* chief, excellent, important
captain *n.* chief, head, commander, master, skipper
capture *v.* seize, arrest, trap, ▷*catch* ★**release**
car *n.* automobile, vehicle, conveyance, carriage, coach
carcass *n.* body, corpse, skeleton
care [1] *v.* take care, beware, heed, mind [2] *n.* attention, protection ★**carelessness**
careful *adj.* heedful, prudent, watchful, ▷*cautious* ★**careless**
careless *adj.* neglectful, slack, casual, thoughtless ★**careful**
carelessness *n.* inaccuracy, negligence, slackness ★**care**
caress *v.* hug, stroke, cuddle, embrace ★**tease**
carriage *n.* car, coach, cab, chariot
carry *v.* bring, convey, lift, support, ▷*bear*
carry on *v.* continue, maintain, persist
carry out *v.* perform, achieve, fulfill, do
cart *n.* wagon, pushcart, van, buggy, barrow
carton *n.* bin, case, casket, crate, ▷*box*
carve *v.* sculpt, cut, chisel, fashion, whittle, ▷*shape*
case *n.* casket, bin, cover, ▷*box*
cash *n.* money, coins, banknotes, coinage CACHE
cask *n.* barrel, keg, drum
cast [1] *v.* mold, form, shape [2] fling, heave, sprinkle, ▷*throw* CASTE
casual *adj.* accidental, chance, random, ▷*occasional* ★**regular**
catch *v.* grasp, seize, arrest, ▷*capture* ★**lose**
catching *adj.* infectious, contagious
cause [1] *v.* bring about, create, provoke [2] *n.* reason, source, origin CAWS
caution *n.* watchfulness, heed, vigilance, wisdom, ▷*care* ★**rashness**
cautious *adj.* careful, discreet, prudent, ▷*watchful* ★**heedless**
cavity *n.* dent, hole, gap, hollow
cease *v.* stop, conclude, end, refrain, terminate ★**begin**
celebrate *v.* commemorate, observe, honor, glorify, rejoice, praise
cell *n.* chamber, cavity, cubicle, compartment SELL
cellar *n.* basement, vault, crypt, cave SELLER
cement [1] *v.* glue, stick, bind, gum, unite [2] *n.* plaster, mortar, adhesive
censor *v.* cut, examine, take out CENSER
censure *v.* blame, rebuke, reprimand, chide, ▷*scold* ★**praise**
center *n.* middle, core, heart, nucleus
ceremony *n.* ritual, custom, performance

certain [1] *adj.* decided, definite, undoubted, ▷*sure* ★**dubious** [2] particular *I had a particular reason for inviting you*, special
certainty *n.* confidence, assurance, trust, sureness ★**doubt**
certificate *n.* document, permit, deed, diploma, testimonial
chafe *v.* rub, rasp, grate, irritate
chain *v.* bind, fetter, shackle, tether, bond
challenge *v.* dare, demand, dispute, defy, object to
chamber *n.* apartment, bedroom, compartment, hollow, room
champion *n.* defender, victor, master, winner ★**loser**
chance [1] *n.* fortune, hazard, luck, gamble, lottery, wager [2] opportunity, occasion, risk ★**certainty**
change *v.* alter, vary, turn, shift, reform, transform ★**conserve**
chant *v.* intone, drone, croon, recite, ▷*sing*
chaos *n.* turmoil, confusion, disorder, pandemonium ★**order**
chapter *n.* clause, division, part, period *It was a period in my life that I will never forget*, phase
character [1] *n.* letter, mark, emblem, device [2] reputation *She had the reputation of being very generous*, temperament, qualities
charge [1] *n.* attack, stampede, advance [2] cost, amount, price [3] accusation, blame *The men were all guilty, but it was Harry Smith who took the blame*, indictment
charm *v.* please, delight, enchant, bewitch, ▷*attract* ★**irritate**
charming *adj.* delightful, appealing, lovely, pleasant, ▷*attractive* ★**ugly**
chart *n.* map, sketch, diagram, plan
chase *v.* hunt, pursue, follow, run after, hurry
chaste *adj.* virgin, pure, virtuous, innocent ★**immodest** CHASED
chastise *v.* punish, whip, flog, beat, scold, tell off
chat *v.* converse, gossip, ▷*talk*
chatter *v.* babble, gossip, ▷*talk*
cheap *adj.* inexpensive, low-priced, bargain, reasonable, inferior ★**expensive**

cheat *v.* swindle, bilk, defraud, fleece, ▷*trick*
check [1] *v.* inspect, compare, examine *The customs officer examined our luggage*, make sure [2] *n.* bill, invoice, reckoning
cheek *n.* audacity, boldness, impertinence, insolence
cheer [1] *v.* comfort, console, elate, buck up, [2] applaud *The audience applauded the leading soprano*, clap, hail
cheerful *adj.* lively, bright, happy, merry, joyful, ▷*happy* ★**sad**
cheery *adj.* blithe, breezy, bright, merry ★**downcast**
cherish *v.* caress, hold close, care for, shelter, treasure
chest [1] *n.* case, coffer, ▷*box* [2] bosom, torso
chew *v.* bite, gnaw, grind, munch, ▷*eat*
chide *v.* scold, criticize, blame, tell off
chief *adj.* main, principal, leading, foremost ★**minor**
child *n.* baby, infant, bairn, juvenile
chilly *adj.* cool, crisp, brisk, cold, unfriendly ★**warm**
chip *v.* & *n.* crack, splinter, dent, flake
chirp *v.* warble, trill, cheep, chirrup, twitter
choice [1] *n.* option *I had no option but to take the job*, preference, alternative [2] *adj.* select, dainty, precious, cherished, special
choke *v.* throttle, suffocate, gag, strangle, ▷*stifle*
choose *v.* pick, elect, decide, fancy, ▷*select* CHEWS

chop *v.* cut, hack, clip, cleave, sever, lop
chubby *adj.* plump, buxom, portly, round, stout ★**slim**
chum *n.* comrade, pal, friend, buddy, companion
chuck *v.* throw, toss, fling, heave, sling
chuckle *v.* cackle, chortle, snigger, giggle, ★**laugh**
chunk *n.* piece, lump, mass, portion, slab
churlish *adj.* brusque, harsh, impolite, morose *Dad had a headache and was in rather a morose mood,* ▷surly ★**polite**
circle [1] *n.* ring, band [2] company, group, class
circular [1] *adj.* round, disc-like [2] *n.* handbill, notice *The notice on the board announced the new play at the theater,* poster
circulate *v.* broadcast, distribute, publicize
cistern *n.* tank, sink, basin, reservoir
cite *v.* mention, specify, name, quote SIGHT, SITE
civil *adj.* polite, courteous, polished, ▷*affable* ★**churlish**
claim *v.* demand, ask, require, insist, call for
clamor *n.* babel, blare, din, row, hubbub, racket, ▷*noise* ★**silence**
clamp *v.* fasten, fix, hold, grasp
clap *v.* applaud, acclaim, cheer
clarify [1] *v.* make clear, explain, simplify [2] cleanse, purify
clash [1] *v.* battle, conflict, quarrel [2] bang, crash, clang, clatter
clasp [1] *v.* grasp, grip, seize, hold, fasten [2] *n.* buckle, catch, pin
class *n.* category, type, sort, grade, group, species
classical *adj.* pure, refined, scholarly, elegant, polished, well-proportioned
classify *v.* grade, sort, arrange, catalog
clean [1] *adj.* pure, fresh, spotless, unsoiled [2] *v.* cleanse, scrub, ▷*wash* ★**dirty**
cleanse *v.* purify, scour, ▷ *clean* ★**defile**
clear [1] *adj.* bright, fair, fine, light ★**dim** [2] distinct, audible, lucid ★**vague** [3] free, open, empty
cleft *n.* crack, cranny, slit, split, aperture
clever *adj.* able, astute, apt, brainy, skillful, talented, ▷*expert* ★**foolish**
cliff *n.* precipice, height, bluff, crag, overhang
climax *n.* crisis, head, summit, turning point
climb *v.* mount, scale, ascend, soar, go up
cling *v.* adhere, attach, embrace, grasp, hold
clip [1] *n.* fastener, clasp [2] *v.* trim, prune, snip, cut
clog *v.* block, dam up, hinder, jam, impede
close [1] *v.* shut, bolt, bar, obstruct *The draperies were thick and obstructed a lot of light,* end [2] *adj.* near, neighboring, adjacent ★**far** [3] heavy, stuffy, uncomfortable
closet *n.* cupboard, cabinet
clothing *n.* garments, dress, attire, raiment
cloud *n.* vapor, fog, billow, haze
clown *n.* buffoon, comedian, jester, joker
club [1] *n.* cudgel, stick, truncheon [2] company, group, society
clue *n.* evidence, inkling, lead, sign CLEW
clump *n.* cluster, group, bunch
clumsy *adj.* awkward, gawky, ungainly, blundering ★**graceful**
clutch *v.* snatch, clasp, grasp, seize, grip
clutter *n.* litter, muddle, mess
coach [1] *n.* bus, car, carriage, vehicle [2] trainer, tutor
coarse [1] *adj.* rough, unrefined, unpolished [2] brutish, rude, uncivil ★**refined** COURSE
coat [1] *n.* jacket, blazer, windbreaker [2] fleece, fur, skin, hide

Clothing

Coats and jackets
anorak
blazer
cardigan
cloak
poncho
raincoat
suit
tuxedo

Tops
blouse
pullover
shirt
sweatshirt
T shirt

Dresses and pants
Bermuda shorts
cocktail dress
dress
evening gown
jeans
jodhpurs
kilt
miniskirt
petticoat
sari
sarong
skirt
slacks

Foot and legwear
boot
clog
galoshes
moccasin
panty hose
sneakers
socks
stockings

Headwear *see page 56*

coax *v.* cajole, wheedle, urge, persuade, beguile *We sat for hours as Aunt Anna beguiled us with stories* ★**dissuade** COKES

coddle *v.* pamper, spoil, indulge, baby, mollycoddle

coffer *n.* casket, case, chest, treasury COUGHER

cog *n.* tooth, prong

coil *v.* twist, wind, loop

coincide *v.* match, agree, accord, synchronize, tally

cold *adj.* cool, chilly, frigid, freezing, frosty, frozen ★ **hot**

collapse *v.* founder, topple, break down, crumple, fall down

collect *v.* accumulate, amass, assemble, save, ▷ *gather* ★**scatter**

collide *v.* crash, smash, hit, strike, meet

colossal *adj.* enormous, gigantic, immense, massive, ▷*huge* ★**tiny**

column [1] *n.* pillar, post, shaft [2] file *The file of soldiers marched on to the parade*, line, procession

combat *v.* battle, contend, contest, oppose, defy ★**submit**

combine *v.* unite, join, link, fuse, merge, mix ★**separate**

come *v.* arrive, appear, enter, reach, advance ★**go**

come by *v.* get, procure, acquire *I acquired a new TV set in the sale*

comfort *v.* cheer, hearten, calm, soothe, console ★**torment**

comfortable *adj.* restful, convenient, cozy, agreeable ★**uncomfortable**

comforting *adj.* cheering, encouraging, consoling

command [1] *v.* order, dictate, direct [2] rule, dominate

commence *v.* start, begin, initiate, originate ★**finish**

comment *v.* mention, remark, observe, point out

commiserate *v.* sympathize, show pity, be sorry for ★**congratulate**

commit *v.* carry out, do, enact, perform, promise, entrust

common [1] *adj.* ordinary, vulgar, habitual, customary [2] public, social, communal

commonplace *adj.* everyday, humdrum, ordinary, obvious ★**rare**
commotion *n.* excitement, flurry, stir, uproar, ▷*fuss*
communicate *v.* tell, disclose, impart, reveal
community *n.* society, partnership, association, ▷*group*
compact *adj.* dense, close, tight, firm, condensed, concise
companion *n.* comrade, friend, chum, colleague, comrade, escort ★**rival**
company *n.* association, league, alliance, business, firm
compare *v.* match, liken, equal, parallel
compartment *n.* cubicle, alcove, bay, cell, carriage
compassion *n.* kindness, mercy, sympathy, charity, understanding, ▷*pity* ★**indifference**
compel *v.* make, coerce, drive, force, urge ★**coax**
compensate *v.* make good, refund, reimburse, repay, reward ★**injure**
compete *v.* contest, contend, rival, strive, oppose
competent *adj.* able, adapted, capable, ▷*clever* ★**incompetent**

Compel

competition *n.* game, match, contest, contest, rivalry, race
compile *v.* amass, put together, unite, ▷*collect*
complacent *adj.* self-satisfied, contented, ▷*smug* ★**diffident**
complain *v.* protest, gripe *They're a miserable couple; always griping about something,* grumble, grouse, ▷*nag* ★**rejoice**
complement *v.* complete, round off, add to, supplement COMPLIMENT
complete [1] *v.* finish, accomplish, achieve [2] *adj.* finished, full, entire
complex *adj.* complicated, intricate, mixed, tangled ★**simple**
complicated *adj.* entangled, involved, ▷*complex*
compliment *v.* flatter, admire, congratulate, ▷*praise* COMPLEMENT ★**insult**
comply *v.* agree to, assent to, abide by, perform, yield ★**refuse**
compose [1] *v.* make up, put together, form, construct, write [2] calm, quell
composure *n.* assurance, calm, confidence ★**consternation**
compound *n.* mixture, alloy, blend, combination
comprehend *v.* grasp, discern, take in, ▷*understand* ★**misunderstand**
compress *v.* condense, contract, abbreviate, ▷*squeeze* ★**expand**
comprise *v.* contain, consist of, include, comprehend
compromise [1] *v.* meet halfway, strike a balance, adjust, agree [2] imperil, weaken, jeopardize
compulsory *adj.* forced, obligatory *Everyone in the school has to go to the meeting; it's obligatory,* required ★**voluntary**
compute *v.* calculate, figure, reckon, estimate
computer *n.* calculator, word processor

comrade *n.* companion, pal, chum, buddy, ▷*friend* ★**enemy**
conceal *v.* bury, camouflage, cover, ▷*hide* ★**reveal**
concede *v.* allow, admit, yield, acknowledge, surrender ★**dispute**
conceit *n.* vanity, self-importance, arrogance, ▷*pride* ★**modesty**
conceited *adj.* proud, vain, arrogant ★**modest**
conceive *v.* create, design, devise *We devised a way of sharpening the scissors*, form, think up
concentrate *v.* focus on, centralize, heed, pay attention
concept *n.* idea, thought, theory, idea, view
concern [1] *v.* affect, touch [2] *n.* affair, matter, interest, business
concerning *prep.* as regards, respecting, about
concise *adj.* brief, condensed, short, ▷*compact* ★**expansive**
conclude [1] *v.* finish, terminate, ▷*end* [2] deduce, judge, reckon, presume
conclusion *n.* result, termination, end
concoct *v.* contrive, hatch, plan, devise, invent
concord *n.* agreement, understanding, good will, harmony ★**discord**
concrete [1] *adj.* actual, definite, real [2] *n.* cement, mortar
concur *v.* approve, agree, coincide, consent ★**disagree**
condemn *v.* blame, denounce, reprove, sentence, disapprove ★**approve**
condense *v.* compress, concentrate, abridge, thicken ★**expand**
condition *n.* shape, way, state, position, plight, situation, ▷*predicament*
condone *v.* overlook, disregard, forgive, excuse ★**censure**
conduct [1] *n.* attitude, bearing, behavior [2] *v.* guide, direct, lead
confederate *n.* accomplice, ally, associate, partner
confer *v.* bestow, grant, award, give, present
conference *n.* discussion, meeting, forum
confess *v.* admit, acknowledge, own up, divulge ★**deny**
confide *v.* tell, divulge, reveal, whisper, entrust
confidence *n.* assurance, belief, boldness, firmness ★**doubt**
confident *adj.* certain, assured, poised, fearless ★**diffident**
confine *v.* restrict, limit, detain, imprison, limit ★**free**
confirm *v.* verify, assure, approve, endorse, attest ★**deny**
confiscate *v.* seize, impound, commandeer *The old house was commandeered by the army*
conform *v.* agree with, comply with, yield, adjust
confound *v.* perplex, mystify, puzzle, baffle, fluster, ▷*bewilder* ★**enlighten**
confront *v.* challenge, defy, face, oppose, menace
confuse *v.* baffle, bemuse, mystify, ▷*bewilder* ★**clarify**
congenial *adj.* companionable, natural, sympathetic, agreeable, ▷*friendly* ★**disagreeable**
congested *adj.* jammed, crowded, clogged, packed, teeming ★**clear**
congratulate *v.* rejoice, compliment, praise, wish one joy ★**commiserate**
congregate *v.* assemble, meet, come together, converge ★**disperse**
congress *n.* meeting, assembly, council, convention
conjecture *v.* guess, surmise, suspect, imagine, assume
connect *v.* unite, join, combine, fasten, link ★**disconnect**
conquer *v.* beat, crush, overcome, overpower, triumph, ▷*defeat* ★**surrender**
conscientious *adj.* moral, scrupulous, careful, diligent, ▷*honest* ★**careless**
conscious *adj.* alert, alive, aware, sensible, responsible ★**unconscious**
consecutive *adj.* chronological, in sequence, successive, continuous
consent *v.* assent, permit, concur, approve, comply, ▷*agree* ★**oppose**
conserve *v.* keep, preserve, protect, save, store up, safeguard ★**squander**

consider *v.* discuss, examine, ponder, reflect *Alone on the island, I reflected on all that had happened*, take account of ★**ignore**

considerable *adj.* abundant, ample, great, large, noteworthy, important ★**insignificant**

consist of *v.* comprise, be composed of, contain, include

consistent *adj.* uniform, constant, regular, steady ★**inconsistent**

console *v.* comfort, cheer, sympathize, soothe, solace ★**upset**

conspicuous *adj.* noticeable, marked, apparent, obvious, prominent ★**inconspicuous**

conspire *v.* plot, intrigue, scheme *He was thrown into a dungeon for his evil plotting*

constant [1] *adj.* regular, stable, uniform, ▷*consistent* [2] loyal, faithful, staunch, true ★**fickle**

consternation *n.* dismay, horror, fear, awe, stupefaction, ▷*alarm* ★**composure**

constitute *v.* compose, comprise, set up, fix, form, establish ★**destroy**

constrict *v.* tighten, strain, tauten, draw together, choke, pinch ★**expand**

construct *v.* erect, compose, compound, assemble, ▷*build* ★**demolish**

consult *v.* ask, ask advice, discuss, confer, debate

consume *v.* use up, absorb, eat up, devour

contact *n.* touch, connection, communication

contagious *adj.* catching, infectious

contain *v.* comprise, consist of, hold, accommodate, enclose

contaminate *v.* pollute, soil, stain, sully, taint, infect

contemplate *v.* think, reflect, deliberate, consider, ponder

contempt *v.* disdain, scorn, disregard, derision ★**admiration**

contend *v.* compete, contest, conflict, strive, struggle ★**concede**

content [1] *adj.* (con-*tent*) satisfied, contented, smug [2] *v.* satisfy, delight, gratify [3] *n.* (*con*-tent) matter, text, subject

contest [1] *n.* (*con*-test) competition, match, tournament [2] *v.* (con-*test*) dispute, argue

continue *v.* go on, keep up, endure, last, persist ★**stop**

contract [1] *v.* (con-*tract*) condense, lessen, shrink [2] *n.* (*con*-tract) agreement, pact, understanding

contradict *v.* deny, dispute, challenge, oppose

contrary *adj.* opposed, adverse, counter, opposite ★**agreeable**

contrast [1] *n.* (*con*-trast) difference, disparity, comparison [2] *v.* (con-*trast*) compare, differ, oppose, distinguish

contribute *v.* donate, present, bestow, provide ★**withhold**

contrive *v.* form, fashion, construct, create, design, invent

control *v.* command, direct, dominate, lead, supervise

convene *v.* call together, rally, meet, muster *We mustered on the dock before boarding the ship*, assemble ★**dismiss**

convenient *adj.* handy, fit, helpful, suitable, accessible ★**awkward**

conversation *n.* talk, chat, communication, discussion

convert *v.* alter, change, transform, adapt

convey *v.* carry, transport, conduct, bear, transmit

convict [1] *n.* (*con*-vict) prisoner, captive, criminal [2] *v.* (con-*vict*) find guilty, condemn

convince *v.* assure, persuade, prove to, win over

cook *v.* boil, broil, heat, warm, steam, fry, stew, bake

cool [1] *adj.* chilly, frigid, ▷*cold* [2] self-composed, calm, relaxed

cooperate *v.* collaborate, combine, aid, assist, join forces

cope (with) *v.* deal, handle, struggle, grapple, manage

copy *v.* duplicate, reproduce, imitate, mimic, simulate

cord *n.* string, rope, twine, line CHORD

cordial *adj.* hearty, sincere, congenial, jovial, affable ★**hostile**

core *n.* heart, kernel, pith, crux *Now we're getting to the crux of the problem!*, center CORPS
corner *n.* angle, bend, crook, cavity, cranny, niche, compartment
corpse *n.* body, carcass, remains
correct *adj.* true, actual, accurate, exact, precise ★**wrong**
correspond [1] *v.* fit, harmonize, agree, coincide [2] write letters
corridor *n.* hallway, passage, aisle
corroborate *v.* confirm, certify, endorse, establish ★**contradict**
corrode *v.* erode, waste, eat away, rust
corrupt [1] *adj.* dishonest, fraudulent, rotten [2] *v.* bribe, deprave, entice
cost [1] *n.* charge, amount, price, outlay [2] penalty, forfeit, sacrifice
costly *adj.* expensive, valuable, precious, dear
costume *n.* suit, outfit, ensemble, attire, dress
cot *n.* bed, bunk, berth
cottage *n.* bungalow, cabin, chalet, shack, lodge
couch *n.* sofa, chaise longue
council *n.* assembly, committee, congress, convention COUNSEL
counsel [1] *n.* lawyer, attorney, advocate [2] *v.* advise, instruct, recommend COUNCIL
count *v.* add up, calculate, check, compute, reckon, tally
counter [1] *n.* token, coin, disk [2] bar, bench [3] *adj.* against, opposed
counterfeit *adj.* forged, fraudulent, fake, bogus *She entered the country on a bogus passport*, false
country [1] *n.* nation, people, realm, state [2] *adj.* rural, backwoods, farmland
couple [1] *n.* pair, brace, two [2] *v.* link, yoke, unite, join, connect
courage *n.* bravery, valor, boldness, gallantry, daring, pluck ★**cowardice**

Cooking utensils

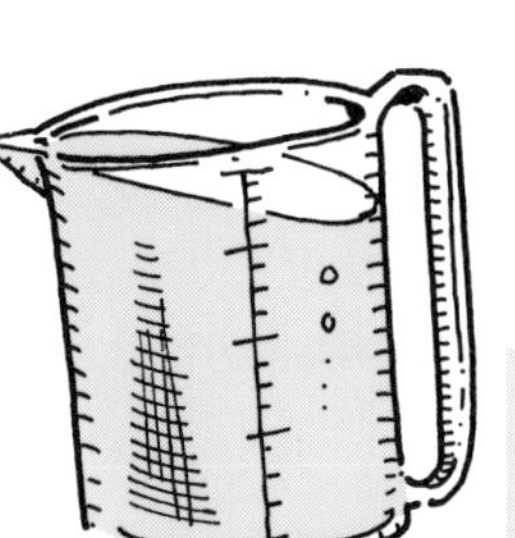

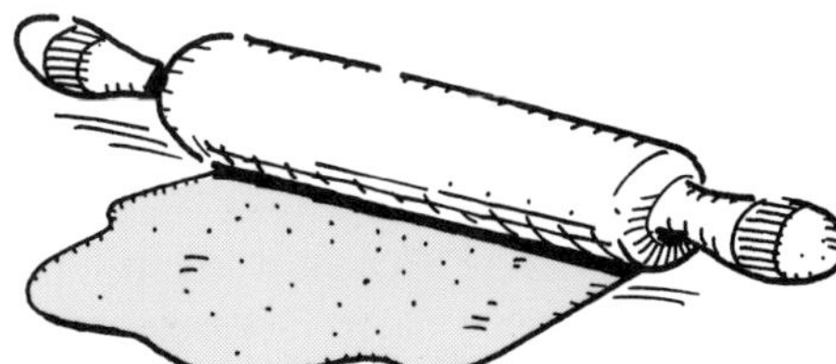

Blender	Grill	Rolling pin
Bottle	Jar	Saucepan
Bowl	Kettle	Saucer
Casserole	Ladle	Sieve
Colander	Lemon juicer	Skillet
Cup	Masher	Spatula
Cutting board	Measuring cup	Spoon
Dish	Pan	Tureen
Frying pan	Peeler	Urn
Funnel	Plate	Waffle iron
Grater	Pot	Whisk
Griddle	Ramekin	Wok

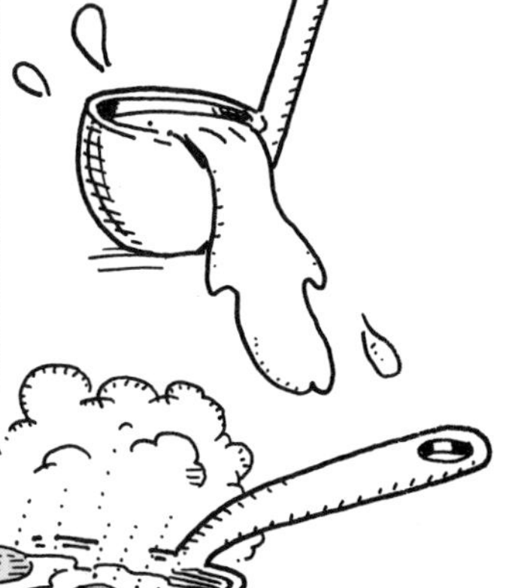

courageous *adj.* brave, bold, fearless, valiant, ▷*plucky* ★**cowardly**
course [1] *n.* route, channel, path, road, track, trail [2] policy, plan, manner COARSE
court [1] *n.* alley, courtyard, atrium, [2] bar, law court, tribunal [3] palace, retinue [4] *v.* make love, woo, flatter
courteous *adj.* considerate, polite, refined, elegant ★**discourteous**
courtesy *n.* politeness, civility, manners, gentility
cove *n.* inlet, bay, creek, firth
cover [1] *v.* conceal, hide, secrete [2] include, embody, incorporate [3] *n.* cap, case, lid, canopy
covet *v.* want, envy, fancy, hanker after, long for, crave
cow [1] *v.* frighten, bully, terrorize, scare, subdue
coward *n.* weakling, craven, funk, sneak ★**hero** COWERED
cowardice *n.* fear, funk, faint-heartedness ★**courage**

cowardly *adj.* fearful, weak, scared, spineless ★**courageous**
cower *v.* cringe, grovel, flinch, crouch
coy *adj.* demure, skittish, blushing, bashful, shy ★**forward**
crack [1] *n.* slit, split, cleft, cranny, crevice, breach [2] *v.* snap, split, splinter
craft [1] *n.* cunning, deceit [2] ability, cleverness, expertise [3] occupation, business [4] boat, ship, plane
crafty *adj.* cunning, artful, wily, shrewd
cram *v.* ram, stuff, squeeze, press
cramp *v.* restrict, obstruct, hinder, confine
crash *v.* bang, clash, clatter, break, fall, topple
crass *adj.* stupid, oafish, boorish, obtuse ★**sensitive**
crave *v.* long for, hanker after, need, yearn for, beg, plead
crawl *v.* creep, drag, slither, grovel
crazy *adj.* insane, mad, beserk, deranged, idiotic ★**sane**
creak *v.* grate, grind, rasp, groan CREEK
crease *n.* fold, pucker, ridge, fold, tuck
create *v.* bring into being, compose, concoct, make, invent
creation invention, handiwork, foundation, production ★**destruction**
creature *n.* animal, beast, being, brute *It was a huge brute, the biggest crocodile I ever saw,* person
credible *adj.* believable, likely, plausible ★**incredible**
credit [1] *n.* acclaim, kudos, merit [2] belief, faith, confidence
creek *n.* bay, bight, cove CREAK
creep *v.* crawl, slither, squirm, wriggle
crest *n.* top, crown, pinnacle
crestfallen *adj.* downcast, dejected, discouraged ★**elated**
crevice *n.* cleft, chink, crack, cranny, gap
crew *n.* team, company, party, gang
crime *n.* misdemeanor, offense, fault, felony
criminal [1] *n.* culprit, convict, felon, crook [2] *adj.* unlawful, wicked
cringe *v.* cower, flinch, duck, shrink, grovel
cripple *v.* disable, mutilate, paralyze, weaken, damage

crisis *n.* climax, turning point, catastrophe, disaster
crisp *adj.* brittle, crumbly, crunchy, firm, crusty
critical *adj.* crucial, all-important, acute, grave
criticize *v.* find fault with, disapprove of, condemn ★**praise**
crony *n.* accomplice, ally, confederate, comrade, chum, ▷*friend*
crooked [1] *adj.* bent, bowed, distorted, twisted [2] dishonest, criminal
crop [1] *n.* harvest, gathering, yield [2] *v.* graze, shorten, browse
cross [1] *adj.* angry, annoyed, crusty [2] *v.* bridge, pass over [3] *n.* crucifix
crouch *v.* stoop, squat, bow, cringe
crow [1] *v.* gloat, shout, brag, bluster [2] *n.* jackdaw, raven
crowd *n.* mob, multitude, flock, assembly, swarm, throng
crowded *adj.* jammed, packed, congested, cramped
crucial *adj.* decisive, critical, acute
crude *adj.* raw, unrefined, rustic, unpolished, ▷*coarse* ★**refined**
cruel *adj.* unkind, brutal, inhuman, ruthless, ▷*savage* ★**kind**
cruise *n.* voyage, sail, crossing CREWS
crumb *n.* bit, morsel, seed, grain, scrap, shred
crumble *v.* decay, grind, powder, crunch
crumple *v.* crinkle, crush, wrinkle, pucker
crunch *v.* chew, grind, masticate, munch ▷*crush*
crush *v.* squash, mash, pound, compress
cry [1] *v.* exclaim, call, shout, shriek [2] weep, bawl, blubber, sob
cuddle *v.* hug, embrace, fondle, cosset, pet, snuggle
cue *n.* hint, key, nod, sign, signal QUEUE
cull *v.* choose, pick, thin out, amass, collect
culprit *n.* criminal, convict, felon, offender, malefactor
cultivated *adj.* refined, civilized, cultured, educated, trained ★**neglected**
cumbersome *adj.* bulky, awkward, clumsy, hefty ★**convenient**
cunning *adj.* artful, astute, crafty ★**gullible**
curb *v.* check, tame, restrain
cure [1] *n.* remedy, medicine, drug [2] *v.* heal, remedy, treat, attend
curious [1] *adj.* odd, peculiar, singular [2] inquisitive, prying, nosy
curl *v.* coil, twist, curve, crimp
current [1] *adj.* present, contemporary, topical, fashionable [2] *n.* stream, course, flow, electrical flow CURRANT
curse [1] *v.* swear, condemn, damn [2] *n.* oath, denunciation
curt *adj.* brusque, blunt, churlish, crusty, gruff, ▷*terse* ★**polite**
curtail *v.* trim, shorten, clip, truncate *It was usually a long movie, but we saw a truncated version,* ▷*abbreviate* ★**lengthen**
curve *n.* loop, hook, curl, twist, wind, coil, ▷*bend*
cushion *n.* pillow, bolster, pad, support
custom *n.* habit, usage, convention, rite, ▷*fashion*
customer *n.* purchaser, buyer, client, patron
cut *v.* carve, whittle, chisel, cleave, sever, gash, slice
cut off *v.* disconnect, interrupt
cute *adj.* charming, attractive, pretty
cutting *adj.* sharp, biting, bitter, sarcastic

D d

dab *v.* blot, swab, touch, pat
dabble *v.* toy, meddle, tinker, trifle, putter
daft *adj.* crazy, silly, innocent, idiotic, cracked, dopey ★**bright**
dagger *n.* knife, dirk, bayonet, stiletto
daily [1] *adj.* everyday, normal, common *It is quite common to see squirrels in the woods* [2] *n.* newspaper
dainty *adj.* delicate, charming, exquisite, choice, tasty
dally *v.* play, trifle, dawdle, linger, loiter
damage *n.* harm, sabotage, vandalism, injury, hurt
damn *v.* curse, swear, condemn, criticize ★**bless**
damp *adj.* humid, clammy, dank, ▷*moist* ★**dry**
damsel *n.* girl, maid, maiden, miss
dance *v.* hop, skip, jump, prance, frolic, gambol
danger *n.* peril, hazard, risk, jeopardy, menace ★**safety**
dangerous *adj.* perilous, precarious, unsafe, risky, hazardous ★**safe**
dangle *v.* hang, swing, sway
dank *adj.* sticky, muggy, moist, soggy, ▷*damp*
dapper *adj.* spruce, natty, neat, stylish, trim, ▷*smart* ★**scruffy**
dare *v.* brave, face, risk, defy, challenge, venture
daring *adj.* adventurous, dashing, bold, fearless, ▷*brave* ★**timid**
dark *adj.* dusky, swarthy, shady, dim, dingy, shadowy ★**light**
darling *n.* pet, love, dear, favorite, beloved, precious
darn *v.* mend, sew, patch, repair
dart [1] *n.* arrow, missile [2] *v.* dash, hurtle *The express train hurtled through the tunnel,* charge, gallop
dash *v.* rush, gallop, run, career, fly, hasten
date [1] *n.* time, point [2] appointment *I have an appointment to see the doctor,* engagement [3] *v.* become old, become dated

Dances

Ballet
Bolero
Bop
Cha-cha
Charleston
Conga
Country dance
Fandango
Flamenco
Fox-trot
Gavotte
Highland fling
Jitterbug
Jive
Mazurka
Minuet
Morris dance
Polka
Polonaise
Quadrille
Quickstep
Rumba
Samba
Square dance
Tango
Tarantella
Two-step
Twist
Waltz

daub *v.* plaster, spread, smear, coat, paint
daunt *v.* intimidate, terrify, scare, confront
dauntless *adj.* fearless, gallant, courageous, ▷*brave* ★**discouraged**
dawdle *v.* linger, loiter, lag, waste time, ▷*dally* ★**hurry**
dawn *n.* beginning, daybreak, daylight, morning, sunrise ★**dusk**
daze *v.* deaden, muddle, blind, dazzle, ▷*bewilder* DAYS
dazzle *v.* blind, glare, confuse, ▷*daze*
dead *adj.* deceased, departed, gone, lifeless, dull ★**alive**
deaden *v.* paralyze, blunt, muffle, drown
deadly *adj.* fatal, lethal, mortal, baleful, venomous
deaf *adj.* hard of hearing, unhearing, heedless
deal *v.* bargain, trade, market, communicate, traffic, give out
dealer *n.* merchant, trader, tradesman
dear [1] *adj.* darling, beloved, loved, cherished *These old records are some of my cherished possessions* [2] expensive, high-priced, costly DEER
death *n.* decease, end of life, mortality ★**life**
debate *v.* argue, discuss, dispute, question, contend
debris *n.* trash, junk, ▷*rubbish*
debt *n.* obligation, debit, dues, liability ★**credit**
decay [1] *v.* decompose, rot *The potatoes had been left too long and had rotted*, spoil [2] decline, sink, dwindle, waste
deceive *v.* dupe, hoax, trick, cheat, mislead, ▷*betray* ★**enlighten**
decent *adj.* respectable, chaste, proper, fair, modest ★**indecent**
decide *v.* determine, rule, judge, resolve
declare *v.* avow, state, profess, proclaim, announce
decline [1] *v.* descend, dwindle *The profits of the business had dwindled*, drop, fall [2] refuse, say no ★**assent** [3] *n.* descent, slope, slant, dip, pitch
decorate *v.* embellish, adorn, ornament
decoy [1] *v.* entice *We were enticed into the café by the smell of roasting coffee*, ensnare, mislead, tempt [2] *n.* lure, bait
decrease *v.* diminish, lessen, wane, decline, reduce ★**increase**
decree *n.* law, edict, manifesto, rule, decision
decrepit *adj.* senile, infirm, crippled, feeble, frail ★**robust**
dedicate *v.* devote, apportion, assign, surrender, pledge
deduce *v.* draw, infer, conclude, glean, surmise, reason
deduct *v.* subtract, take from, remove, withdraw ★**add**
deed [1] *n.* act, feat, stunt [2] document, paper, contract *Greta Garbo was under contract to the film studio*
deep [1] *adj.* profound *Mary and John were profoundly happy*, bottomless, low [2] learned, wise, sagacious
deface *v.* disfigure, deform, injure, mar, blemish ★**adorn**
defeat *v.* beat, conquer, overcome, triumph, vanquish ★**triumph**
defect *n.* flaw, fault, weak point, blemish, error
defective *adj.* imperfect, faulty, deficient, insufficient ★**perfect**
defend *v.* protect, guard, fortify, support, sustain, uphold ★**attack**
defer *v.* postpone, put off, adjourn, waive, yield ★**hasten**
defiant *adj.* mutinous, rebellious, resistant, aggressive ★**submissive**
deficient *adj.* wanting, imperfect, defective, faulty ★**superfluous**
defile *v.* taint, infect, pollute, sully, disgrace ★**cleanse**
define *v.* explain, interpret, designate, mark out, specify ★**obscure**
definite *adj.* clear, certain, clear-cut, distinct, ▷*sure* ★**vague**
deform *adj.* misshape, distort, contort, twist, warp
defraud *v.* fleece, swindle, embezzle, diddle, ▷*cheat*
defy *v.* resist, withstand, disregard, challenge, disobey ★**obey**
degrade *v.* humble, debase, corrupt, downgrade, cheapen ★**improve**

degree *n.* grade, step, measure, rate, scale *The rebellion turned into a full-scale war,* class

dejected *adj.* depressed, downcast, crestfallen, disheartened, ▷*gloomy* ★**elated**

delay *v.* postpone, put off, detain, halt, hinder, impede ★**hurry**

deliberate [1] *adj.* willful, calculated, intentional, planned ★**unintentional** [2] *v.* reflect, contemplate, discuss

delicate *adj.* dainty, refined, soft, luxurious, modest, fragile, tender ★**harsh**

delicious *adj.* palatable, luscious, mellow, savory, choice, ▷*scrumptious* ★**unpleasant**

delight *n.* enjoyment, pleasure, rapture, bliss, ▷*happiness* ★**displease**

delightful *adj.* enjoyable, cheery, enchanting, lovely, ▷*agreeable* ★**horrible**

deliver [1] *v.* transfer, hand over, bear *I bear good news of your family,* carry, convey [2] free, liberate, release

delude *v.* cheat, hoax, hoodwink, mislead, ▷*deceive* ★**guide**

deluge *n.* inundation, swamp, spate, ▷*flood*

demand [1] *v.* request, ask, appeal, entreat [2] badger, pester, nag *The children have been nagging me to take them to the park*

demeanor *n.* bearing, manner, conduct, air

demented *adj.* distracted, foolish, insane, ▷*mad* ★**sane**

demolish *v.* destroy, wreck, ruin, smash, overthrow, knock down ★**build up**

demon *n.* fiend, imp, devil, evil spirit

demonstrate *v.* prove, exhibit, illustrate, ▷*show*

demote *v.* degrade, downgrade, relegate ★**promote**

demur *v.* hesitate, object, protest, doubt, waver ★**consent**

demure *adj.* coy, sedate, staid, sober, prudish, discreet ★**indiscreet**

den [1] *n.* nest, cave, haunt, lair [2] hideaway, retreat *This little room is my retreat, where I can sit and think,* study

denote *v.* designate, indicate, mean, show, point out

denounce *v.* decry, defame, attack, brand, ▷*accuse* ★**praise**

dense [1] *adj.* thick, solid, stout, compact ★**sparse** [2] stupid, thick, stolid, obtuse ★**clever** DENTS

dent *n.* notch, cavity, chip, dimple, hollow

deny [1] *v.* refuse, reject, repudiate [2] disagree with *I am afraid that I disagree with what you say,* oppose, contradict ★**admit**

depart *v.* quit, go, retire, withdraw, vanish, ▷*leave* ★**arrive**

department *n.* section, division, office, branch, province

depend on *v.* lean on, rely upon, trust in

depict *v.* describe, sketch, portray, outline, draw

deplorable *adj.* distressing, disastrous, shameful, scandalous ★**excellent**

deplore *v.* regret, lament, mourn ★**praise**

deport *v.* banish, exile, expel, oust

deposit *v.* drop, lay, place, put, bank, entrust, save ★**withdraw**

depot [1] *n.* warehouse, storehouse [2] terminus, station

depraved *adj.* corrupted, immoral, evil, sinful, vile *After calling me vile names, he left* ★**upright**

depreciate [1] *v.* devalue, lessen, lose value *From the moment it was bought the car began losing value,* reduce [2] belittle, disparage, deride ★**appreciate**

depress [1] *v.* dishearten, dispirit, cast down ★**cheer** [2] flatten, push down

depressed *adj.* dispirited, disheartened, despondent, fed up

deprive *v.* take away, rob, starve, divest *The traitor had been divested of all her honors* ★**bestow**

depth *n.* pit, shaft, well, chasm, gulf, abyss

deputy *n.* agent, delegate, lieutenant, assistant, councillor

derelict *adj.* abandoned, deserted *The **Mary Celeste** sailing ship was found deserted in the Atlantic,* forlorn

deride *v.* laugh at, jeer at, ridicule, ▷*mock* ★**praise**

derive *v.* develop *Many English words developed from Norman-French,* obtain, arise from, originate

descend *v.* fall, drop, lower, decline, collapse, ▷*sink* ★**ascend**
describe *v.* depict, portray, detail, define, tell
desert [1] *n.* (*dez*-ert) wasteland, wilderness [2] *adj.* desolate, arid, barren [3] *v.* (dez-*ert*) forsake, leave, ▷*abandon*
deserve *v.* be worthy of, merit, warrant, be entitled to ★**forfeit**
design *n.* drawing, painting, plan, pattern, scheme
desirable [1] *adj.* agreeable, pleasing, good [2] attractive, alluring, adorable
desire [1] *v.* wish, require, need, want, crave [2] long for, yearn after, pine for *My sister lived abroad, but always pined for home* ★**detest**
desist *v.* abstain, avoid, break off, cease, end
desolate *adj.* lonely, forlorn, miserable, wretched, alone ★**cheerful**
despair *n.* depression, misery, hopelessness, sorrow, ▷*gloom* ★**hope**
desperate *adj.* drastic, reckless, frantic, rash, wild ★**hopeful**
despicable *adj.* contemptible, low, detestable, degrading ★**noble**
despise *v.* abhor, detest, loathe, look down upon, ▷*hate* ★**prize**
despite *prep.* in spite of, notwithstanding
despondent *adj.* depressed, dispirited, brokenhearted, ▷*miserable* ★**hopeful**
destination *n.* goal, terminus, end, objective, journey's end
destiny *n.* fate, lot, fortune, future, prospect, doom
destitute *adj.* poor, needy, bankrupt, penniless, poverty-stricken ★**wealthy**
destroy *v.* ruin, demolish, spoil, smash, exterminate, ▷*wreck* ★**create**
destruction *n.* desolation, downfall, ruin, defeat, havoc ★**creation**
detach *v.* separate, part, divide, loosen, undo ★**attach**
detail *n.* item, fact, circumstance, point
detain *v.* delay, retard, restrain, arrest, hold up ★**release**
detect *v.* notice, discover, observe, scent, track down ★**hide**

deter *v.* prevent, hold back, check, stop, ▷*detain* ★**encourage**
deteriorate *v.* become worse, worsen, corrode, decline, decompose ★**improve**
determine *v.* find out, decide, identify, choose, regulate
detest *v.* abhor *Lucy was a peaceful woman and abhorred violence*, loathe, despise, ▷*hate* ★**adore**
devastate *v.* lay waste, ravage, overwhelm, ▷*destroy*
develop *v.* mature, ripen, grow up, evolve, extend ★**restrict**
deviate *v.* diverge, differ, vary, contrast, wander ★**continue**
device *n.* apparatus, contrivance, instrument, appliance
devil *n.* imp, evil spirit, demon, fiend, Satan
devious *adj.* tricky, sly, subtle, cunning, roundabout ★**forthright**
devise *v.* contrive, fashion, form, plan, conceive
devoid *adj.* barren, empty, free, without, lacking ★**endowed**
devote *v.* allocate, allot, give, assign, dedicate
devoted *adj.* dedicated, devout, loyal, caring, ardent ★**indifferent**

devour *v.* swallow, gulp, gorge, consume, ▷*eat*
devout *adj.* pious, devoted, religious, faithful, passionate ★**insincere**
dexterous *adj.* able, active, deft, nimble, ▷*skillful* ★**clumsy**
diagram *n.* outline, plan, sketch, draft, chart, drawing
dictate *v.* speak, utter, say, instruct, ordain, command
die *v.* expire, finish, end, pass away, perish, cease ★**live** DYE
differ [1] *v.* vary, contrast, diverge *In this case, my views diverge strongly from yours* [2] argue, conflict, clash
difference *n.* variance, distinctness, divergence, subtlety ★**agreement**
different *adj.* contrary, variant, distinct, original, unusual ★**same**
difficult *adj.* hard, puzzling, baffling, complex, laborious ★**easy**
difficulty *n.* trouble, bother, predicament, ★**plight**
diffident *adj.* bashful, reserved, retiring, timid, unsure, ▷*shy* ★**confident**
dig *v.* burrow, excavate, grub, delve, scoop
digest [1] *v.* (di-*gest*) absorb, assimilate, dissolve [2] *n.* (*di*-gest) *n.* abridgment, condensation, précis
digit [1] *n.* number, figure, cipher [2] finger, toe, thumb
dignified *adj.* grave, majestic, noble, lofty, grand ★**undignified**
dignity *n.* grandeur, merit, fame, gravity, nobility
dilapidated *adj.* neglected, unkempt, crumbling, decayed
dilemma *n.* quandary, plight, difficulty, predicament
dilute *v.* water down, weaken, reduce, thin
dim *adj.* dark, faint, pale, gloomy, ▷*obscure* ★**distinct**
diminish *v.* reduce, lessen, decrease, become smaller ★**enhance**
din *n.* uproar, racket, babble, ▷*noise* ★**quiet**
dingy *adj.* murky, dark, dreary, somber, gloomy, ▷*dismal* ★**bright**
dip *v.* sink, subside, immerse, plunge
dire *adj.* alarming, appalling, awful, horrible, ▷*terrible* DYER
direct [1] *adj.* straight, even, blunt, candid [2] *v.* aim, level, train, point
direction *n.* course, trend, way, track, route
dirt *n.* impurity, filth, grime, muck, soil
dirty *adj.* unclean, impure, filthy, sordid, squalid, nasty ★**clean**
disable *v.* cripple, lame, maim, disarm
disadvantage *n.* inconvenience, burden, damage, loss, obstacle ★**advantage**
disagree *v.* differ, revolt, decline, refuse, dissent, argue ★**agree**
disagreeable *adj.* unpleasant, obnoxious, unwelcome, offensive ★**agreeable**

Dogs

Afghan Hound
Airedale Terrier
Basenji
Bassett Hound
Beagle
Bloodhound
Borzoi
Boxer
Bulldog

disappear *v.* vanish, dissolve, fade, melt, depart, expire ★**appear**

disappoint *v.* frustrate, disillusion, let down, dismay, dissatisfy ★**please**

disapprove *v.* condemn, denounce, criticize, reproach ★**approve**

disaster *n.* calamity, catastrophe, accident, misfortune ★**triumph**

disbelief *n.* incredulity, distrust, doubt, suspicion ★**belief**

discard *v.* eliminate, get rid of, reject, scrap *Once we got a new car, I scrapped the old one,* throw away ★**adopt**

discern *v.* note, discover, distinguish

discharge 1 *v.* dismiss, give notice to, expel 2 detonate, emit, fire

disciple *n.* follower, learner, pupil, attendant

discipline *n.* correction, training, self-control, obedience

disclaim *v.* repudiate, disown, renounce, deny, reject ★**acknowledge**

disclose *v.* discover, show, reveal, expose, betray, ▷*divulge* ★**conceal**

disconcert *v.* abash, confuse, confound, upset, baffle ★**encourage**

disconnect *v.* separate, detach, cut off, sever, uncouple ★**connect**

disconsolate *adj.* distressed, sad, forlorn, melancholy, desolate, ▷*unhappy* ★**cheerful**

discontented *adj.* displeased, disgruntled, unsatisfied, reluctant ★**content**

discord *n.* disagreement, strife ★**concord**

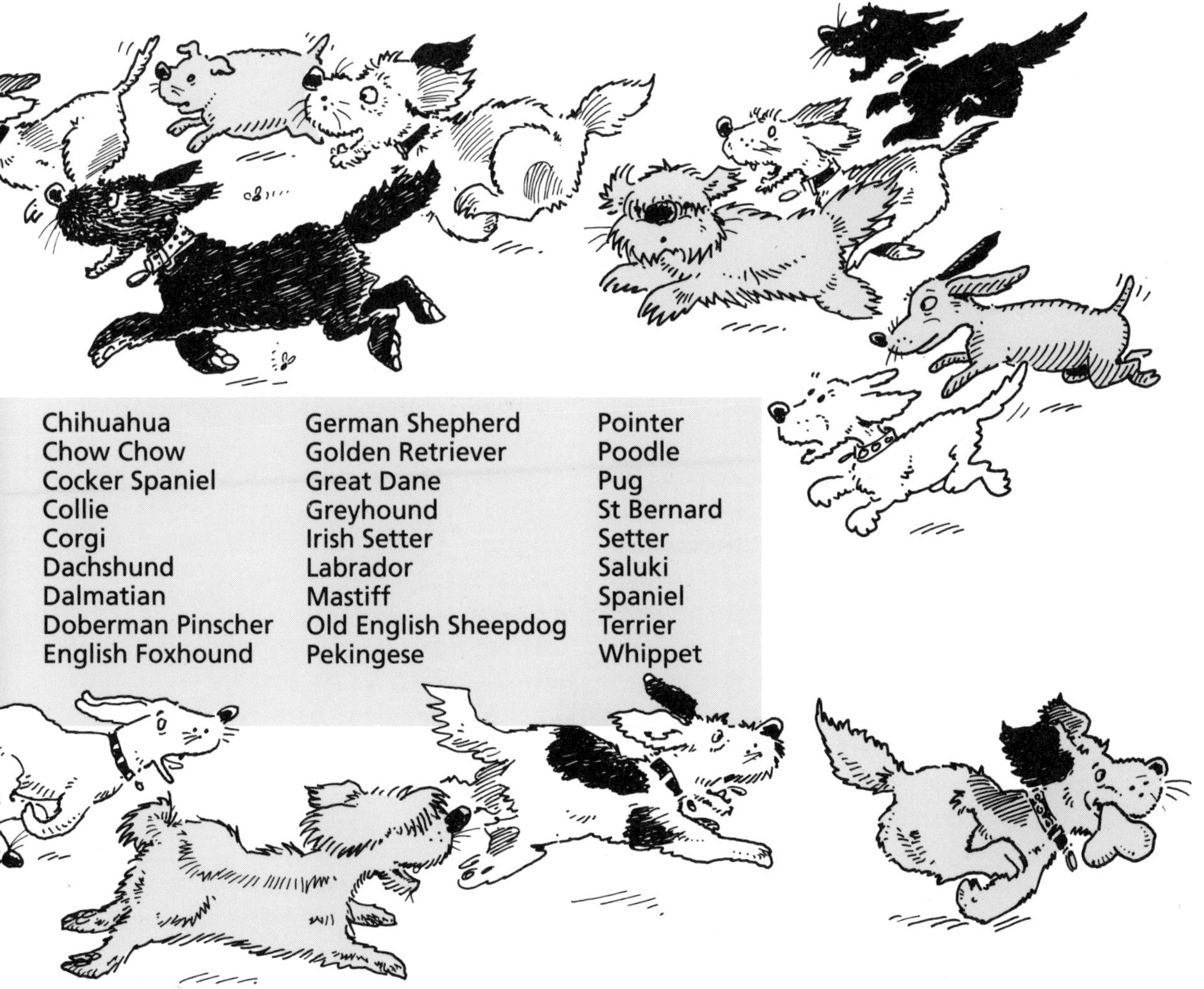

Chihuahua
Chow Chow
Cocker Spaniel
Collie
Corgi
Dachshund
Dalmatian
Doberman Pinscher
English Foxhound
German Shepherd
Golden Retriever
Great Dane
Greyhound
Irish Setter
Labrador
Mastiff
Old English Sheepdog
Pekingese
Pointer
Poodle
Pug
St Bernard
Setter
Saluki
Spaniel
Terrier
Whippet

discourage *v.* depress, dishearten, dismay, dispirit *Today everything went wrong, and I am very dispirited*, put off ★**encourage**
discouraged *adj.* crestfallen, daunted, depressed, downcast ★**encouraged**
discourteous *adj.* blunt, crude, churlish, outspoken, abrupt ★**courteous**
discover *v.* locate, surprise, unearth, uncover, ▷*find* ★**conceal**
discreet *adj.* prudent, cautious, careful, tactful, sensible ★**indiscreet** DISCRETE
discriminate *v.* distinguish, penetrate, favor, judge, assess ★**confound**
discuss *v.* confer, consider, talk over, debate, argue
disdain *n.* ridicule, scorn, contempt, derision ★**admiration**
disease *n.* infection, contagion, illness, plague, ailment, sickness
disfigure *v.* blemish, deface, deform, mar, scar, spoil ★**adorn**
disgrace *n.* scandal, dishonor, shame, infamy, stigma ★**honor**
disguise *v.* conceal, mask, falsify, cloak, deceive, fake
disgust [1] *n.* revulsion, loathing, distaste *The room was messy, and I viewed it with distaste* [2] *v.* repel, revolt, nauseate ★**admire**
dish *n.* plate, platter, bowl
dishearten *v.* depress, cast down, deter, deject, ▷*discourage* ★**encourage**
dishonest *adj.* deceitful, unscrupulous, shady, crooked ★**honest**
disintegrate *v.* crumble, molder, decompose, rot, fall apart ★**unite**
dislike *v.* hate, loathe, detest, abhor, abominate, ▷*despise* ★**like**
dismal *adj.* dreary, ominous, cheerless, depressing, ▷*hopeless* ★**cheerful**
dismiss *v.* banish, discard, abandon, dispel, repudiate, release ★**appoint**
disobey *v.* rebel, transgress, resist, defy, ignore ★**obey**
disorder *n.* confusion, disarray, commotion, chaos ★**order**
dispel *v.* diperse, drive away, dismiss, allay, scatter ★**collect**
dispense *v.* distribute, arrange, allocate, supply, measure out ★**accept**
disperse *v.* scatter, separate, break up, spread abroad, distribute ★**gather**
display *v.* show, exhibit, unfold, expose, flaunt *He wears expensive clothes, which he flaunts to his companions*, flourish, ▷*reveal* ★**hide**
displease *v.* annoy, anger, irritate, upset, vex ★**please**
dispose *v.* arrange, place, position, regulate, order
dispose of *v.* discard, dump, destroy, eliminate, throw away ★**keep**
dispute [1] *n.* (dis-*pute*) conflict, quarrel, argument [2] *v.* (*dis*-pute) argue, refute, contend
disregard *v.* overlook, misjudge, despise, ignore, snub ★**heed**
disreputable *adj.* discreditable, dishonorable, disgraceful, ▷*shameful* ★**honorable**
dissect *v.* examine, scrutinize, analyze, dismember
dissent *n.* disagreement, difference, repudiation, opposition ★**assent**
dissimilar *adj.* different, diverse, unlike, various ★**similar**
dissolve *v.* melt, thaw, break up, fade
dissuade *v.* deter, discourage, warn, put off ★**persuade**
distance *n.* extent, remoteness, range, reach, span, stretch
distinct [1] *adj.* separate, independent, detached [2] clear, conspicuous, lucid ★**hazy**
distinguish *v.* discern, discover, differentiate
distinguished *adj.* important, notable, great, famed, celebrated ★**ordinary**
distort *v.* deform, misshape, twist, bend, buckle
distract [1] *v.* beguile, bewilder, disturb, confuse [2] entertain
distress *v.* harass, embarrass, trouble, grieve, ▷*worry* ★**soothe**
distribute *v.* give out, deliver, disperse, circulate, ▷*dispense* ★**collect**

Domesticated animals

Camel
Canary
Cat
Cattle
Chicken
Dog
Donkey
Duck
Elephant
Goat
Goose
Horse
Parakeet
Parrot
Pig
Pigeon
Sheep

district *n.* area, community, locality *Pat and Mike have moved to a new locality,* neighborhood, region

distrust *v.* suspect, discredit, doubt, disbelieve ★**trust**

disturb *v.* annoy, bother, disquiet, unsettle, upset, confuse ★**calm**

dither *v.* waver, hesitate, falter, oscillate

dive *v.* plunge, pitch, swoop, descend, drop

diverse *adj.* different, various, dissimilar, numerous, separate ★**identical**

divert [1] *v.* alter, change, deflect [2] entertain, gratify

divest *v.* disrobe, undress, strip

divide *v.* separate, dissect, part, divorce, distribute, apportion, split ★**join**

division *n.* portion, fragment, section, compartment, department

divorce *v.* annul, cancel, separate, divide, part, split up

divulge *v.* betray, disclose, tell, announce, broadcast, uncover

dizzy *adj.* giddy, confused, shaky, wobbling, muddled, staggering

do [1] *v.* carry out, perform, act [2] be adequate, suffice

do away with *v.* destroy, abolish, eliminate, kill

do up, *v.* fasten, tie, fix

docile *adj.* amenable, tame, meek, orderly, manageable ★**uncooperative**

doctrine *n.* article, belief, creed, dogma, teaching

document *n.* paper, deed, certificate, form

dodge *v.* avoid, parry, duck, elude, fend off

dogged *adj.* obstinate, morose, sullen, persistent, steadfast ★**docile**

doleful *adj.* dismal, woebegone, depressing, rueful, sad, ▷*gloomy* ★**merry**

domestic [1] *adj.* homey, household *The children always help with the household jobs,* family, internal [2] domesticated, tame

dominant *adj.* masterful, superior, supreme, prevalent ★**subordinate**

dominate *v.* rule, control, direct, tyrannize, overbear ★**yield**

donation *n.* gift, present, contribution

doom *n.* judgment, fate, verdict, destiny, destruction

door *n.* entrance, doorway, gate, gateway, portal

dose *n.* draft, potion, quantity, amount

doubt *v.* hesitate, waver, demur, suspect, mistrust, be dubious ★**trust**

doubtful *adj.* suspicious, dubious, indefinite, uncertain, unclear ★**certain**

dour *adj.* austere, dreary, grim, hard, severe ★**cheery**

dowdy *adj.* dull, plain, dingy, frumpish, ▷*shabby* ★**elegant**

downcast *adj.* crestfallen, downhearted, dejected, ▷*miserable* ★**happy**

downfall *n.* ruin, overthrow, misfortune, disgrace, failure
downright *adj.* blunt, candid, absolute, forthright, straightforward
doze *v.* snooze, slumber, sleep, nod off, drowse
drab *adj.* colorless, cheerless, dull, gloomy, gray, ▷*dreary* ★**bright**
draft *v.* sketch, outline, draw, design, plan
drag *v.* draw, pull, haul, tug, tow, lug
drain [1] *v.* draw, strain, drip, percolate, empty, dry, drink up [2] *n.* conduit, sewer, pipe
dramatic *adj.* theatrical, exciting, surprising, sensational ★**ordinary**
drape *v.* hang, suspend, droop, cover
drastic *adj.* extreme, dire, desperate, harsh, radical ★**mild**
draw [1] *v.* pull, tug, drag, haul [2] sketch, design, depict, portray
drawback *n.* weakness, shortcoming, failing, defect, handicap ★**advantage**
dread *n.* fear, terror, horror, alarm, awe, dismay, ▷*fright* ★**confidence**
dreadful *adj.* fearful, terrible, horrible, alarming, ▷*awful* ★**comforting**
dream *n.* trance, vision, fancy, reverie, fantasy, illusion
dreary *adj.* dingy, gloomy, somber, cheerless, ▷*dismal* ★**bright**
drench *v.* saturate, soak, steep, flood
dress *n.* clothing, vestments, costume, garb, apparel, attire
dress up *v.* play-act, don costumes
drift *v.* float, flow, wander, stray, meander *The little stream meandered through lush countryside*
drill [1] *v.* teach, exercise, train, discipline [2] bore, penetrate, pierce
drink *v.* imbibe, swallow, absorb, quaff, sip
drip *v.* drop, ooze, percolate, drizzle, trickle
drive [1] *v.* make, compel, force, oblige, prod, goad [2] propel, direct, operate, actuate
drivel *n.* nonsense, babble, twaddle, bunkum, gibberish
drizzle *v.* dribble, mizzle, shower, spit, ▷*rain*
droll *adj.* whimsical, comical, comic, ▷*funny*
droop *v.* flag, sink, decline, languish, drop, bend, wilt
drop [1] *v.* fall, sink, dip, plunge, plummet [2] *n.* droplet, globule, drip
drown *v.* sink, immerse, swamp, submerge, extinguish
drowsy *adj.* sleepy, somnolent, dazed, tired
drudge *v.* toil, labor, struggle, plod, slave
drug *v.* dope, deaden, sedate, stupefy, poison
dry [1] *adj.* arid, parched, moistureless, dried up ★**wet** [2] uninteresting, boring, tedious, prosaic, dull
dubious *adj.* suspicious, fishy, suspect, untrustworthy, ▷*doubtful* ★**trustworthy**
duck [1] *n.* waterfowl [2] *v.* plunge, submerge, dip, dodge, lurch
due [1] *adj.* owing, unpaid, payable [2] just, fair, proper [3] scheduled, expected DEW
duel *n.* combat, contest, battle, swordplay
duffer *n.* blunderer, bungler, booby, dolt
dull [1] *adj.* stupid, stolid, obtuse, dimwitted [2] blunt, not sharp [3] boring, uninteresting, tedious
dumb [1] *adj.* silent, speechless, mute [2] foolish, stupid, ▷*dull* ★**intelligent**
dummy [1] *n.* mannequin, puppet, doll [2] blockhead, dimwit [3] *adj.* artificial, fake, false
dump *v.* deposit, ditch, empty, throw away
dunce *n.* dimwit, dolt, blockhead, duffer, ignoramus ★**genius**
dungeon *n.* cell, prison, jail, vault
dupe *v.* cheat, defraud, deceive, outwit
duplicate *n.* copy, facsimile, replica, reproduction
durable *adj.* lasting, enduring, permanent, stable, reliable ★**fragile**
dusk *n.* twilight, nightfall, evening, gloaming ★**dawn**
dusty *adj.* grimy, dirty, filthy, grubby ★**polished**
duty [1] *n.* obligation, responsibility, allegiance, trust, task [2] impost, tax, excise
dwell *v.* stop, stay, rest, linger, tarry, live, reside
dwell on *v.* emphasize, linger over, harp on
dwindle *v.* diminish, decrease, decline, waste, shrink, become smaller ★**increase**
dye *n.* pigment, coloring matter, color, stain, tint DIE

E e

eager *adj.* avid, enthusiastic, ambitious, ardent, zealous, ▷*keen* ★**indifferent**
early *adj.* advanced, forward, soon ★**late**
earn *v.* make money, deserve, merit, rate, win, acquire ★**spend** URN
earnest *adj.* serious, sincere, determined, eager, zealous ★**flippant**
earth [1] *n.* soil, dust, dry land [2] world, globe, sphere
ease *n.* calm, repose, quiet, peace, dexterity ★**difficulty**
easy *adj.* effortless, smooth, simple, practicable ★**difficult**
eat *v.* consume, dine, chew, swallow, gorge
ebb *v.* flow back, fall back, recede, decline, wane ★**flow**
eccentric *adj.* queer, strange, odd, erratic, whimsical, ▷*peculiar* ★**normal**
echo *v.* vibrate, reverberate, imitate
economical *adj.* moderate, reasonable, frugal, ▷*thrifty* ★**expensive**
ecstasy *n.* joy, happiness, delight, elation, ▷*bliss* ★**torment**
edge *n.* border, rim, brink, fringe, margin, tip, ▷*end*
edible *adj.* eatable, comestible, safe, wholesome ★**inedible**
edit *v.* revise, correct, adapt, censor, publish
educate *v.* instruct, teach, tutor, coach, train
educated *adj.* learned, cultured, erudite, literate, well-bred ★**illiterate**
eerie *adj.* weird, unearthly, uncanny, awesome
effect [1] *n.* outcome *What was the outcome of your interview?*, end, result [2] *v.* cause, make, bring about, accomplish
effective *adj.* operative, serviceable, competent ★**useless**
efficient *adj.* competent, proficient, able, ▷*effective* ★**inefficient**
effort *n.* exertion, toil, labor, accomplishment, ▷*feat*
eject *v.* drive out, force out, expel, evict, oust, discharge
elaborate *adj.* complex, elegant, ornate, intricate ★**simple**
elated *adj.* excited, gleeful, joyous, overjoyed, ▷*pleased* ★**downcast**

Eating verbs

bolt breakfast
chew chomp consume
devour dig in dine drink
eat eat up
feast feed finish off
gobble gorge gulp guzzle
imbibe
lap up lunch
masticate munch
nibble nosh
partake peck at pick at
quaff
relish
sample savor set to sip slurp
snack swallow sup swig swill
taste tuck in
wash down wine and dine
wolf down

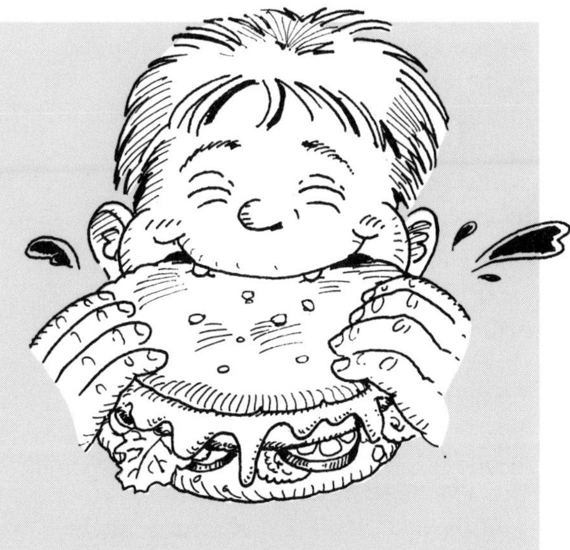

elderly *adj.* old, aged, ancient ★**youthful**
elect *v.* choose, determine, vote, select, pick
elegant *adj.* refined, luxurious, polished, classical, ▷*graceful* ★**inelegant**
elementary *adj.* easy, effortless, basic, clear, ▷*simple* ★**complex**
elevate *v.* raise, erect, hoist, upraise, ▷*lift* ★**lower**
eligible *adj.* qualified, suitable, acceptable, proper, ▷*fit* ★**unfit**
eliminate *v.* do away with, abolish *The government has abolished many old laws*, exterminate, erase, delete ★**keep**
elude *v.* evade, avoid, depart, dodge, escape
embarrass *v.* abash, confuse, disconcert, fluster, shame
emblem *n.* badge, mark, brand, sign, crest, device
embrace [1] *v.* hug, squeeze, cuddle, caress, hold [2] include *The census figures include new arrivals this year*, encompass, enclose
emerge *v.* come out, exit, appear, arise, turn up ★**disappear**
emergency *n.* crisis, danger, extremity, predicament, ▷*plight*
eminent *adj.* famous, noted, renowned, well-known, esteemed, ▷*important* ★**unknown**
emit *v.* give off, belch, radiate, discharge, eject, vent ★**absorb**
emotion *n.* sentiment, feeling, fervor, passion
emotional *adj.* affected, sensitive, responsive, temperamental ★**cold**
emphasize *v.* accentuate, accent, intensify, ▷*stress* ★**understate**
employ *v.* engage, hire, retain, apply, adopt, ▷*use*
employee *n.* worker, workman, staff member, jobholder
empty [1] *adj.* bare, barren, vacant *That house has been vacant for months*, hollow, unoccupied ★**full** [2] *v.* discharge, drain, unload, pour out ★**fill**
enchant *v.* enthrall, bewitch, delight, gratify, ▷*charm* ★**bore**
enclose *v.* surround, encircle, encompass, contain, include ★**open**
encounter *v.* come upon, meet, experience, face
encourage *v.* cheer, hearten, console, comfort, support, ▷*urge* ★**dissuade**
encroach *v.* intrude, transgress, overstep, trespass, infringe
end [1] *n.* conclusion, finish, limit, boundary *This river marks the boundary of the county* [2] *v.* complete, close, terminate, ▷*finish* ★**start**
endanger *v.* hazard, imperil, jeopardize, ▷*risk* ★**protect**
endeavor *v.* aspire, aim, strive, struggle, try, ▷*aim*
endless *adj.* ceaseless, continuous, everlasting, limitless
endorse *v.* undersign, uphold, support, guarantee, vouch for ★**disapprove**
endow *v.* settle upon, invest, award, bequeath, provide, ▷*bestow* ★**divest**
endowed *adj.* talented, gifted, enhanced
endure *v.* bear, tolerate, suffer, go through, experience, cope with
enemy *n.* foe, adversary, rival, antagonist, opponent ★**friend**
energetic *adj.* dynamic, lively, vigorous, brisk, ▷*active* ★**sluggish**
energy *n.* vigor, endurance, stamina, vitality, force, power
enforce *v.* apply, administer, carry out
engage [1] *v.* employ, hire, charter, rent [2] occupy *That new book has occupied my mind for weeks*, oblige, operate [3] pledge, betroth
engine *n.* machine, device, motor, turbine, appliance
engrave *v.* etch, stipple, incise, sculpture, carve, chisel
engrossed *adj.* absorbed, fascinated, enthralled ★**bored**
enhance *v.* intensify, strengthen, amplify, improve ★**decrease**
enigma *n.* riddle, puzzle, cryptogram, mystery, problem
enjoy *v.* like, be fond of, delight in, appreciate, savor, ▷*relish* ★**detest**
enjoyable *adj.* likable, amusing, delicious, ▷*agreeable* ★**disagreeable**

Engines

Diesel engine
Internal combustion engine
Jet engine
Piston engine
Steam engine
Turbojet engine
Turboprop engine
Wankel engine

enlarge *v.* amplify, make bigger, expand, extend, magnify, increase, broaden, ▷*swell* ★**shrink**

enlighten *v.* inform, teach, explain to, educate, instruct ★**confuse**

enlist *v.* conscript, employ, engage, muster, sign up, volunteer

enmity *n.* animosity, acrimony, bitterness, hostility, antagonism, antipathy, ▷*hatred* ★**friendship**

enormous *adj.* immense, vast, tremendous, massive, ▷*huge* ★**tiny**

enough *adj.* sufficient, adequate, ample, plenty ★**insufficient**

enrage *v.* aggravate, incite, incense, infuriate, ▷*anger* ★**soothe**

enrich *v.* decorate, embellish, adorn, improve, adorn ★**impoverish**

enroll *v.* sign up, enlist, register, accept, admit ★**reject**

enslave *v.* bind, conquer, dominate, overpower, yoke ★**free**

ensue *v.* develop, follow, result, arise, ▷*happen* ★**precede**

ensure *v.* confirm, guarantee, insure, protect, secure

entangle *v.* tangle, snarl, ensnare, complicate, ▷*bewilder* ★**extricate**

enter *v.* go in, arrive, enroll, invade, commence, penetrate ★**leave**

enterprise *n.* endeavor, adventure, undertaking, concern, establishment

entertain *v.* amuse, charm, cheer, please, divert, beguile ★**bore**

enthrall *v.* captivate, charm, entrance, fascinate ★**bore**

enthusiasm *n.* fervor, ardor, interest, hobby, passion, eagerness

entice *v.* attract, beguile, coax, lead on, wheedle

entire *adj.* complete, intact, total, whole, full ★**partial**

entirely *adj.* absolutely, wholly, utterly *Our old dog came home, utterly tired and exhausted,* altogether ★**partially**

entitle [1] *v.* allow, authorize, empower *As president, I am empowered to sign this document,* enable [2] call, christen, term

entrance [1] *n.* (*en*-trance) way in, access *There is an access to the garden on the far side,* doorway, gate, opening [2] *v.* (en-*trance*) bewitch, captivate, charm ★**repel**

entreat *v.* beg, beseech, implore, ask

entry *n.* access, admission, access ▷*entrance* ★**exit**

envelop *v.* wrap, wind, roll, cloak, conceal, enfold

envious *adj.* jealous, grudging, covetous *Arlene cast a covetous eye at my new jacket,* resentful ★**content**

environment *n.* surroundings, neighborhood, vicinity, background

envy *v.* covet, grudge, desire, crave, resent

episode *n.* occasion, affair, circumstance, happening, installment

equal [1] *adj.* matching, like, alike, same ★**different** [2] fit *Is Joe really fit for this job?*

equip *v.* furnish, provide, supply, fit out, rig

equipment *n.* stores, supplies, outfit, tackle *When we arrived at the lake, Sam found he'd left his fishing tackle behind,* gear

equivalent *adj.* equal, comparable, alike, similar, interchangeable ★**unlike**

era *n.* epoch, age, generation, period, time

eradicate *v.* uproot, weed out, remove, stamp out, ▷*abolish*

erase *v.* cancel, rub out, obliterate, eliminate, ▷*delete* ★**mark**

erect [1] *adj.* upright, upstanding, rigid *The tent had a rigid metal frame* ★**relaxed** [2] *v.* build, construct, put up ★**demolish**

err *v.* be mistaken, blunder, go astray, mistake, misjudge, sin ★**correct**
errand *n.* mission, assignment, duty, job, ▷*task*
erratic *adj.* eccentric, irregular, unstable, unreliable ★**stable**
erroneous *adj.* untrue, false, faulty, inaccurate, ▷*wrong* ★**correct**
error *n.* mistake, fault, flaw, fallacy, untruth, ▷*blunder* ★**truth**
erupt *v.* blow up, explode, burst, vent, ▷*discharge* ★**absorb**
escape *v.* break free, get away, dodge, elude, evade, ▷*flee* ★**capture**
escort [1] *n.* (*es*-cort) guard, conductor, aide, attendant, procession [2] *v.* (es-*cort*) accompany, conduct
especially *adv.* chiefly, principally, notably
essay [1] *n.* effort, trial [2] theme, manuscript, composition *Whoever writes the best composition gets a prize*
essence [1] *n.* extract, juice, perfume [2] substance *He spoke well, but there was no substance in his speech*, core, pith, character
essential *adj.* necessary, needed, vital, requisite ★**superfluous**
establish *v.* situate, place, station, found, organize, set up ★**upset**
estate *n.* property, land, fortune, inheritance
esteem *v.* honor, respect, admire, ▷*like* ★**dislike**
estimate *v.* consider, calculate, figure, assess, reckon
estrange *v.* alienate, antagonize, separate ★**unite**
eternal *adj.* endless, ceaseless, forever, immortal, undying ★**temporary**
evacuate *v.* leave, desert, quit, ▷*abandon* ★**occupy**
evade *v.* elude, avoid, get away from, escape from ★**face**
evaporate *v.* vanish, dissolve, disappear, condense, dry up
even [1] *adj.* smooth, plane, flat, flush [2] balanced, equal ★**uneven** [3] yet, still
evening *n.* eve, eventide, sunset, ▷*dusk* ★**morning**
event *n.* occurrence, incident, happening
ever *adv.* always, evermore, perpetually, forever ★**never**
everlasting *adj.* continual, endless, permanent, lasting ★**temporary**
everyday *adj.* common, frequent, daily, familiar ★**occasional**
everything *n.* all, the whole, the lot
evict *v.* expel, eject, cast out, remove, kick out
evidence *n.* appearance, proof, sign, token, testimony
evident *adj.* obvious, apparent, plain, visible, conspicuous ★**uncertain**
evil *v.* wicked, sinister, wrong, bad, hurtful, sinful ★**good**
exact *adj.* accurate, precise, definite, correct, ▷*right* ★**inexact**
exaggerate *v.* magnify, overstate, overestimate, amplify ★**modify**
examine *v.* check, inspect, scrutinize, test, quiz, question
example *n.* case, sample, specimen, pattern, model, illustration
exasperate *v.* provoke, anger, annoy, aggravate ★**soothe**
excavate *v.* mine, quarry, shovel, dig up, discover, unearth ★**bury**
exceed *v.* excel, surpass, better, beat, outstrip
excel *v.* outdo, ▷*exceed*
excellent *adj.* admirable, good, superb, exquisite, ▷*splendid* ★**inferior**
except *prep.* with the exception of, barring, save, saving, omitting
exceptional *adj.* unique, unusual, rare *Margaret has a rare gift for the piano*, uncommon ★**common**
excess *n.* too much, extreme, glut, extravagance, extreme, ▷*surplus* ★**scarcity**
exchange *v.* trade, barter, swap, convert, change
excite *v.* inflame, inspire, provoke, rouse, thrill ★**quell**
excited *adj.* ablaze, wild, ecstatic, frantic, thrilled ★**bored**
exclaim *v.* state, say, utter, ejaculate, declare, cry out

exclude *v.* bar, shut out, prevent, boycott, forbid, leave out ★**include**

exclusive *adj.* only, personal, choice, particular, special ★**inclusive**

excuse *v.* forgive, pardon, absolve, exempt, release ★**accuse**

execute *v.* accomplish, do, carry out *The work was carried out just as I had expected*, achieve [2] put to death, hang

exempt *v.* excuse, release, discharge, relieve, exonerate

exercise [1] *n.* performance, lesson, lecture, training [2] *v.* apply, train, practice *We have been practicing our tennis for months*

exert *v.* apply, exercise, strain, struggle, toil

exhale *v.* breathe out, expel, expire ★**inhale**

exhaust [1] *v.* use up *We have used up all our butter*, consume, deplete, empty [2] overtire, fatigue, weaken

exhibition *n.* spectacle, show, fair, pageant, display

exhilarate *v.* invigorate, animate, stimulate, thrill ★**discourage**

exile *v.* deport, banish, relegate, transport, dismiss

exist *v.* be, live, breathe, subsist, stand

exit *n.* way out, outlet, egress, door

expand *v.* inflate, spread, dilate, extend, amplify, ▷*swell* ★**contract**

expansive *adj.* affable, genial, friendly, open, comprehensive

expect *v.* look out for, anticipate, assume, foresee, contemplate

expedition [1] *n.* outing, excursion, exploration, quest *As a child I spent long hours in the library in the quest for knowledge* [2] speed, dispatch, alacrity

expel *v.* evict, eject, discharge, throw out ★**admit**

expend *v.* spend, lay out, waste, consume, use up, ▷*exhaust* ★**save**

expensive *adj.* costly, high-priced, valuable, rich ★**cheap**

experience [1] *n.* training, practice, wisdom, knowledge [2] *v.* encounter, try, undergo, endure

experiment *n.* trial, test, check, venture

expert *n.* specialist, master, authority, professional ★**novice**

expire [1] *v.* breathe out, exhale [2] die, lapse *The lease on this house will lapse at the end of the year*, run out ★**begin**

explain *v.* elucidate, spell out, define, expound, teach ★**mystify**

explanation *n.* definition, outline, answer, meaning

explode *v.* detonate, blow up, go off, burst, discharge

exploit [1] *n.* deed, feat, act, stunt [2] *v.* take advantage of, profit by

export *v.* ship, send out, send abroad

expose *v.* show, reveal, exhibit, present, lay bare, betray ★**cover**

express [1] *v.* phrase, voice, put into words, utter [2] squeeze out [3] *adj.* speedy, fast

expression [1] *n.* phrase, idiom, sentence, statement [2] look, countenance, appearance

exquisite *adj.* dainty, subtle, fine, refined, ▷*beautiful* ★**coarse**

extend *v.* stretch, reach, lengthen, ▷*expand* ★**shorten**

extent *n.* breadth, expanse, width, bulk, mass, reach, duration

exterior [1] *n.* outside, surface [2] *adj.* external, outer, outdoor ★**interior**

extinct *adj.* defunct, dead, exterminated ★**living**

extinguish *v.* put out, blow out, abolish, destroy, quench ★**establish**

extract *v.* take out, select, remove, withdraw ★**insert**

extraordinary *adj.* unusual, incredible, strange, uncommon, marvelous ★**common**

extravagant *adj.* wasteful, reckless, prodigal, lavish ★**rational**

extreme [1] *adj.* excessive, outrageous, intense ★**moderate** [2] farthest, final, remote

extricate *v.* loose, loosen, remove, retrieve, pull out

exultant *adj.* rejoicing, jubilant, joyous, triumphant, ▷*elated* ★**depressed**

F f

fable *n.* myth, legend, story, fantasy ★**fact**
fabric *n.* cloth, textile, material
fabulous *adj.* imaginary, legendary *Robin Hood was a legendary figure because he never really existed,* mythical, marvelous, ▷*wonderful*
face [1] *n.* countenance, visage [2] front, frontage, façade *Although it was a new building, the old façade remained* [3] *v.* confront, be opposite
facetious *adj.* frivolous, jocular, humorous, witty, comical, ▷*funny* ★**serious**
facility *n.* ease, readiness, quickness, adroitness, knack
facsimile *n.* replica, copy, repro, photocopy
fact *n.* truth, deed, occurrence, event, reality, actuality ★**fiction**
factory *n.* plant, mill, works, shop
factual *adj.* true, actual, accurate, correct, ▷*real* ★**false**
fad *n.* craze, fashion, passion, desire, mania *My sister has a mania for teddy bears,* vogue
fade *v.* discolor, bleach, dwindle, dim
fail *v.* collapse, fall, miss, trip, lose, flop ★**succeed**
failing *n.* frailty, weakness, fault, flaw, ▷*defect* ★**advantage**
failure *n.* collapse, crash, fiasco, downfall ★**success**
faint [1] *adj.* indistinct *The writing was so indistinct that we could hardly read it,* soft, low, dim, feeble [2] *v.* swoon, pass out, collapse FEINT
fair [1] *adj.* just, equal, reasonable ★**unfair** [2] mediocre *He was not a good piano player, just mediocre,* middling, moderate [3] blonde, light-skinned, beautiful
faith *n.* trust, confidence, belief, fidelity, creed
faithful [1] *adj.* loyal, constant, staunch, true ★**faithless** [2] accurate, dependable *My watch is very dependable; it keeps accurate time* ★**inaccurate**
faithless *adj.* false, unfaithful, untrue ★**faithful**
fake *adj.* false, fictitious, pretended, ▷*bogus* ★**genuine**
fall [1] *v.* fall down, stumble, drop [2] decline, dwindle *My mother's shares had dwindled and were worth much less,* lower ★**rise**
fall down *v.* stumble, lose one's balance
fall through *v.* collapse, fail, founder *The family business had foundered during the recession*
fallacy *n.* flaw, fault, mistake, illusion, deception
false [1] *adj.* untrue, counterfeit, fake, inaccurate [2] dishonest, disloyal ★**reliable**
falsehood *n.* lie, fiction, fable, fabrication, untruth, fib ★**truth**
falter *v.* reel, totter, stumble, waver, tremble
fame *n.* glory, distinction, honor, eminence, renown
familiar [1] *adj.* common, frequent, well-known [2] intimate *Joe and Mary are intimate friends of mine,* close, dear
famine *n.* scarcity, hunger, shortage, starvation
famished *adj.* hungry, starving, ravenous
famous *adj.* famed, well-known, celebrated, legendary *My grandmother was very attractive: her beauty was legendary* ★**unknown**
fan *v.* ventilate, cool, blow, stimulate
fanatic *n.* enthusiast, zealot, follower, fan
fanciful *adj.* romantic, fantastic, imaginary, unreal ★**ordinary**
fancy [1] *adj.* decorative, beautiful, ornamental [2] *v.* desire, hanker after *I had been hankering after a sea trip all year,* yearn
fantastic *adj.* strange, bizarre, unfamiliar, romantic, ▷*fanciful* ★**ordinary**
far *adj.* distant, faraway, remote ★**near**
fare [1] *v.* manage *I managed quite well while my parents were abroad,* get along, happen [2] *n.* charge, cost, fee [3] food, meals, menu
farewell *n.* goodbye, parting, adieu *We bade our hosts adieu as we drove off*
farm [1] *v.* cultivate, raise, grow [2] *n.* farmstead, homestead, holding *We owned a small holding of land in the west*
fascinate *v.* bewitch, beguile, enthrall, engross ★**bore**

fashion [1] *n.* style, fad, mode, manner [2] *v.* form, carve, sculpt, devise
fast [1] *adj.* rapid, quick, speedy, brisk [2] *v.* starve, famish, go hungry
fasten *v.* fix, tie, attach, bind, hitch, truss **★unfasten**
fat *adj.* stout, corpulent *Uncle Harry was a corpulent old man,* ▷*plump* **★thin** [2] *n.* grease, oil, tallow
fatal *adj.* deadly, lethal, destructive, mortal **★harmless**
fate *n.* fortune, destiny, future, lot, portion
fathom *v.* unravel, understand, follow, comprehend
fatigue [1] *n.* tiredness, weariness [2] *v.* tire, exhaust, languish *The passengers from the shipwreck languished in an open boat*
fault [1] *n.* defect, flaw, imperfection [2] blame, responsibility, error
faulty *adj.* imperfect, defective, unreliable, unsound **★perfect**
favor [1] *n.* boon, courtesy, benefit [2] *v.* indulge, prefer, approve **★disapprove**
favorite [1] *n.* choice, darling, preference [2] *v.* best-liked, chosen, preferred
fawn *v.* crouch, crawl, grovel FAUN
fear [1] *n.* fright, alarm, terror, panic, shock **★courage** [2] *v.* dread, be afraid, doubt
fearful *adj.* timid, anxious, alarmed, worried, ▷*afraid* **★courageous**
fearless *adj.* gallant, courageous, daring, valiant *Despite her illness, my mother made a valiant effort to recover,* ▷*brave* **★timid**
feast *n.* banquet, repast, dinner
feat *n.* deed, exploit, achievement, performance, stunt FEET
feature *n.* mark, peculiarity, distinction, characteristic
fee *n.* charge, commission, cost
feeble *adj.* frail, faint, flimsy, puny, ▷*weak* **★strong**
feed *v.* nourish, sustain, foster, nurture *These plants must be nurtured if they are to survive*
feel *v.* touch, handle, perceive, comprehend, know, suffer

feign *v.* fake, pretend, act, sham FAIN
feint *n.* bluff, pretense, dodge, deception FAINT
fellow *n.* companion, comrade, associate, colleague
female *adj.* feminine, womanly, girlish, maidenly **★male**
fence [1] *n.* barrier, paling, barricade [2] *v.* dodge, evade, parry *The morning attack was parried by the defenders,* duel
ferocious *adj.* fierce, savage, brutal, grim, vicious **★gentle**
fertile *adj.* fruitful, productive, rich, abundant **★barren**
fervent *adj.* warm, passionate, enthusiastic, zealous ▷*ardent*

festival *n.* celebration, carnival, fête, jubilee
festive *adj.* convivial, jovial, sociable, gleeful, cordial ★**somber**
fetch *v.* bear, bring, carry, deliver, convey
fête *n.* bazaar, carnival, fair, festival
fetter *v.* manacle, handcuff, shackle, restrain
feud *n.* dispute, grudge, conflict, discord ★**harmony**
fever *n.* illness, infection, passion, excitement
few *adj.* scant, scanty, meager, paltry, not many
fiasco *n.* washout, calamity, disaster, failure
fib *n.* lie, falsehood, untruth
fickle *adj.* unstable, changeable, faithless, disloyal ★**constant**
fiction *n.* stories, fable, myth, legend, invention ★**fact**
fidelity *n.* faithfulness, loyalty, allegiance *I owe allegiance to my family and my country* ★**treachery**
fidget *v.* be nervous, fret, fuss, jiggle, squirm
field *n.* farmland, grassland, green, verdure, meadow, prairie
fiend *n.* devil, demon, imp, beast, brute
fiendish *adj.* atrocious, cruel, devilish, diabolical
fierce *adj.* barbarous, cruel, brutal, merciless, ▷*savage* ★**gentle**
fiery *adj.* passionate, inflamed, excitable, flaming ★**impassive**
fight *n.* & *v.* conflict, argument, encounter, combat, contest, battle
figure [1] *n.* symbol, character, numeral [2] form, shape, model [3] *v.* calculate, reckon *Bella has reckoned the amount correctly*
filch *v.* steal, thieve, sneak, purloin *Someone has purloined the letters from our mailbox*
file [1] *v.* scrape, grind, grate, rasp [2] *n.* binder, case, folder
fill *v.* load, pack, cram, replenish, occupy ★**empty**
filter *v.* sieve, sift, refine, clarify, screen, percolate PHILTER
filth *n.* impurity, dirt, soil, slime, smut ★**purity**
filthy *adj.* unclean, impure, nasty, foul, ▷*dirty* ★**pure**
final *adj.* terminal, closing, ultimate, conclusive, ▷*last*
find *v.* discover, achieve, locate, obtain, perceive, meet with *Our plans met with the approval of the committee* ★**lose** FINED
fine [1] *adj.* thin, minute, smooth, slender [2] excellent, sharp, keen, acute [3] *n.* forfeit, penalty
finesse *n.* skill, competence, deftness
finger [1] *v.* feel, grope, handle, touch [2] *n.* digit, thumb, pinkie
finish *v.* accomplish, complete, close, conclude, ▷*end* ★**begin**
fire [1] *n.* blaze, conflagration, heat [2] *v.* ignite, light, discharge
firm [1] *adj.* stable, steady, solid, substantial [2] *n.* company, business
first *adj.* beginning, earliest, initial, chief, principal
fishy *adj.* suspicious, dubious, doubtful ★**honest**
fissure *n.* breach, cleft, crack, cranny FISHER
fit *adj.* suitable, fitting, able, trim, hale, healthy
fitting *adj.* proper, suitable, appropriate, correct ★**unsuitable**
fix [1] *v.* repair, mend, attach, fasten [2] *n.* predicament, jam, pickle, plight *After the earthquake, the town was in a desperate plight*
flabby *adj.* baggy, drooping, feeble, sagging, slack
flag [1] *v.* droop, languish, dwindle, fail [2] banner, ensign, colors *The regimental colors were flying at half-mast*
flagrant *adj.* blatant, bold, brazen, arrant ★**secret**
flair *n.* knack, talent, faculty, ability, gift FLARE
flame *n.* fire, blaze, radiance
flap *v.* agitate, flutter, wave, swing, dangle
flare [1] *v.* blaze, burn, glare, flash, glow [2] *n.* signal, beacon FLAIR
flash *v.* gleam, glimmer, sparkle, twinkle, scintillate
flat [1] *adj.* level, smooth, even, horizontal [2] *n.* apartment, chambers
flatter *v.* blandish, toady, soft-soap, butter up, curry favor *He gives me presents, but only to curry favor with me* ★**criticize**

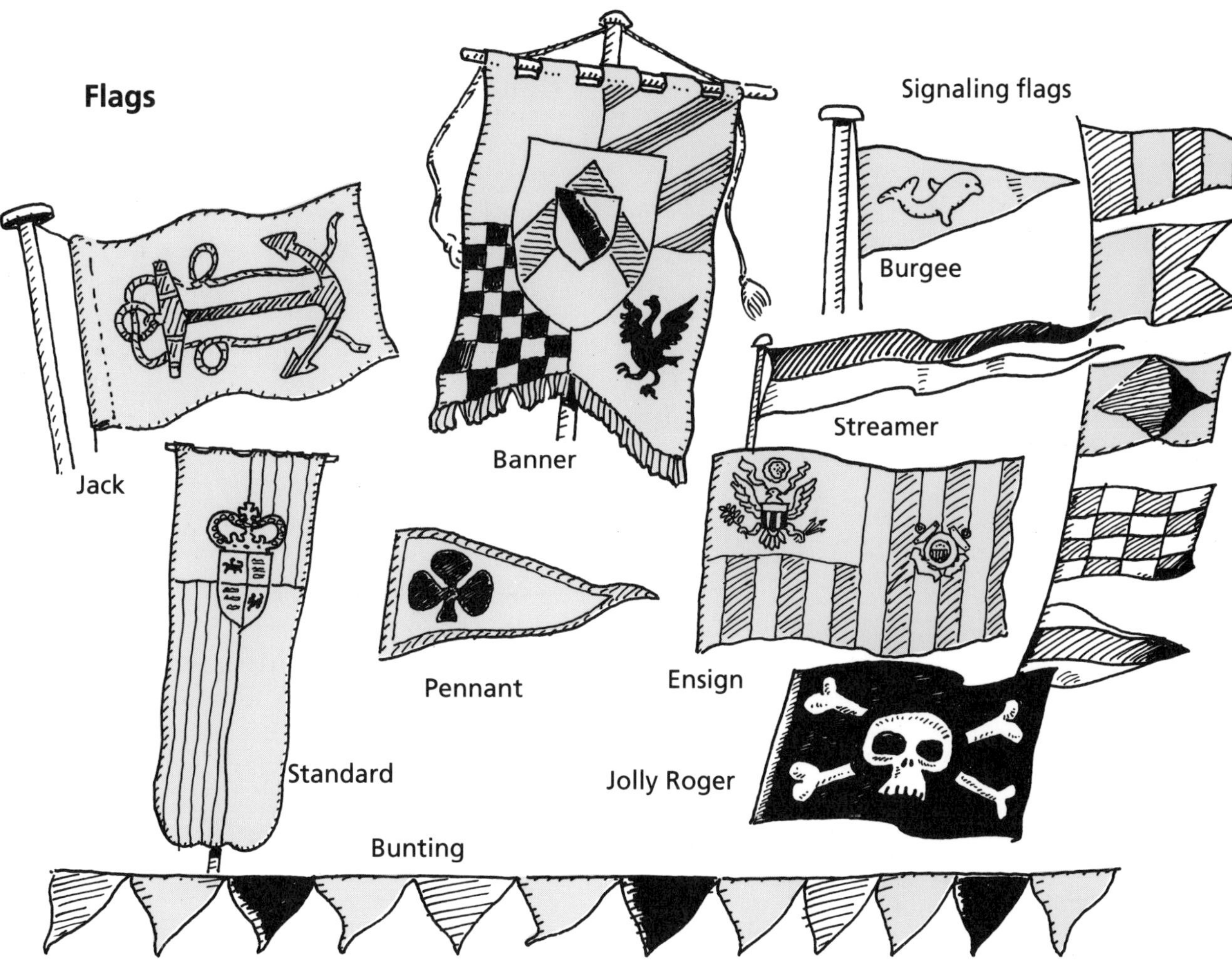

flavor *n.* taste, savor, tang, aroma, quality
flaw *n.* fault, defect, blemish, mark, weakness
flawless *adj.* perfect, immaculate, faultless, sound ★**imperfect**
flee *v.* escape, abscond, run away, bolt, vanish ★**stay** FLEA
fleet [1] *adj.* rapid, speedy, quick, nimble, ▷*swift* ★**slow** [2] navy, armada, flotilla *A flotilla of gunboats sailed up the river*
fleeting *adj.* passing, brief, momentary, temporary ★**lasting**
flexible *adj.* pliant, pliable, supple, elastic
flicker *v.* blaze, glitter, flare, burn, sparkle
flimsy *adj.* slight, meager, fragile, trivial ★**sturdy**
flinch *v.* cower, cringe, shrink, wince *I had twisted my ankle, and winced with pain as I climbed from the hill*
fling *v.* throw, pitch, cast, heave, ▷*hurl*
flippant *adj.* saucy, pert, brash, impudent, glib ★**earnest**
float *v.* drift, glide, hover, sail, swim
flock *n.* herd, drove, crush, group
flog *v.* beat, chastise, flay, lash, spank
flood *v.* deluge, engulf, inundate *The town was inundated after the river overflowed*, drown
floor *n.* deck, base, bottom, platform, level, story
flop *v.* flap, fall, drop, droop, fall flat
florid *adj.* ruddy, flushed, red, ornate ★**pale**
flounce *v.* bounce, fling, jerk, spring, bob
flounder [1] *v.* bungle, fail, falter, fumble [2] *n.* flatfish
flour *n.* meal, bran, farina FLOWER
flourish [1] *v.* shake, brandish, flaunt [2] blossom, bloom, prosper, ▷*thrive*
flow *v.* run, stream, glide, sweep, swirl, ▷*gush* FLOE

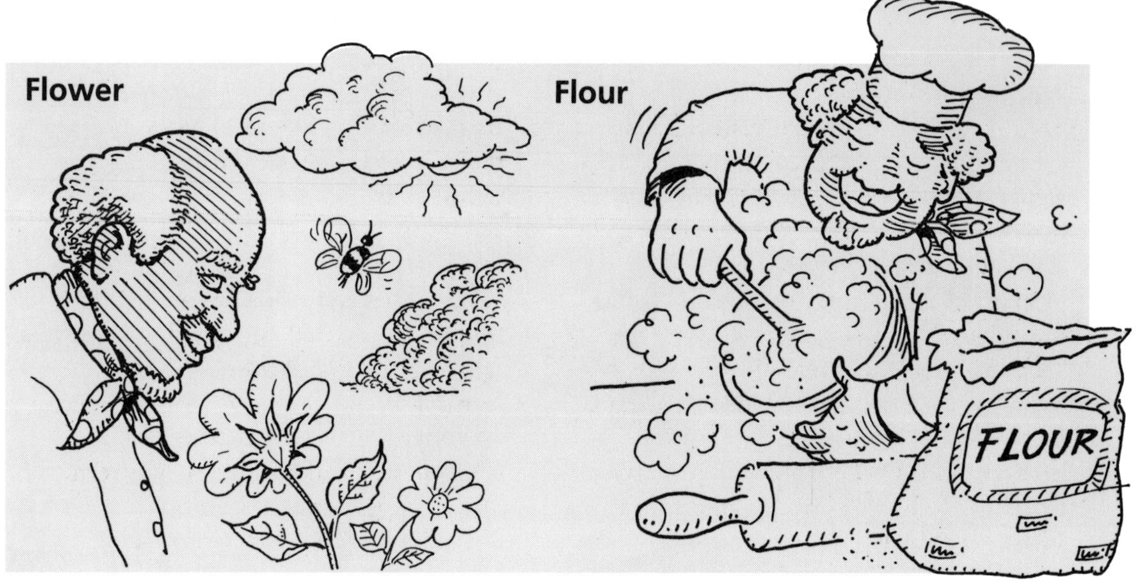

flower *n.* & *v.* blossom, bloom, bud FLOUR
fluent *adj.* vocal, facile, articulate *Sally is very articulate, and has a great command of language,* flowing, fluid
fluid *adj.* watery, flowing, liquid, runny ★**solid**
flummox *v.* baffle, confuse, fluster, confound, ▷*bewilder* ★**enlighten**
flush [1] *v.* glow, bloom, blush [2] douse, drench, rinse [3] *adj.* level, even
fluster *v.* bother, confuse, perturb, ▷*fuss* ★**calm**
flutter *v.* wave, flap, flop, flitter, hover, flit
fly [1] *v.* take flight, glide, soar, float [2] escape, hasten [3] *n.* winged insect
foam *n.* froth, scum, lather, suds, surf
foe *n.* enemy, opponent, rival, adversary ★**friend**
fog *n.* mist, vapor, haze, cloud
foil [1] *v.* defeat, overcome, elude [2] *n.* sheet metal, film, flake
fold *n.* & *v.* crease, hem, seam, crimp, pleat FOALED
follow [1] *v.* pursue, succeed, come after [2] understand, catch on to
folly *n.* silliness, foolishness, absurdity, craziness, ▷*nonsense* ★**wisdom**
fond *adj.* tender, loving, caring, ▷*affectionate* ★**hostile**
fondle *v.* pet, stroke, cuddle, caress, coddle
food *n.* nourishment, nutriment, provender, provisions, fare
fool [1] *n.* idiot, dunce, clown, blockhead, simpleton [2] *v.* deceive, trick, swindle
foolhardy *adj.* reckless, impetuous, madcap, ▷*rash* ★**cautious**
foolish *adj.* absurd, ridiculous, daft, ▷*silly* ★**wise**
for *prep.* on behalf of, toward, because of ★**against** FORE, FOUR
forbid *v.* bar, ban, prohibit, deter, hinder, prevent ★**allow**
force [1] *n.* energy, strength, might, power [2] *v.* make, compel, coerce *It's no use, you can't coerce me into flying home,* push
fore *adj.* first, front, leading FOR, FOUR
forecast *v.* foresee, predict, foretell, prophesy
foreign *adj.* alien, strange, remote, exotic, outlandish ★**domestic**
foremost *adj.* chief, leading, principal, uppermost
forfeit *v.* abandon, give up, lose, relinquish, sacrifice ★**reward**
forge [1] *v.* counterfeit, falsify, copy, imitate [2] construct, form, make, fashion
forgery *n.* fake, dud, counterfeit, imitation, phony
forget *v.* overlook, neglect, lose sight of ★**remember**
forgive *v.* pardon, absolve, reprieve, let off, overlook ★**blame**

forlorn *adj*. lonely, desolate, miserable, wretched ★**hopeful**
form [1] *v.* make, fabricate, fashion, contrive, create [2] *n*. manner, fashion, style [3] shape, figure *Models need to have excellent figures*
formal *adj*. stiff, solemn, ceremonial, ritualistic, aloof ★**informal**
former *adj*. earlier, previous, prior ★**later**
formidable *adj*. awful, terrible, alarming, terrifying, serious ★**trivial**
forsake *v.* abandon, give up, desert, discard, leave, ▷*quit* ★**resume**
forth *adv.* ahead, forward, onward, outward
forthright *adj*. frank, candid, direct, bald, blunt ★**devious**
forthwith *adv.* immediately, directly, at once, instantly ★**soon**
fortify [1] *v.* strengthen, confirm, corroborate, hearten [2] garrison, protect, buttress *The old house was crumbling, and the walls needed to be buttressed* ★**weaken**
fortitude *n*. courage, endurance, bravery, composure, ▷*strength* ★**cowardice**
fortunate *adj*. happy, felicitous, auspicious, rosy, ▷*lucky* ★**unfortunate**
fortune [1] *n*. affluence, wealth, treasure [2] chance, destiny, fate
forward [1] *adv.* onward, forth, ahead, before [2] *adj*. progressive, bold, audacious ★**modest** [3] advance, send, transmit
foster [1] *v.* help, promote, aid [2] care for, cherish, nurse
foul *adj*. mucky, nasty, filthy, dirty, murky ★**fair** FOWL
found *v.* create, build, erect, establish
foundation *n*. establishment, base, basis, groundwork *You will soon pick up Spanish, for you already have the groundwork*
fountain *n*. spring, well, reservoir, source
fowl *n*. bird, chicken, poultry FOUL
foxy *adj*. crafty, slick, cunning, tricky, ▷*artful* ★**naive**
fraction *n*. portion, part, division, ▷*fragment*
fracture *n*. break, cleft, crack, fissure, opening, ▷*split*
fragile *adj*. brittle, frail, delicate, dainty, ▷*flimsy* ★**robust**
fragment *n*. portion, bit, chip, morsel, piece, ▷*fracture*
fragrance *n*. aroma, smell, odor, ▷*scent*
frail *adj*. weak, feeble, infirm, ▷*fragile*
frame *n*. framework, casing, shape, mount, chassis
frank *adj*. sincere, candid, open, honest, blunt, ▷*truthful* ★**insincere**
frantic *adj*. excited, furious, distracted, wild, mad, ▷*frenzied* ★**calm**
fraud *n*. deceit, fake, extortion, swindle, ▷*forgery*
fraudulent *adj*. sham, fake, counterfeit, ▷*bogus* ★**genuine**
fray *n*. combat, contest, battle, brawl, ▷*rumpus*
freak *adj*. abnormal, bizarre *A snowstorm in the tropics would be bizarre*, queer, odd, unusual ★**common**
free [1] *adj*. unhindered, at liberty, liberated, unrestricted [2] gratuitous, gratis, without cost [3] *v.* let loose, unleash, release
freeze *n*. ice, frost, refrigerate FREES, FRIEZE
frenzied *adj*. agitated, excited, furious, hysterical *Lisa became hysterical when she saw the spider*, ▷*frantic* ★**placid**
frequent *adj*. repeated, numerous, recurrent, common, ▷*regular* ★**rare**
frequently *adv.* often, many times, commonly ★**rarely**
fresh *adj*. new, young, vigorous, blooming, recent, wholesome ★**stale**
fret *v.* worry, harass, irritate, torment, ▷*vex* ★**calm**
friction [1] *n*. rubbing, grating, contact, abrasion [2] ill-feeling, discord, dispute
friend *n*. companion, associate, ally, crony *On Saturdays, my father plays cards with some of his cronies*, pal, ▷*chum*
friendly *adj*. affable, amicable, kindly, cordial, ▷*genial* ★**hostile**
friendship *n*. affection, fellowship, fondness, harmony, ▷*concord* ★**enmity**
fright *n*. alarm, dread, dismay, terror, ▷*fear* ★**calm**
frighten *v.* daunt, dismay, scare, alarm, ▷*terrify* ★**reassure**

frightful *adj.* alarming, shocking, ghastly, ▷*horrible* ★**pleasant**
frigid *adj.* cool, chilly, icy, frozen, wintry ★**warm**
fringe *n.* edge, border, limits, outskirts
frisky *adj.* lively, spirited, playful, active ★**quiet**
frivolous *adj.* frothy, facetious, flippant, foolish, ▷*trivial* ★**serious**
frock *n.* robe, dress, gown, smock
frolic *v.* gambol, caper, frisk, sport
front *n.* fore, brow, forehead, face, façade, beginning ★**back**
frontier *n.* border, boundary, edge, limit
frosty *adj.* chilly, frigid, frozen, freezing, ▷*cold* ★**warm**
froth *n.* scum, bubbles, ▷*foam*
frown *v.* glower, grimace, glare, ▷*scowl* ★**smile**
frugal *adj.* thrifty, economical, careful, sparing *We were poor in the old days and needed to be sparing with our money,* ▷*meager* ★**wasteful**

Futile

I shall go in for the race but it's a forlorn hope I shall win!

fruitful *adj.* fertile, productive, flourishing ★**barren**
fruitless *adj.* unprofitable, sterile, barren, pointless ★**fruitful**
frustrate *v.* thwart, balk, foil, hinder, defeat ★**fulfill**
fugitive *n.* escapee, runaway, deserter
fulfill *v.* perform, render, please, accomplish, achieve ★**frustrate**
full *adj.* loaded, packed, laden, charged, abundant, complete ★**empty**
fumble *v.* grope, spoil, mismanage, flail, ▷*bungle*
fun *n.* sport, frolic, gaiety, jollity, entertainment, amusement
function [1] *n.* service, purpose, activity [2] affair, party, gathering [3] *v.* act, operate, work
fund *n.* stock, supply, pool, store, treasury *The city treasury has a good surplus this year*
fundamental *adj.* basic, essential, primary, essential ★**unimportant**
funny *adj.* comical, droll, amusing, ridiculous, ▷*humorous* ★**solemn**
furious *adj.* agitated, angry, fierce, intense, ▷*frantic* ★**calm**
furnish [1] *v.* supply, provide, offer [2] equip, fit out
furrow *n.* groove, channel, hollow, seam, rib
further [1] *adj.* extra, more, other, supplementary, [2] *v.* advanced, aid, hasten
furtive *adj.* secretive, sly, hidden, ▷*stealthy* ★**open**
fury *n.* anger, frenzy, ferocity, passion, ▷*rage* ★**calm**
fuse *v.* melt, smelt, combine, merge, solder, ▷*join*
fuss *n.* stir, excitement, tumult, bustle, ▷*ado* ★**calm**
fussy *adj.* busy, faddish, fastidious, finicky, exacting ★**plain**
futile *adj.* useless, in vain, hopeless, barren, forlorn *I'll enter the race, but it's a forlorn hope that I could win,* ineffective ★**effective**
future *adj.* forthcoming, coming, impending, eventual
fuzzy *adj.* murky, foggy, misty, unclear

G g

gain *v.* get, win, acquire, attain, profit
gale *n.* storm, wind, hurricane, tornado, cyclone
gallant *adj.* courageous, noble, chivalrous, ▷*brave*
gallop *v.* dash, run, career, rush
gamble *v.* bet, risk, wager, chance GAMBOL
gambol *v.* prance, romp, frisk, frolic, ▷*jump* GAMBLE
game [1] *n.* sport, pastime, contest, competition ★**work** [2] *n.* quarry, prey
gang *n.* crew, team, troop, crowd, cluster, party
gap *n.* space, blank, hole, break, cranny, chink, opening, crack, interval
gape *v.* yawn, stare, gaze, gawk, ▷*look*
garbage, *n.* trash, rubbish, refuse, waste, slops
garden *n.* yard, patio, park
garment *n.* clothes, dress, attire, robe, costume, ▷*clothing*
garret *n.* attic, loft, back room
gas *n.* vapor, fume, mist, smoke
gasp *v.* gulp, pant, choke, ▷*breathe*
gate *n.* door, portal, gateway GAIT
gather [1] *v.* collect, pick up, pick, draw, amass, assemble, flock, hoard, acquire ★**disperse** [2] *v.* understand *I understand that you have been elected treasurer of the club*, assume, judge
gathering *n.* meeting, assembly, function, affair, company, collection
gaudy *adj.* flashy, cheap, tawdry, loud, showy
gaunt, *adj.* thin, lean, skinny, spare, ▷*haggard* ★**robust**
gauge [1] *n.* measure, meter, rule [2] *v.* judge, measure, estimate *We must estimate what the weather conditions will be*, probe GAGE
gaze *v.* stare, look, regard, contemplate
gear *n.* tackle, array, accessories, machinery, harness, equipment
gem *n.* jewel, stone, treasure
general *adj.* normal, usual, habitual, customary, total, whole ★**local**
generous *adj.* free, liberal, kind ★**selfish**
genial *adj.* cheerful, cheery, sunny, hearty, cordial, pleasant ▷*jolly* ★**cold**
genius *n.* brilliance, prowess, talent, power, skill, cleverness, brains ★**stupidity**
genteel *adj.* refined, polished, civil, courteous, well-bred, polite, elegant ★**boorish**
gentle [1] *adj.* easy, mild, soft, kind, moderate, tender, humane [2] *adj.* gradual, faint, feeble, slight *The field had a slight slope as it came down to the river*
genuine [1] *adj.* real, authentic, true, sound [2] *adj.* sincere, honest, candid, frank ★**false**
germ *n.* microbe, seed, embryo, nucleus
gesture *n.* sign, signal, motion, nod, shrug, movement
get [1] *v.* acquire, obtain, gain, win, receive, secure, achieve, inherit ★**forfeit** [2] *v.* understand, catch on *It took little Johnny some time to catch on to what I meant*, fathom, figure out, learn
get up *v.* arise, awake, awaken
get rid of *v.* discard, reject, throw away, scrap
ghastly *adj.* shocking, hideous, horrible, fearful, terrible, frightful
ghost *n.* spook, spirit, specter, banshee, phantom, apparition
ghostly *v.* uncanny, haunted, eerie, weird
giant *adj.* mammoth, huge, colossal, enormous, tremendous, immense, ▷*big, gigantic* ★**tiny**
gibber *v.* gabble, prattle, jabber
gibberish *n.* nonsense, drivel, rubbish
gibe *v.* jeer, sneer, scoff, deride, ▷*taunt*
giddy *adj.* dizzy, whirling, reeling, unsteady, wild, reckless
gift [1] *n.* present, donation, bounty, boon [2] *n.* talent, skill *Her skill was so great that I knew she must have been born with it*, ability, power
gigantic *adj.* stupendous, titanic, colossal, ▷*giant* ★**minute**
giggle *v.* chuckle, chortle, cackle, snicker, ▷*laugh*
gingerly *adv.* carefully, daintily, warily, cautiously

girder *n.* rafter, joist, beam
girl *n.* maid, maiden, miss, damsel, young woman, lass, wench
girlish *adj.* maidenly, dainty, feminine
girth *n.* circumference, perimeter, fatness, breadth
gist *n.* essence, substance, kernel, nub, pith
give [1] *v.* donate, grant, distribute, bestow [2] bend, yield *The wooden footbridge soon yielded under his weight and crashed into the stream*, relax, recede [3] produce, yield [4] pronounce, utter, emit ★**take**
give back *v.* return, restore
give forth *v.* emit, send out, radiate
give in *v.* surrender, quit, yield
give off *v.* belch, emit, exude
give up *v.* surrender, give in, relinquish, hand over
giver *n.* donor, bestower, presenter
glad *adj.* joyful, joyous, delighted, pleased, ▷*happy* ★**sorry**
gladden *v.* make happy, gratify, delight, elate, ▷*please* ★**grieve**
gladly *adv.* freely, readily, cheerfully, willingly
glamour *n.* romance, interest, fascination, attraction, enchantment
glance [1] *n.* look, glimpse, peep [2] *v.* peer, notice [3] *v.* brush, graze, shave *The bullet merely grazed his head*
glare [1] *v.* blaze, glow, flare, sparkle, dazzle [2] frown, glower, stare
glaring [1] *adj.* sparkling, dazzling [2] *adj.* blatant, notorious, conspicuous
glass *n.* tumbler, goblet, beaker, mirror, looking glass
glaze *v.* polish, gloss, burnish, varnish
gleam *v.* sparkle, glitter, flash, glisten, twinkle
glee *n.* jollity, gaiety, elation, triumph, ▷*happiness*
glib *adj.* fluent, slick, smooth, facile, talkative
glide *v.* slide, slither, slip, soar, sail, skate, skim
glimmer *v.* sparkle, scintillate, flicker, glow, gleam
glimpse *v.* spy, spot, glance, view
glisten *v.* shine, glitter, glow, gleam
glitter *v.* gleam, sparkle, flash, glint, glisten, scintillate
gloat *v.* whoop, exult, crow, revel, triumph
globe *n.* ball, sphere, planet, earth, world
gloom *n.* darkness, gloaming, dusk, shadow, dimness, bleakness ★**light**
gloomy *adj.* cheerless, black, dark, bleak, cloudy, overcast, dismal, dour, glum, melancholy, ▷*dreary* ★**happy**
glorious *adj.* brilliant, lustrous, noble, exalted, renowned, ▷*splendid* ★**dull**
glory *n.* brilliance, radiance, pride, ▷*splendor*
gloss *n.* luster, sheen, shimmer, polish, ▷*glaze*
glossy *adj.* shiny, burnished, sleek, slick, polished
glow *n.* & *v.* glare, glitter, bloom, blush, flush, shine, gleam, twinkle
glower *v.* frown, stare, scowl, glare
glue [1] *n.* paste, gum, cement, mucilage, adhesive, rubber [2] *v.* stick, fasten
glum *adj.* sullen, sulky, morose, miserable, dejected, downcast, ▷*gloomy*
glut *n.* abundance, plenty, too much, surplus
glutton *n.* gorger, stuffer, crammer, pig, gormandizer, gourmand
gnash *v.* grind, chomp, bite, crunch
gnaw *v.* chew, nibble, bite, champ, consume
go [1] *v.* walk, pass, move, travel, depart, proceed [2] *v.* stretch, reach, extend *The prairie extended as far as the mountain range*
go after *v.* pursue, chase, follow
go ahead *v.* progress, proceed, continue
go away *v.* leave, depart, vanish, disappear
go back *v.* return, resume, withdraw
go by *v.* pass, elapse, vanish
go in *v.* enter, advance, invade, penetrate
go in for *v.* enter, take part, participate, compete
go off *v.* explode, blow up, depart
go on *v.* continue, advance, proceed, move ahead, keep up
go up *v.* climb, mount, rise, ▷*ascend*
goad *v.* prod, incite, impel, drive, urge, sting, worry
goal *n.* target, ambition, aim, object, destination
gobble *v.* devour, gorge, swallow, gulp, bolt
goblin *n.* sprite, demon, gnome, elf

God *n.* the Creator, the Father, the Almighty, Jehovah, the Divinity, the Holy Spirit, King of Kings, the Supreme Being

godless *adj.* unholy, unclean, wicked, savage, profane ★**righteous**

golden *adj.* excellent, precious, brilliant, bright

good [1] *adj.* excellent, admirable, fine [2] favorable, *Spring is a favorable time to clean the house* advantageous, profitable [3] righteous, moral, true *My neighbors are nice, considerate people* [4] clever, skillful, expert [5] fit, proper, suited ★**bad**

goodness *n.* excellence, merit, worth, honesty, kindness, ▷*virtue* ★**evil**

goods *n.* wares, commodities, cargo, load, material, belongings

gorge [1] *v.* swallow, gulp, devour, ▷*eat* [2] *n.* canyon, glen, valley

gorgeous *adj.* beautiful, ravishing, stunning, superb, magnificent

gossip *v.* chat, chatter, prattle, tittle-tattle

gouge *v.* excavate, groove, dig out

govern *v.* rule, reign, manage, direct, guide, control, conduct, command

government *n.* rule, administration, supervision, parliament

governor *n.* director, manager, leader, chief, overseer, head of state

gown *n.* robe, dress, frock

grace *n.* elegance, refinement, polish, symmetry, ▷*beauty*

graceful *adj.* beautiful, lovely, shapely, refined, ▷*elegant*

gracious *adj.* amiable, kind, suave, urbane, affable, elegant ★**churlish**

grade [1] *n.* class, rank, degree [2] *n.* slope, gradient, incline, slant

gradual *adj.* by degrees, step by step, continuous, little by little ★**sudden**

graft [1] *v.* splice, insert, bud, plant [2] *n.* bribery, corruption

grain *n.* fiber, crumb, seed, particle, atom, bit, drop

grand *adj.* splendid, impressive, stately, magnificent, wonderful, superb

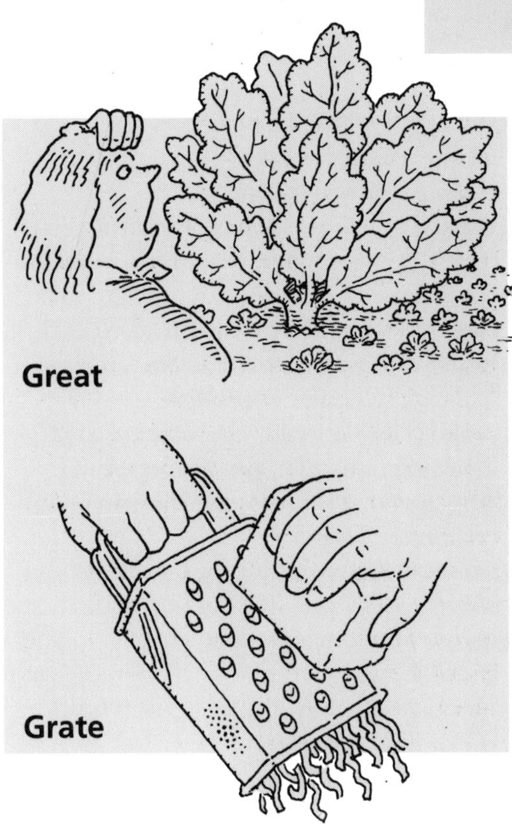

grandeur *n.* magnificence, splendor, majesty, lordliness

grant [1] *n.* bounty, award, subsidy [2] *v.* bestow, donate *We all donated some money to help the earthquake victims*, confer, give

grapple *v.* struggle, tussle, wrestle, seize, grasp, clutch

grasp [1] *v.* grip, seize, take, grab, hold [2] *v.* understand, comprehend

grasping *adj.* greedy, avaricious, covetous, miserly ★**generous**

grate [1] *v.* rasp, file, jar, clash, rub, grind [2] *v.* annoy, irritate, vex [3] *n.* fireplace GREAT

grateful *adj.* thankful, appreciative, obliged, indebted

gratify *v.* delight, satisfy, please, content, enchant, indulge, favor ★**displease**

gratitude *n.* thankfulness, appreciation, obligation

grave [1] *adj.* solemn, sober, momentous, dignified, majestic [2] *adj.* essential, important *I have important news to reveal* [3] *n.* tomb, vault, shrine

gravity [1] *n.* seriousness, solemnity, importance, significance [2] *n.* force, gravitation, weight

graze [1] *v.* scrape, brush, shave, glance [2] browse, crop, bite GRAYS
grease *n.* fat, suet, tallow, oil
great [1] *adj.* large, considerable, bulky, huge, ample [2] important, elevated, noted *Here is a list of noted citizens of this town* [3] main, chief, principal GRATE
greedy *adj.* gluttonish, voracious, grasping, selfish, acquisitive ★**unselfish**
green [1] *adj.* emerald, jade, turquoise [2] ungrown, immature, raw *During the war, many recruits to the army were raw country lads,* untrained ★**expert**
greet *v.* welcome, accost, hail, salute, salaam, address
grief *n.* woe, sadness, regret, distress, anguish, ▷*sorrow* ★**joy**
grievance *n.* injury, hardship, complaint, wrong, trial ★**boon**
grieve *v.* lament, deplore, mourn, sorrow, be sad, afflict, hurt ★**rejoice**
grievous *adj.* lamentable, deplorable, grave, critical, severe, mortal
grill [1] *v.* fry, broil [2] *n.* grating, grid
grim [1] *adj.* serious, stern, harsh, solemn, dour, forbidding [2] horrid, dreadful, terrible, ▷*somber* ★**mild**
grime *n.* smut, soil, dust, soot, ▷*dirt*
grin *n.* & *v.* smile, beam, smirk, simper
grind [1] *v.* scrape, file, crush, powder [2] sharpen, whet, grate
grip *v.* grasp, grab, snatch, clasp, seize, ▷*hold* ★**loosen**
grisly *adj.* horrid, horrible, dreadful, ghastly, ▷*grim*
grit [1] *n.* powder, dust, sand, gravel [2] nerve, mettle, pluck, ▷*courage*
groan *v.* moan, complain, grumble, creak GROWN
groom [1] *n.* husband, bridegroom [2] stable-boy, servant, hostler [3] *v.* spruce, tidy, preen
groove *n.* furrow, ridge, corrugation, channel, rut, score
grope *v.* feel, handle, finger, manipulate, touch, pick

Groups of Animals

a chatter of parakeets
a drey of squirrels
a drove of cattle
a flock of birds
a herd of elephants
a mob of kangaroos
a pack of wolves
a pride of lions
a school of porpoises
a sloth of bears
a swarm of bees
a troop of monkeys
a colony of seals
a cete of badgers
a skulk of foxes
a litter of cats

gross [1] *adj.* large, bulky, unwieldy, massive [2] coarse, vulgar, crude [3] outrageous, glaring, flagrant *The car driver was arrested for a flagrant disregard of the safety rules*
grotesque *adj.* deformed, malformed, misshapen, freakish, abnormal, bizarre
ground [1] *n.* dry land, soil, earth, dust [2] bottom, base, foundation
grounds [1] *n.* foundation, cause, basis, excuse [2] dregs, sediment, silt [3] garden, parkland, estate

Growls, grunts, and other animal noises

Bees buzz	Lions roar
Cats meow	Mice squeak
Cows moo	Owls hoot
Dogs bark	Pigs grunt
Dogs also growl	Roosters crow
Ducks quack	Snakes hiss
Horses neigh	Wolves howl

group [1] *n.* division, section, branch [2] gang, throng, cluster, bunch, class, set
grovel *v.* fawn, crouch, crawl, toady, cringe, wallow, cower
grow [1] *v.* increase, advance, expand, extend, develop, raise [2] sprout, germinate, shoot
growl *v.* snarl, snap, threaten, thunder
growth *n.* expansion, development, advance, ▷*increase*
grow up *v.* mature, develop, ripen
grubby *adj.* messy, dirty, mucky
grudge *n.* & *v.* hate, envy, dislike, spite
gruesome *adj.* frightful, hideous, ghastly, ▷*grisly*
gruff *adj.* husky, throaty, croaky, blunt, churlish, crusty, curt ***affable**
grumble *v.* complain, snivel, murmur, growl, protest
grumpy *adj.* disgruntled, dissatisfied, surly, sour, irritable, sullen ***affable**
grunt *n.* & *v.* snort, groan ***growl**
guarantee *n.* warranty, assurance, security, pledge
guard [1] *n.* protector, sentry, guardian, watchman [2] *v.* protect, defend, watch over, shelter, shield
guess *v.* surmise, conjecture, judge, think, suspect, suppose
guest *n.* visitor, caller GUESSED
guide [1] *n.* pilot, director, leader, controller [2] *v.* steer, navigate, lead, direct, manage, conduct *Our teacher conducted us to the bus, and we all climbed aboard*
guild *n.* club, trade union, association, federation, fellowship, band, society
guile *n.* knavery, foul play, trickery, deceit, cunning, fraud ***honesty**
guilty *adj.* blameworthy, sinful, wicked, wrong ***innocent**
guise *n.* garb, pose, posture, role, aspect *The motel manager's aspect was a little too friendly; we did not trust him*, appearance GUYS
gulch *n.* valley, gully, ravine
gulf [1] *n.* bay, basin, inlet [2] chasm, opening, abyss, depths
gullible *adj.* credulous, innocent, naive, trusting
gully *n.* trench, ditch, channel, ravine
gulp *v.* swallow, consume, guzzle, devour
gun *n.* rifle, cannon, revolver, pistol, automatic, shotgun
gurgle *v.* ripple, murmur, purl, babble
gush *v.* stream, spurt, spout, flow, run, pour out
gust *n.* blast, blow, squall, wind
gusto *n.* relish, zest, eagerness, zeal, pleasure
gutter *n.* moat, ditch, dike, drain, gully, channel, groove
guzzle *v.* gulp, imbibe, drink, swill, quaff

H h

habit [1] *n.* custom, practice, routine, way, rule [2] mannerism *Jim had a mannerism of holding his ear as he thought*, addiction, trait
hack *v.* chop, mangle, gash, slash
hackneyed *adj.* stale, trite, commonplace, tired ★**new**
hag *n.* crone, harridan, witch, virago *I know I have a temper, but Julia is a real virago*
haggard *adj.* drawn, wan, pinched, thin, ▷*gaunt* ★**hale**
haggle *v.* bargain, barter, bicker, dispute ★**yield**
hail [1] *v.* salute, call to, accost, welcome, greet [2] *n.* shower, storm, torrent *Last summer it rained torrents* HALE
hair *n.* locks, mane, tresses, strand
hale *adj.* hearty, robust, sound, fit, ▷*healthy* ★**ill** HAIL
half *n.* division, fraction, segment
hall *n.* entrance, foyer, corridor, lobby, vestibule *The landlord provided a table and chair for the apartment house vestibule* HAUL
hallow *v.* sanctify, consecrate, bless, dedicate, make holy
hallucination *n.* illusion, fantasy, delusion, mirage, dream ★**reality**
halt *v.* end, pause, rest, cease, ▷*stop* ★**start**
halting *adj.* faltering, hestitating, wavering, awkward ★**fluent**
hammer [1] *v.* beat, pound, bang [2] *n.* mallet, gavel *The leader banged his gavel on the desk and called for order*
hamper [1] *v.* hinder, interfere, impede, curb ★**aid** [2] *n.* basket, creel *We watched the fishermen carrying creels of herring*, crate
hand [1] *v.* give, pass, present, yield [2] *n.* fist, palm
handicap *n.* defect, disability, drawback, restriction ★**advantage**
handicraft *n.* skill, hobby, art, workmanship, craft, occupation
handle [1] *n.* shaft, holder, grip [2] *v.* feel, touch, finger, work, wield

Habitations

Apartment
Bungalow
Cabin
Castle
Chalet
Chateau
Cottage
Flat
Hacienda
Igloo
Lodge
Mansion
Palace
Ranch-house
Shack
Shanty
Villa

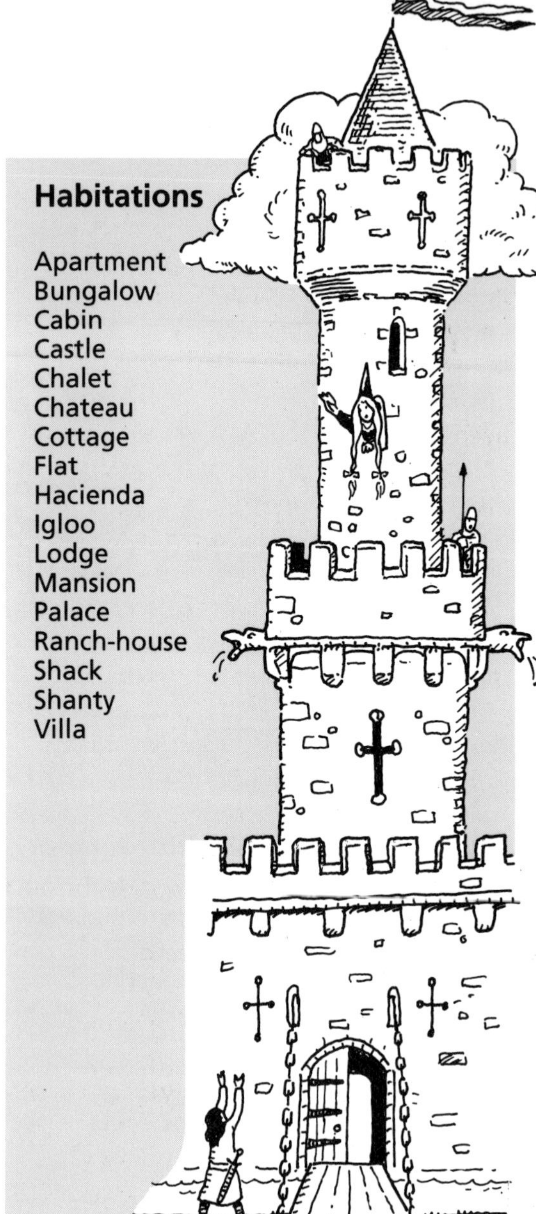

handsome [1] *adj.* good-looking, graceful, attractive [2] generous, lavish *Aunt Betsy is always so lavish with presents for the children,* HANSOM
handy *adj.* ready, convenient, deft, skilled ★**clumsy**
hang *v.* dangle, suspend, sag, droop, swing
hanker for *v.* long for, yearn for, crave, desire ★**dislike**
haphazard *adj.* accidental, random, aimless, casual, ▷*chance* ★**deliberate**
hapless *adj.* ill-fated, luckless, unlucky, ▷*miserable* ★**lucky**
happen *v.* occur, take place, come about, result

happening *n.* event, incident, occurrence, occasion
happiness *n.* delight, ecstasy, gaiety, joy, enjoyment, ▷*bliss* ★**unhappiness**
happy *adj.* cheerful, blithe, content, joyous, jubilant, ▷*merry* ★**unhappy**
harass *v.* beset, annoy, upset, bother, ▷*distress* ★**assist**
harbor [1] *n.* port, anchorage, mooring [2] refuge, shelter, safety *At last we were back in the safety of our home* [3] *v.* give shelter to
hard [1] *adj.* firm, stony, rocky, solid ★**soft** [2] difficult, tough *I had a very tough problem to solve*, perplexing ★**easy** [3] stern, severe
hardly *adv.* seldom, rarely, scarcely, slightly
hardship *n.* trouble, suffering, want, ▷*difficulty* ★**ease**
hardy *adj.* rugged, sturdy, tough, healthy, rugged, ▷*robust* ★**weak**
hark *v.* listen, hear, ▷*listen*
harm [1] *n.* damage, mischief, ruin, wrong, abuse, sin [2] *v.* abuse, blemish, hurt *I'm sorry, I didn't mean to hurt you*, injure ★**benefit**
harmful *adj.* injurious, evil, wicked, damaging ★**harmless**
harmless *adj.* safe, gentle, innocuous, innocent ★**harmful**
harmony *n.* agreement, conformity, accord, unity, goodwill ★**discord**
harp [1] *n.* lyre, stringed instrument [2] *v.* (on) dwell upon *I tried to forget our quarrel, but Carol continued to dwell upon it*, allude to
harrow *v.* agonize, taunt, distress, torture, harry, ▷*harass* ★**hearten**
harsh [1] *adj.* jarring, coarse, rough [2] severe, strict, ruthless ★**mild**
harvest *v.* plow, harrow, reap, pluck
hash [1] *n.* mess, confusion, muddle [2] hot pot, stew, goulash
hassle *n.* argument, bother, difficulty, squabble, struggle ★**peace**
haste *n.* rush, bustle, dispatch, urgency, swiftness, ▷*hurry* ★**delay**
hasten *v.* hurry, hustle, quicken, accelerate, speed up ★**dawdle**
hasty *adj.* hurried, rushed, abrupt, indiscreet ★**deliberate**
hate *v.* abhor, detest, loathe, ▷*despise* ★**like**
hateful *adj.* abominable, loathsome, odious, despicable ★**pleasing**
haughty *adj.* arrogant, disdainful, scornful, snobbish ★**humble**
haul *v.* pull, draw, tug, drag, heave HALL
have *v.* possess, occupy, own, receive, take in
haven *n.* harbor, port, refuge, retreat, sanctum *This is my inner sanctum, the room where I relax alone*, shelter
havoc *n.* wreckage, ruin, destruction, disorder, mayhem
hay *n.* pasture, soilage, grass, straw HEY
haze *n.* cloud, vapor, fog, mist, vagueness HAYS
hazy *adj.* foggy, misty, murky, vague, uncertain ★**clear**
head [1] *n.* visage, skull, cranium, pate [2] *adj.* chief, main, principal
heading *n.* caption, headline, title, inscription
headlong *adj.* rough, dangerous, reckless, ▷*rash*
heal *v.* soothe, treat, cure, mend, restore HEEL, HE'LL
healthy *adj.* fine, fit, hearty, sound, vigorous, ▷*hale* ★**sick**
heap *n.* pile, mass, mound, collection
hear *v.* listen to, hearken, overhear HERE
hearten *v.* assure, encourage, embolden, inspire ★**dishearten**
heartless *adj.* brutal, callous, cold, ▷*unkind* ★**kind**
hearty *adj.* cordial, sincere, earnest, honest, jovial ★**cold**
heat [1] *n.* warmth, temperature [2] passion, ardor, fervor *She spoke with great fervor about what she believed*
heave *v.* fling, cast, hurl, hoist, pull, tug
heavenly *adj.* beautiful, blessed, divine, lovely ★**hellish**
heavy *adj.* weighty, hefty, ponderous, loaded ★**light**
hectic *adj.* excited, fast, frenzied, wild, ▷*frantic* ★**leisurely**
heed *v.* listen, pay attention, follow, respect ★**ignore**

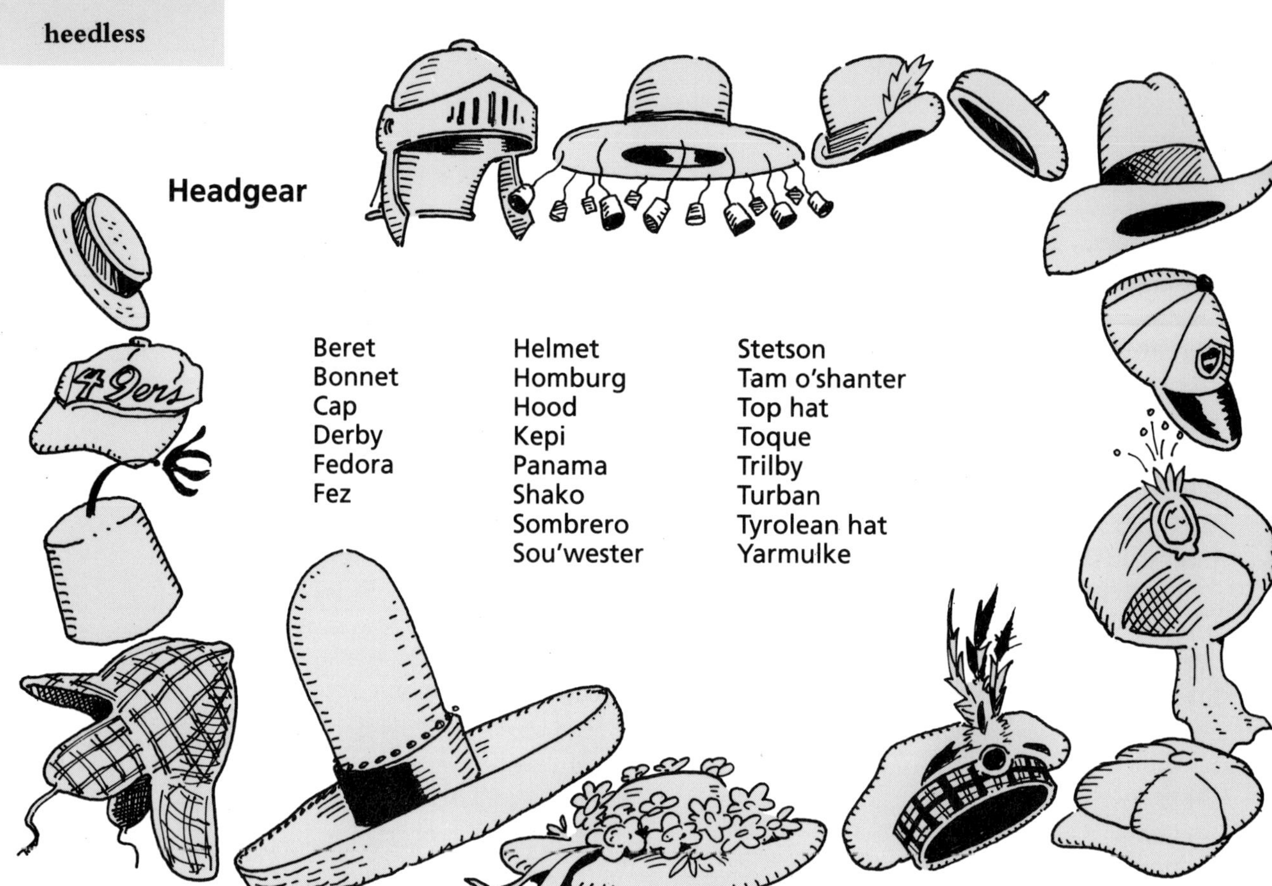

heedless *adj.* thoughtless, reckless, unwary, ▷*careless*

height *n.* altitude, stature, top, apex, peak ★**depth**

hellish *adj.* abominable, awful, inhuman, fiendish ★**heavenly**

help [1] *n.* aid, support, assistance [2] *v.* lend a hand *We all lent a hand in building the hut,* aid, assist ★**hinder**

helpful *adj.* caring, considerate, ▷*useful* ★**useless**

helping *n.* ration, portion, piece, serving *Mike would like a second helping. He's still hungry,* share

helpless *adj.* incapable, powerless, unfit, forlorn, ▷*weak* ★**strong**

hem *n.* edge, border, fringe, margin

hence *adv.* accordingly, thus, therefore, henceforward

herd *n.* crowd, crush, flock, group, mass, mob, horde HEARD

here *adv.* present, attending, hereabouts, in this place HEAR

heritage *n.* inheritance, legacy, birthright, tradition

hermit *n.* recluse, solitary, monk

hero *n.* champion, daredevil, star, idol, conqueror ★**villain**

heroic *adj.* bold, fearless, lion-hearted, gallant, ▷*brave* ★**cowardly**

heroine *n.* celebrity, goddess *Mary Pickford was a goddess of the silent screen,* idol, star. lead

hesitate *v.* falter, dither, doubt, wait

hew *v.* chop, cut, fashion, carve, sculpt HUE

hidden *adj.* concealed, covered, veiled, unseen ★**open**

hide *v.* conceal, cover, obscure, bury, cloak ★**reveal** HIED

hideous *adj.* repulsive, unsightly, gruesome, horrible, ▷*ugly* ★**beautiful**

hiding *n.* beating, thrashing, caning

high [1] *adj.* tall, towering, lofty, elevated [2] shrill *The referee blew his whistle, which had a shrill tone,* treble, strident [3] expensive, costly, dear ★**low**

highbrow *adj.* brainy, educated, intellectual

hijack *v.* raid, kidnap, seize, snatch, steal
hike *v.* walk, ramble, tramp
hilarious *adj.* amusing, gleeful, jocular, entertaining, ▷*funny* ★**serious**
hill *n.* hummock, rise, climb, height, elevation, slope
hinder *v.* hamper, impede, obstruct, retard, frustrate, ▷*handicap* ★**help**
hindrance *n.* impediment, obstruction, check, barrier ★**aid**
hint *n.* clue, inkling *We had just an inkling of what was in store*, whisper, tip, suggestion
hire *v.* charter, rent, lease, retain, engage ★**dismiss** HIGHER
hiss *v.* boo, hoot, jeer, deride, whistle, ▷*ridicule* ★**applaud**
history *n.* narration, account, saga, story, chronicle *The new book is a chronicle of the last war*
hit [1] *v.* strike, slap, beat, batter, whack [2] collide, strike, clash ★**miss** [3] *n.* stroke, collision, blow [4] success, triumph
hitch [1] *v.* attach, connect, fasten [2] *n.* delay, hold-up, problem, snag *The work went smoothly for hours, until we hit a snag*
hoard *v.* accumulate, save, collect, treasure ★**squander** HORDE
hoarse *adj.* raucous, croaky, husky, throaty ★**mellow** HORSE
hoax *n.* trick, deception, fraud, leg-pull, joke, spoof
hobble *v.* dodder, falter, shuffle, stagger
hobby *n.* pastime, amusement, recreation, interest
hoist *v.* lift, raise, erect, heave
hold [1] *v.* have, possess, own, retain, keep, grasp [2] contain, accommodate *This cabin can accommodate four people* [3] stop, arrest [4] *n.* fortress, keep, storeplace HOLED
hole *n.* aperture, slot, perforation, opening, cavity WHOLE
hollow [1] *adj.* concave, empty, vacant [2] insincere, artificial [3] *n.* basin, depression *Water had accumulated in a small depression*, crater, channel
holy *adj.* sacred, pure, consecrated, blessed, hallowed ★**wicked** WHOLLY
home *n.* house, dwelling, homestead
homely [1] *adj.* humble, unpretentious, comfortable, modest [2] ordinary, plain, simple [3] unattractive, plain
honest *adj.* upright, fair, sincere, honorable ★**devious**
honesty *n.* integrity, honor, sincerity, morality ★**dishonesty**
honor *n.* morality, honesty, reputation, integrity, uprightness ★**disgrace**
honorable *adj.* honest, respectable, high-minded, virtuous ★**dishonest**
hook *n.* clasp, link, catch, fastener, barb *The fishing line ended in a number of small barbs*
hoop *n.* loop, ring, band, circle
hoot *v.* call, cry, howl, shout, shriek, yell
hop *v.* jump, leap, skip, spring, vault, caper
hope *v.* anticipate, envision, envisage, desire, expect, foresee ★**despair**
hopeful *adj.* expectant, confident, optimistic ★**pessimistic**
hopeless *adj.* despairing, desperate, downhearted, unattainable ★**hopeful**
horde *n.* crowd, gang, band, throng, swarm *We were suddenly attacked by a swarm of hornets*
horrible *adj.* awful, atrocious, frightful, ghastly, ▷*horrid* ★**agreeable**
horrid *adj.* beastly, bloodcurdling, dreadful, frightening, ▷*horrible* ★**pleasant**
horror *n.* dread, fear, fright, outrage, panic, loathing ★**attraction**
horse *n.* mount, charger, hack, stallion, mare, filly, colt, foal HOARSE
hose [1] *n.* tubing, pipe [2] socks, stockings HOES
hospitable *adj.* sociable, neighborly, charitable, welcoming ★**hostile**
host [1] *n.* landlord, innkeeper [2] army, band, legion, horde
hostile *adj.* unfriendly, antagonistic, alien, malevolent ★**friendly**
hot [1] *adj.* warm, fiery, scalding, roasting, heated ★**cold** [2] pungent, peppery, sharp
hotel *n.* inn, hostelry *The stagecoach pulled in to a local hostelry for refreshment*, tavern, motel, resort
house *n.* home, residence, dwelling, abode
hovel *n.* cabin, shed, den, shack, shanty

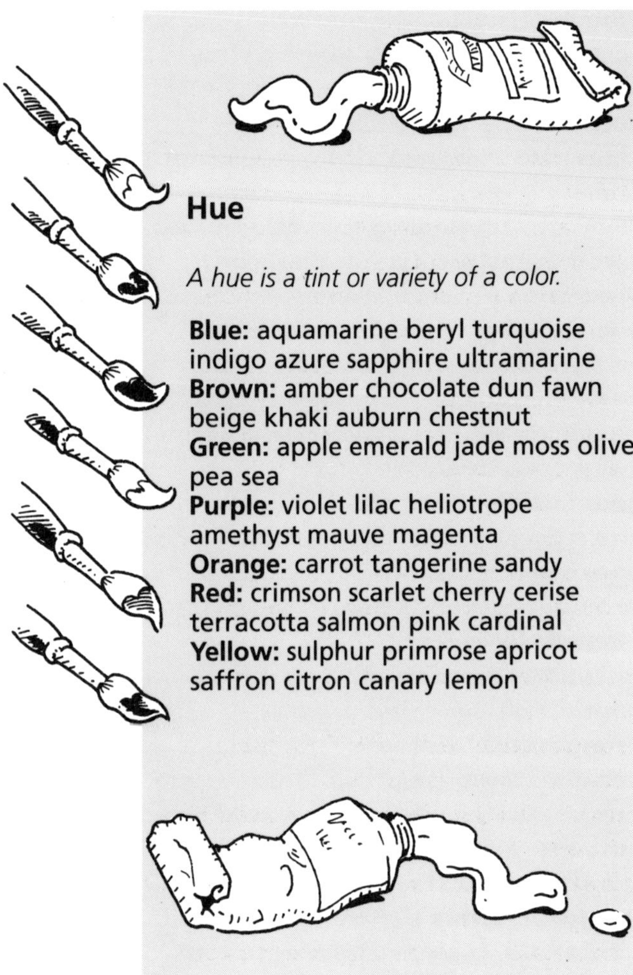

Hue

A hue is a tint or variety of a color.

Blue: aquamarine beryl turquoise indigo azure sapphire ultramarine
Brown: amber chocolate dun fawn beige khaki auburn chestnut
Green: apple emerald jade moss olive pea sea
Purple: violet lilac heliotrope amethyst mauve magenta
Orange: carrot tangerine sandy
Red: crimson scarlet cherry cerise terracotta salmon pink cardinal
Yellow: sulphur primrose apricot saffron citron canary lemon

hover *v.* fly, float, hang, dither, dally, linger
howl *v.* hoot, cry, bellow, shriek, ▷*scream*
hub *n.* center, axis, focal point, pivot
hubbub *n.* babel, bedlam, chaos, clamor, uproar, ▷*row* ★**calm**
huddle *v.* cluster, flock, gather, herd, nestle ★**separate**
hue *n.* color, dye, shade, tinge, tint HEW
huff *n.* anger, passion, mood, pique *My cousin stormed off in a fit of pique,* ▷*sulk*
hug *v.* clasp, embrace, enfold, ▷*cuddle*
huge *adj.* enormous, monstrous, colossal, immense, ▷*vast* ★**tiny**
hum *v.* drone, croon, buzz, pulsate, throb
human *adj.* reasonable, understandable, mortal, ▷*humane* ★**inhuman**
humane *adj.* benign, forgiving, gentle, lenient, kind ★**inhumane**
humble *adj.* low, lowly, meek, unassuming, ▷*modest* ★**arrogant**
humbug *n.* bluff, bunkum, claptrap *The salesman's goods were cheap, and he talked a lot of claptrap about them,* quackery, trickery
humdrum *adj.* monotonous, commonplace, everyday, boring, ▷*dreary* ★**exceptional**
humid *adj.* clammy, damp, moist, wet, vaporous ★**dry**
humiliate *v.* embarrass, humble, abash, degrade, deflate ★**boost**
humor [1] *n.* comedy, fun, banter, whimsy [2] *v.* flatter, coax, pamper, spoil
humorous *adj.* amusing, droll, comical, whimsical, ▷*funny* ★**serious** HUMERUS
hunch [1] *n.* feeling, guess, idea, inkling [2] *v.* crouch, curl up, squat *We squatted in the long grass, where we were out of sight*
hunger [1] *n.* craving, desire, starvation [2] *v.* crave, desire, hanker
hungry *adj.* famished, starving, voracious
hunt *v.* chase, seek, scour, search, stalk, trail
hurdle *n.* barrier, fence, hedge, obstruction
hurl *v.* cast, fling, heave, pitch, throw, propel, toss
hurry *v.* dash, hustle, quicken, accelerate, ▷*hasten* ★**dally**
hurt [1] *v.* harm, wound, pain, sting, suffer [2] upset, annoy, distress [3] *adj.* rueful, sad, offended
hurtful *adj.* cutting, cruel, distressing, wounding ★**kind**
hurtle *v.* chase, charge, dash, rush, speed, tear
hush *v.* calm, quiet down, soothe ★**disturb**
husky *adj.* croaking, gruff, harsh, ▷*hoarse*
hustle *v.* bustle, speed, hasten, ▷*hurry*
hut *n.* cabin, shelter, shanty, shack
hymn *n.* anthem, chant, carol, psalm HIM
hypnotize *v.* mesmerize, fascinate, spellbind *We stood spellbound as we watched the trapeze artist,* bewitch
hypocrite *n.* fraud, deceiver, impostor, mountebank
hysterical [1] *adj.* distraught, mad, delirious, beside oneself [2] comical, hilarious, farcical ★**calm**

I i

icy *adj.* freezing, frozen, cold, frigid, frosty

idea *n.* notion, thought, belief, fancy, impression, image

ideal *adj.* perfect, absolute, supreme, best, model, complete

identical *adj.* same, alike, twin, duplicate, equal ★**different**

identify *v.* detect, recognize, know, distinguish, spot

identity *n.* existence, self, singularity, individuality

idiot *n.* imbecile, moron, fool, dimwit, dolt

idiotic *adj.* crazy, stupid, simple, fatuous, ▷*foolish* ★**sane**

idle [1] *adj.* unoccupied, unemployed, unused [2] lazy, frivolous, sluggish ★**active** IDOL

idol [1] *n.* image, icon, god, fetish [2] hero, favorite, star *Buster Keaton was a star of the silent movies* IDLE

ignite *v.* kindle, set light to, spark off, catch fire

ignorant *adj.* unknowing, ill-informed, unread, stupid, dumb ★**wise**

ignore *v.* disregard, neglect, omit, overlook, pass over ★**note**

ill [1] *adj.* ailing, diseased, frail, infirm, sick, poorly ★**well** [2] hostile, malicious *Cinderella's sisters were cruel and malicious*, evil, harmful ★**fortunate**

ill-mannered *adj.* coarse, crude, boorish, uncivil, ▷*rude* ★**polite**

ill-tempered *adj.* bad-tempered, curt, irritable ★**good-tempered**

ill-treat *v.* abuse, harm, injure, neglect, oppress ★**care for**

ill will *n.* animosity, hard feelings, dislike, hatred, hostility, ▷*malice* ★**good will**

illegal *adj.* unlawful, wrong, villainous, illicit, contraband ★**legal**

illegible *adj.* unreadable, indecipherable, obscure, indistinct ★**legible**

illegitimate *adj.* illegal, unlawful, improper, wrong ★**legitimate**

illiterate *adj.* uneducated, unlearned, unread, untaught ★**literate**

illness *n.* ailment, attack, complaint, disease, disorder

illuminate *v.* brighten, clarify, enlighten, light up ★**darken**

illusion *n.* apparition, fancy, fantasy, mirage, deception ★**reality**

illustration *n.* picture, drawing, explanation, sketch

image *n.* likeness, effigy, portrait, replica, reflection, double

imaginary *adj.* unreal, fanciful, fantastic, visionary ★**real**

imagination *n.* idea, notion, thought, illusion, conception, fancy, vision, impression ★**reality**

imagine *v.* assume, believe, invent, pretend, think up, ▷*visualize*

imbecile *n.* blockhead, fool, idiot, bungler, dolt

imitate *v.* emulate, follow, reproduce, simulate, mock, ▷*copy*

immaculate *adj.* clean, spotless, faultless, stainless, ▷*pure* ★**spoiled**

immature *adj.* callow, raw, crude, childish, unripe ★**mature**

immediate [1] *adj.* instant, instantaneous, prompt [2] nearest, next, neighboring *As children, my mother and father lived in neighboring houses* ★**distant**

immediately *adv.* at once, directly, without delay, forthwith

immense *adj.* tremendous, enormous, vast, ▷*huge* ★**tiny**

immerse *v.* plunge, dip, douse, submerge, ▷*sink*

imminent *adj.* impending, approaching, looming, close

immobile *adj.* at rest, at a standstill, motionless ★**moving**

immodest *adj.* shameless, barefaced, indelicate, improper ★**modest**

immoral *adj.* evil, unscrupulous, vicious, vile, depraved, ▷*wicked* ★**moral**

immortal *adj.* undying, eternal, everlasting, constant ★**mortal**

immune *adj.* privileged, exempt, resistant, safe ★**susceptible**
imp *n.* rogue, villain, scamp, demon, evil spirit, elf
impact *n.* blow, shock, stroke, collision, crash, knock
impair *v.* destroy, spoil, devalue, cheapen, harm, ▷*hinder* ★**enhance**
impart *v.* communicate, render, bestow, disclose *I am unable to disclose where I heard that story,* ▷*tell*
impartial *adj.* unbiased, candid, fair-minded, impersonal ★**prejudiced**
impatient *adj.* intolerant, irritable, hasty, curt ★**patient**
impede *v.* hamper, interfere with, obstruct, ▷*hinder* ★**aid**
impel *v.* goad, incite, urge, actuate, push, ▷*drive* ★**dissuade**
impending *adj.* approaching, coming, forthcoming, looming ★**remote**
imperfect *adj.* defective, unsound, blemished, flawed, ▷*faulty* ★**perfect**
imperial *adj.* superior, august, majestic, lofty, regal
imperious *adj.* arrogant, domineering, overbearing ★**humble**
impersonal *adj.* aloof, detached, remote, neutral ★**friendly**
impersonate *v.* ape, imitate, mimic, masquerade as, pose as
impertinent *adj.* insolent, impudent, discourteous, ▷*saucy* ★**polite**
impetuous *adj.* sudden, unexpected, impulsive, spontaneous, ▷*hasty* ★**careful**
implement [1] *v.* accomplish, bring about, fulfill *To visit Japan was a dream that I was able to fulfill* [2] *n.* instrument, tool, gadget
implicate *v.* connect, entangle, involve, throw suspicion on ★**absolve**
implicit *adj.* involved, indicated, understood, tacit
implore *v.* beseech, entreat, beg, crave, plead
imply *v.* hint at, intimate, insinuate, ▷*suggest* ★**declare**
impolite *adj.* discourteous, ill-mannered, ▷*rude* ★**polite**
import [1] *v.* bring in, carry in [2] *n.* meaning, purport *When I grew old enough I realized the purport of my mother's advice,* sense
important *adj.* notable, outstanding, serious, substantial, ▷*great* ★**trivial**
imposing *adj.* impressive, massive, magnificent, ▷*stately* ★**modest**
impossible *adj.* hopeless, not possible, unworkable, unacceptable ★**possible**
impostor *n.* impersonator, masquerader, deceiver, bluffer, pretender
impoverish *v.* bankrupt, diminish, weaken, ruin, beggar ★**enrich**
impractical *adj.* impossible, unworkable, idealistic, unusable ★**practical**
impress [1] *v.* influence, affect, sway, inspire [2] emboss *She wore a crown of gold embossed with diamonds,* engrave, indent
impression [1] *n.* belief, concept, fancy, effect [2] dent, imprint, stamp, printing *The book had sold 5,000 copies, and a new printing was planned*
imprison *v.* jail, lock up, confine, ★**free**
improbable *adj.* doubtful, unlikely, implausible, ▷*dubious* ★**probable**
impromptu *adj.* improvised, spontaneous, ad lib, unrehearsed ★**planned**
improper [1] *adj.* erroneous, false, unsuitable [2] immoral *My parents always taught me that lying and cheating were immoral,* indecent, ▷*wrong* ★**proper**
improve *v.* make better, repair, restore, improve upon, refine ★**diminish**
impudent *adj.* impertinent, audacious, brazen, disrespectful, ▷*rude* ★**polite**
impulse *n.* motive, drive, force, inclination, urge
impulsive *adj.* sudden, unexpected, reckless, ▷*impetuous* ★**cautious**
impure *adj.* contaminated, corrupted, foul, corrupt ★**pure**
inaccessible *adj.* remote, isolated, unattainable ★**accessible**
inaccurate *adj.* erroneous, incorrect, imprecise, ▷*faulty* ★**accurate**
inactive *adj.* inert, static, dormant, quiet, unoccupied ★**active**

inadequate *adj.* deficient, unequal, incapable, ▷*unfit* ★**adequate**
inane *adj.* absurd, ridiculous, stupid, senseless, ▷*silly* ★**sensible**
inappropriate *adj.* improper, wrong, incorrect, unsuitable, unfitting ★**appropriate**
inattentive *adj.* unheeding, indifferent, careless, neglectful ★**attentive**
incapable *adj.* helpless, inadequate, unable, unfit, weak ★**capable**
incense [1] *v.* (in-*cense*) enrage, infuriate, annoy [2] *n.* (*in*-cense) fragrance *We walked through fields where the fragrance of wild flowers was wonderful*, aroma, perfume
incentive *n.* motive, impulse, drive, spur, lure
incident *n.* event, happening, episode, circumstance, occurrence
incidental *adj.* casual, chance, accidental, random, minor
incite *v.* encourage, urge, drive, goad, impel, provoke, ▷*prompt* ★**restrain**
incline [1] *n.* (*in*-cline) slant, slope, grade, gradient [2] *v.* (in-*cline*) tend, verge, lean to, bias, favor
inclined *adj.* liable, prone, disposed, favorable
include *v.* contain, cover, incorporate, embody, comprise ★**exclude**
inclusive *adj.* comprehensive, all-embracing ★**exclusive**
income *n.* earnings, royalty, revenue, receipts, profits ★**expenses**
incomparable *adj.* brilliant, first-class, superb, ▷*unrivaled* ★**ordinary**
incompetent *adj.* incapable, inadequate, inept, helpless, ▷*clumsy* ★**competent**
incomplete *adj.* unfinished, partial, imperfect, wanting ★**complete**
incomprehensible *adj.* unintelligible, perplexing, puzzling ★**comprehensible**
inconceivable *adj.* incredible, unlikely, strange, ▷*extraordinary* ★**comprehensible**
inconsiderate *adj.* tactless, careless, insensitive, ▷*thoughtless* ★**considerate**
inconsistent *adj.* incongruous, unstable, unpredictable ★**consistent**
inconspicuous *adj.* indistinct, faint, hidden, ordinary ★**conspicuous**
inconvenient *adj.* annoying, awkward, difficult, troublesome ★**convenient**
incorrect *adj.* erroneous, imprecise, mistaken, ▷*wrong* ★**correct**
increase [1] *v.* add to, boost, magnify, heighten [2] *n.* addition *We heard the news today that Emily has had an addition to her family*, rise, enhancement ★**decrease**
incredible *adj.* unbelievable, amazing, far-fetched, wonderful ★**ordinary**
incriminate *v.* implicate, accuse, indict, ▷*blame* ★**acquit**
indecent *adj.* immodest, improper, impure, coarse ★**decent**
indeed *adv.* actually, truly, really, very much, positively
indefinite *adj.* uncertain, unsure, unreliable, dubious, ▷*vague* ★**certain**
indelicate *adj.* coarse, immodest, tasteless, ▷*unseemly* ★**delicate**
independent *adj.* free, self-reliant, separate, self-governing ★**dependent**
indicate *v.* show, point out, denote, suggest, symbolize, flag, signal
indifference *n.* disinterest, unconcern, apathy, coldness ★**interest**
indifferent *adj.* careless, cold, casual, apathetic, listless ★**interested**
indignant *adj.* annoyed, resentful, wrathful, ▷*angry* ★**pleased**
indirect *adj.* devious, roundabout, incidental ★**direct**
indiscreet *adj.* incautious, thoughtless, ill-advised, ▷*hasty* ★**discreet**
indiscriminate *adj.* confused, bewildered, careless, ▷*random* ★**deliberate**
indispensable *adj.* necessary, crucial, vital, ▷*essential* ★**unnecessary**
indistinct *adj.* faint, dim, unclear, obscure, murky, ▷*vague* ★**distinct**
individual [1] *adj.* single, odd, special, exclusive [2] *n.* person, being *The inhabitants of the planet were strange green beings*, creature
indulge *v.* gratify, humor, pamper, satisfy, spoil

industrious *adj.* busy, hard-working, diligent, conscientious, ▷*lazy*
inedible *adj.* deadly, poisonous, harmful, uneatable ★**edible**
inefficient *adj.* negligent, incapable, ▷*incompetent* ★**efficient**
inelegant *adj.* awkward, ungainly, crude, coarse, ▷*clumsy* ★**elegant**
inept *adj.* awkward, absurd, unskilled, ▷*clumsy* ★**skillful**
inert *adj.* inactive, passive, static, sluggish, listless, dead ★**alive**
inevitable *adj.* unavoidable, certain, sure, necessary ★**uncertain**
inexact *adj.* imprecise, inaccurate, ▷*erroneous* ★**exact**
inexpensive *adj.* low-priced, reasonable, economical, ▷*cheap* ★**expensive**
inexperienced *adj.* inexpert, unskilled, untrained, ▷*inept* ★**experienced**
infallible *adj.* perfect, unerring, faultless, ▷*reliable* ★**faulty**
infamous *adj.* notorious, shady, scandalous, shameful, disgraceful ★**glorious**
infant *n.* baby, child, little one, toddler
infatuated *adj.* in love, beguiled, fascinated, smitten ★**indifferent**
infect *v.* contaminate, blight, defile, pollute
infectious *adj.* catching, contagious
infer *v.* reason, conclude, judge, understand
inferior *adj.* second-rate, lesser, lower, poor, mediocre, imperfect ★**superior**
infinite *adj.* eternal, unending, endless, immense, unbounded
infirm *adj.* weak, feeble, frail, senile, decrepit ★**healthy**
inflame *v.* inspire, provoke, excite, stimulate, arouse ★**cool**
inflate *v.* expand, dilate, swell, pump up, blow up ★**deflate**
inflict *v.* apply, burden, deal, deliver, force
influence [1] *n.* authority, control, guidance, force [2] *v.* affect, impress, inspire *After Annie visited the old city, she was inspired to write a poem*, prejudice
inform *v.* tell, let know, acquaint, warn, enlighten
informal *adj.* casual, easy, familiar, relaxed, simple ★**formal**
information *n.* knowledge, news, intelligence, advice
infrequent *adj.* unusual, uncommon, occasional, ▷*rare* ★**frequent**
infringe *v.* disobey, violate, encroach, trespass, flout
infuriate *v.* anger, enrage, madden, incense, vex, ▷*annoy* ★**calm**
ingenious *adj.* clever, resourceful, shrewd, adroit, inventive ★**clumsy**
ingenuous *adj.* honest, open, simple, trusting, sincere ★**artful**
ingratiate *v.* curry favor, flatter, grovel, toady *We all disliked the new schoolmate, for she was always toadying the teacher*

We all disliked the new schoolmate, for she was always toadying the teacher.

ingredient *n.* component, element, part, factor
inhabit *v.* live in, dwell in, reside in, dwell, occupy
inhale *v.* breathe in, inspire, sniff, suck in ⋆**exhale**
inherit *v.* succeed to, acquire, take over, receive
inhospitable *adj.* unfriendly, desolate, unkind, unsociable ⋆**hospitable**
inhuman *adj.* barbaric, brutal, beastly, heartless, savage
inhumane *adj.* callous, cruel, pitiless, ruthless, ▷*inhuman* ⋆**humane**
initiate *v.* start, launch, teach, instruct, train, ▷*begin*
initiative *n.* ambition, drive, enterprise, resourcefulness
inject *v.* inoculate, infuse, vaccinate
injure *v.* hurt, mar, spoil, wound, blemish, deform, disfigure
inkling *n.* suspicion, impression, notion, clue
inlet *n.* bay, gulf, basin, bight, estuary, harbor
inn *n.* hotel, hostelry, tavern IN
innocent *adj.* guiltless, faultless, stainless, virtuous, blameless ⋆**guilty**
inoffensive *adj.* harmless, safe, gentle, quiet, ▷*innocent* ⋆**malicious**
inquire *v.* ask, examine, inspect, check, question
inquisitive *adj.* nosy, snooping, eager, inquiring, ▷*curious*
insane *adj.* demented, mad, frenzied, crazy, wild, lunatic ⋆**sane**
inscribe *v.* write, stamp, cut, carve, etch
inscription *n.* heading, caption, legend, epitaph, label
insecure *adj.* perilous, unsafe, hazardous, dangerous, unconfident, uncertain ⋆**secure**
insensible [1] *adj.* unconscious, stunned, knocked out *The reigning champion was knocked out in the third round* [2] insensitive, numb, stupefied
insensitive *adj.* impassive, indifferent, thick-skinned, unruffled, insensible ⋆**sensitive**
inseparable *adj.* indivisible, devoted, intimate, close
insert *v.* put in, inset, introduce, place, interleave ⋆**remove**
inside *adv.* indoors, inner, inward, within ⋆**outside**
insight *n.* awareness, intelligence, judgment, knowledge, ▷*wisdom*
insignificant *adj.* unimportant, non-essential, meager, irrelevant, ▷*humble* ⋆**important**
insincere *adj.* pretended, deceptive, dishonest, two-faced, false ⋆**sincere**
insinuate *v.* suggest, imply, signify, get at, intimate
insipid *adj.* tasteless, flat, flavorless, bland, banal ⋆**tasty**
insist *v.* assert, maintain, request, require, demand, persist ⋆**waive**
insolent *adj.* impudent, impertinent, discourteous, insulting, fresh, rude ⋆**respectful**
inspect *v.* examine, check, oversee, supervise, superintend
inspiration *n.* motive, stimulus, brain wave, ▷*encouragement*
inspire *v.* hearten, prompt, provoke, excite, ▷*encourage* ⋆**deter**
install *v.* establish, plant, set, position, fix, introduce
instance *n.* example, case, occasion, occurrence INSTANTS
instant [1] *adj.* immediate, instantaneous *I pressed the button, and there was an instantaneous explosion*, rapid [2] *n.* moment, minute, flash, jiffy
instantly *adv.* at once, right away, immediately, now, ▷*forthwith* ⋆**later**
instead *adv.* alternatively, preferably, rather
instead of *adv.* in place of, in one's place, on behalf of
instinct *n.* ability, knack, intuition, feeling, sixth sense
institute [1] *n.* association, college, establishment, organization [2] *v.* begin, start *The people raised enough money to start a new social club*, found, open
instruct *v.* teach, direct, order, educate, coach, drill, train

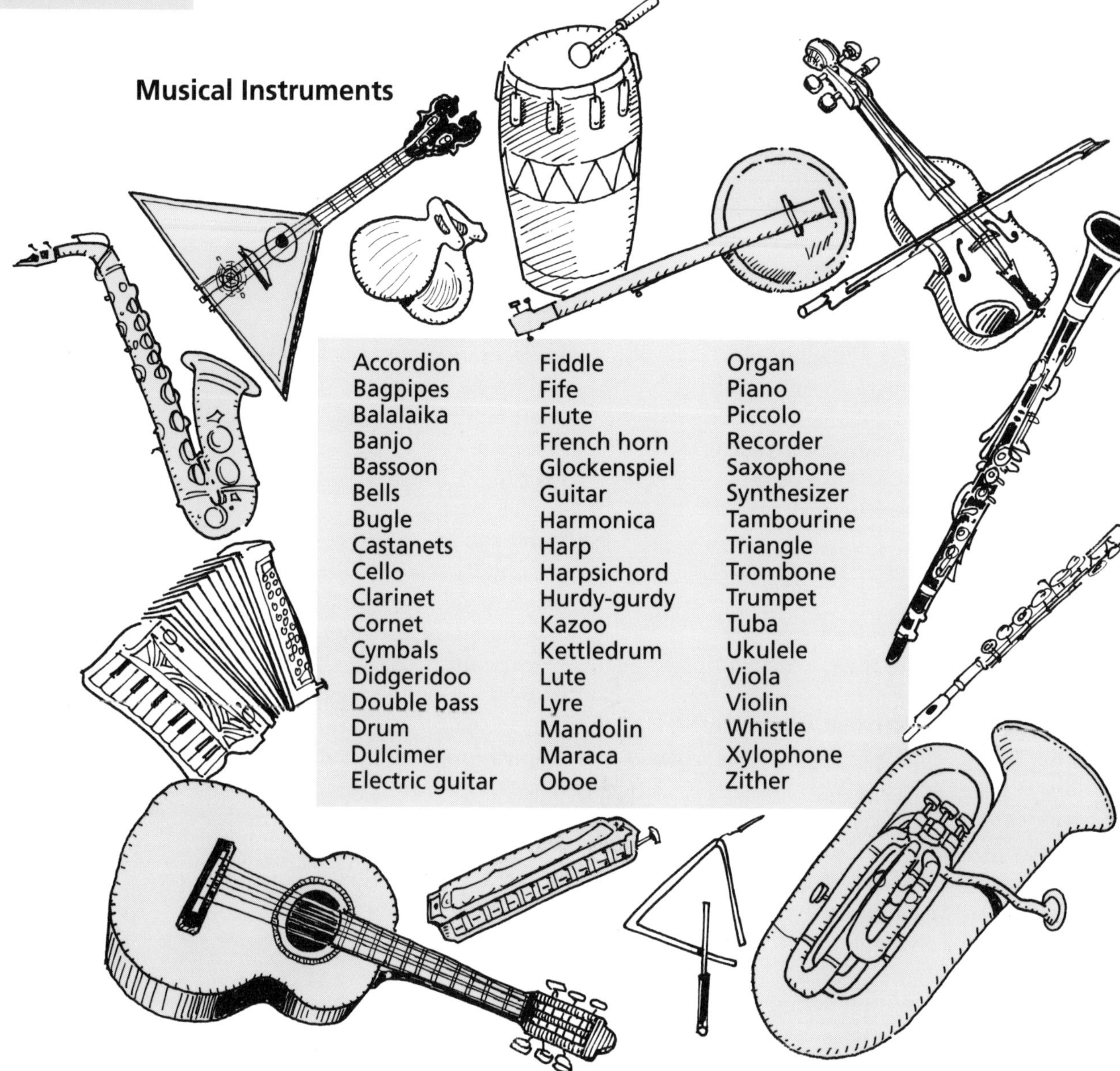

instrument *n.* device, gadget, implement, contraption, tool

insufferable *adj.* unbearable, intolerable, impossible ★**tolerable**

insufficient *adj.* inadequate, lacking, scanty, wanting, ▷*sparse* ★**sufficient**

insulate *v.* protect, shield, isolate, set apart

insult *n.* & *v.* slander, slight, snub, abuse, outrage ★**compliment**

insure *v.* guarantee, protect, warrant, assure

intact *adj.* whole, unharmed, uncut, complete, in one piece, sound ★**damaged**

integrity *n.* honor, uprightness, honesty, goodness, purity ★**dishonesty**

intellectal *adj.* scholarly, studious, thoughtful, ▷*intelligent* ★**foolish**

intelligent *adj.* acute, astute, brainy, brilliant, intellectual, ▷*clever* ★**stupid**

intend *v.* mean, aim, determine, ordain, plan, project

intense *adj.* extreme, ardent, earnest, forcible, passionate, ▷*keen* ★**mild** INTENTS

intention *n.* aim, intent, project, design, notion, end, goal

intercept *v.* stop, arrest, delay, obstruct, ▷*thwart*

interest *n.* appeal, fascination, zest, activity, concern ★**boredom**

interesting *adj.* appealing, fascinating, absorbing, entertaining ★**boring**
interfere *v.* meddle, intrude, interrupt, butt in, tamper ★**assist**
interior *adj.* internal, innermost, inside, inward ★**exterior**
interlude *n.* pause, interval, intermission, spell, recess
internal *adj.* inner, inward, ▷*interior* ★**external**
interpret *adj.* explain, define, construe
interrogate *v.* question, examine, ask, inquire, quiz, ▷*investigate*
interrupt *adj.* break in, butt in, interject, disturb, hold up
interval *n.* space, period, term, intermission, ▷*interlude*
intervene *v.* break in, interrupt, intrude, ▷*interfere*
interview *n.* conference, inquiry, consultation, talk
intimate [1] *adj.* near, close, familiar, private, secret ★**distant** [2] *v.* hint at, suggest *I started to play the violin at school, and my teacher suggested I take it up for a living*, ▷*insinuate*
intimidate *v.* daunt, overawe, cow, bully, frighten, browbeat ★**persuade**
intolerant *adj.* bigoted, unfair, small-minded, dogmatic ★**tolerant**
intoxicated *adj.* drunk, inebriated, tipsy
intrepid *adj.* fearless, heroic, unafraid, bold, gallant, ▷*fearless*
intricate *adj.* complex, complicated, elaborate, tricky ★**simple**
intrigue [1] *n.* plot, scheme, affair, liaison [2] *v.* attract, enchant *The hotel's location was enchanting*, captivate, scheme
introduce [1] *v.* put in, insert, inject [2] acquaint, present
intrude *v.* interrupt, interfere, invade, trespass ★**withdraw**
inundate *v.* flood, deluge, engulf, immerse, submerge, swamp *We advertised for a new assistant and were swamped with replies*
invade *v.* break in, penetrate, assault, assail, ▷*enter* ★**withdraw** INVEIGHED
invalid [1] *adj.* (in-*val*-id) null, void *These tickets are void, for they were left over from last year*, false, useless [2] *n.* (*in*-valid) patient, sufferer, sick person
invaluable *adj.* precious, costly, priceless, valuable ★**worthless**
invent *v.* fabricate, conceive, devise, make up, originate
invention *n.* creation, gadget, contrivance, discovery
investigate *v.* explore, examine, research, inquire, search, study
invisible *adj.* hidden, concealed, out of sight, unseen, masked ★**visible**
invite *v.* ask, beckon, attract, summon, urge, encourage ★**force**
involve *v.* comprise, complicate, entangle, include, take in
inward *adj.* hidden, inner, internal, secret, inside ★**outward**
irate *adj.* incensed, cross, annoyed, furious, infuriated, ▷*angry* ★**calm**
irksome *adj.* annoying, irritating, disagreeable ★**pleasing**
ironic *adj.* satirical, derisive, mocking, scornful
irregular *adj.* uncertain, unsettled, disordered, singular, ▷*odd* ★**regular**
irrelevant *adj.* immaterial, unnecessary, unrelated ★**relevant**
irresistible *adj.* charming, compelling, overpowering, fascinating ★**resistible**
irresponsible *adj.* undependable, unreliable, feckless, flighty ★**responsible**
irritable *adj.* bad-tempered, edgy, fretful, peevish, ▷*cross* ★**cheerful**
irritate *v.* annoy, vex, irk, offend, provoke, ▷*bother* ★**please**
island *n.* isle, islet, key, atoll, cay
issue [1] *v.* flow, ooze, bring out, circulate, publish [2] *n.* edition, printing, publication *My book of poems was ready for publication*, impression [3] problem, question
itch [1] *v.* prickle, tingle, irritate [2] *n.* impulse, motive, desire *I have always had a strong desire to work on the land*
item *n.* point, particular, thing, object, article

J j

jab *v.* poke, prod, push, stab, dig
jabber *v.* chatter, gabble, mumble, babble
jacket *n.* coat, jerkin, cover, case, sheath
jagged *adj.* rough, broken, snagged, notched, uneven ★**smooth**
jail *n.* prison, penitentiary, lock-up, brig
jam [1] *n.* jelly, preserves, conserve, marmalade [2] *v.* crowd, pack *All the buses were full, and we were packed in like sardines!*, crush, squeeze JAMB
jar [1] *n.* jug, beaker, ewer, vase, pitcher, pot [2] *v.* jog, rattle, grate *That singer's voice really grates on me*, grind
jaunt *n.* & *v.* trip, journey, cruise, travel, tour
jaunty *adj.* lighthearted, showy, dapper, spruce, debonair
jealous *adj.* envious, covetous, grudging
jealousy *n.* envy, covetousness, distrust, spite
jeer *v.* laugh at, deride, mock, ridicule, insult, ▷*taunt*
jeopardy *n.* peril, risk, hazard, plight, ▷*danger* ★**safety**
jerk *n.* & *v.* yank, pull, drag, jog, jolt, tug

Jewels

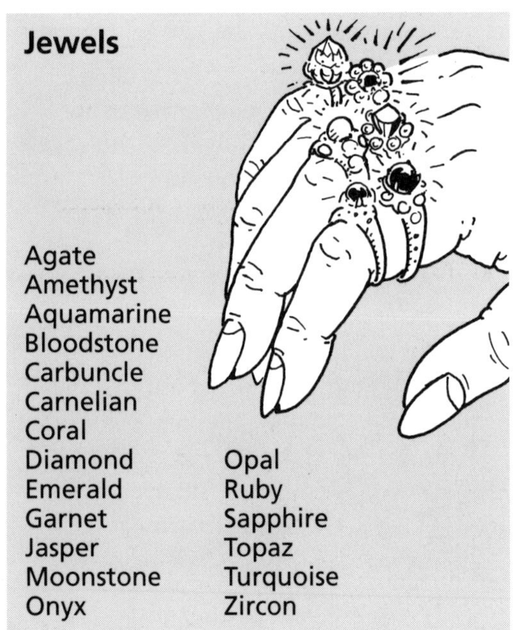

Agate
Amethyst
Aquamarine
Bloodstone
Carbuncle
Carnelian
Coral
Diamond
Emerald
Garnet
Jasper
Moonstone
Onyx
Opal
Ruby
Sapphire
Topaz
Turquoise
Zircon

jersey *n.* pullover, sweater
jest *n.* joke, jape, spoof, banter, chaff
jester *n.* clown, buffoon, merry-andrew, prankster, comedian
jet *n.* & *v.* spurt, squirt, flow, gush
jetty *n.* wharf, dock, quay, pier
jewel *n.* gem, stone, trinket, charm, locket
jibe *v.* mock, scoff, scorn, sneer, taunt, ▷*jeer*
jiffy *n.* instant, flash, minute, moment
jilt *v.* abandon, brush off, desert, drop, forsake
jingle *v.* tinkle, clink, chink, ring, jangle
job *n.* task, work, chore, place, office, post, position
jocular *adj.* gleeful, hilarious, witty, humorous, jolly, ▷*funny* ★**serious**
jog [1] *v.* prod, nudge, shove, shake [2] canter, trot, run, sprint
join [1] *v.* unite, link, combine, connect, attach ★**separate** [2] enlist, sign up *Gaby and Bill have signed up for tennis lessons*
joint [1] *n.* junction, knot, union, connection [2] *adj.* shared, united, mutual *It's in our mutual interest to keep expenses down*
joke *n.* gag, trick, frolic, lark, jape, game, prank, ▷*jest*
jolly *adj.* jovial, cheerful, blithe, frisky, ▷*merry* ★**sad**
jolt *n.* & *v.* jar, shock, shove, rock, jerk, bump
jostle *v.* push, shove, shoulder, thrust, elbow
jot [1] *n.* atom, bit, grain, particle [2] *v.* note, scribble, take down
journal [1] *n.* ledger, account book [2] diary, newspaper, magazine *I've just become editor of the natural history society's magazine*
journey *n.* excursion, trip, tour, jaunt, ramble
jovial *adj.* jolly, festive, cordial, affable, cheerful, ▷*merry* ★**sad**
joy *n.* rapture, enchantment, delight, pleasure, charm, ▷*bliss* ★**sorrow**
joyful *adj.* joyous, enjoyable, pleasurable, happy, jovial, delighted ★**sorrowful**
jubilant *adj.* exultant, gleeful, happy, overjoyed, excited ★**depressed**
judge [1] *n.* justice, magistrate, referee, umpire [2] *v.* assess *We can ask the jeweler to assess the value of the pearls and bracelets*, decide, find, appraise, estimate

judgment [1] *n.* decision, opinion, verdict *The jury gave a verdict of "not guilty,"* decree, finding [2] intelligence, understanding, valuation

judicious *adj.* prudent, discreet, expedient, wise ★**indiscreet**

jug *n.* beaker, ewer, urn, vase, ▷*jar*

juggle *v.* conjure, manipulate

juice *n.* essence, extract, sap, fluid, nectar

jumble *n.* medley, mixture, muddle, tangle, clutter

jump *v.* spring, bound, hop, skip, vault, ▷*leap*

junction [1] *n.* intersection, combination, joint, connection [2] crossroads, railroad connection

jungle *n.* forest, bush, wilderness

junior *adj.* lesser, lower, younger, subordinate ★**senior**

junk *n.* trash, debris, rubbish, waste, clutter, litter, scrap, garbage

just [1] *adj.* sound, regular, orderly, exact, fair, honest, impartial [2] *adv.* exactly, precisely *Our meal cost 46 francs precisely*

justice *n.* equity, impartiality, fairness, right ★**injustice**

justify *v.* vindicate, acquit, condone, uphold, legalize

jut *v.* bulge, extend, stick out, overhang, project *The projecting eaves of the chalet kept the garden shaded* ★**recede**

juvenile [1] *adj.* adolescent, youthful, young, childish ★**mature** [2] *n.* boy, girl, child, youngster, youth

K k

keen [1] *adj.* eager, ardent, earnest, diligent [2] sharp, acute, fine *This razor has a very fine blade* ★**dull**

keep [1] *v.* hold, retain, collect, possess ★**abandon** [2] care for, maintain, shelter *We have arranged to shelter the refugees* [3] *n.* castle, fort, stronghold

keeper *n.* jailer, warden, attendant, caretaker, janitor

keeping *n.* compliance, obedience, accord *Your behavior is not in accord with our rules*

keep on *v.* continue, go on, endure, persist ★**give up**

keepsake *n.* souvenir, token, memento, reminder

keg *n.* barrel, cask, tub, drum, container

ken *n.* grasp, grip, understanding, mastery, knowledge

kerchief *n.* scarf, headscarf, shawl, neckcloth

kernel *n.* core, heart, hub, center, gist, nub COLONEL

kettle *n.* boiler, cauldron, cooking pot, tea-kettle

key [1] *n.* opener [2] solution, clue, answer [3] cay, isle, inlet atoll [4] *adj.* essential, fundamental QUAY

kick [1] *v.* boot, strike with foot, hit [2] complain, grumble, rebel *The country folk rebelled against the building of the new road,* resist

kidnap *v.* abduct, capture, seize, snatch, steal

kill *v.* slay, assassinate, destroy, massacre, slaughter, ▷*murder*

killjoy *n.* spoilsport, wet blanket *I'm not asking Pete to the party, he's such a wet blanket,* grouch, complainer ★**optimist**

kin *n.* race, kindred, offspring, kind, family, relative

kind [1] *adj.* gentle, kindly, genial, good-natured, amiable ★**unkind** [2] *n.* style, character, sort, variety

kindle [1] *v.* light, ignite, set fire to [2] inflame *The mayor's words only inflamed the people even more,* excite, provoke, rouse

A Little Knowledge is a Dangerous Thing – and Other Misquotes

Many of the familiar quotations we use from literature, history or the world of entertainment are incorrect or adaptations of the original. Greta Garbo did not say "I want to be alone." Her true words were: "I like to be alone." Shakespeare did not say "Discretion is the better part of valor." The correct quotation is: "The better part of valor is discretion". Here are some more, with the correct original version printed in italic type:

From the King James Bible
Pride goes before a fall
Pride goeth before destruction and an haughty spirit before a fall

Money is the root of all evil
For the love of money is the root of all evil
(Timothy)

To go the way of all flesh
And, behold, this day I am going the way of all earth. (Joshua)

From Shakespeare
Alas, poor Yorick: I knew him well.
Alas, poor Yorick; I knew him, Horatio...
(Hamlet)

O Romeo. Romeo! wherefore art thou, Romeo?
O Romeo. Romeo! wherefore art thou Romeo? (Romeo and Juliet)
(Note the position of the comma. "Wherefore" means "why" not "where.")

To gild the lily
... to gild refined gold, to paint the lily...
(King John)

Screw your courage to the sticking-point
But screw your courage to the sticking-place

All that glitters is not gold
All that glisters is not gold
(The Merchant of Venice)

kindness *n.* good nature, charity, amiability, affection, tenderness ★**cruelty**

king *n.* monarch, sovereign, majesty, ruler, emperor

kink [1] *n.* knot, loop, bend, coil [2] freak, eccentricity, whim *This strange tower was built as the result of a whim by the old lady*

kiss *v.* salute, embrace, buss

kit *n.* set, outfit, baggage, effects, gear, rig

knack *n.* flair, talent, ability, genius, gift, ▷*skill*

knave *n.* cheat, rascal, villain, scamp, scoundrel, ▷*rogue* NAVE

knead *v.* form, squeeze, mold, shape, press NEED

kneel *v.* bend the knee, genuflect *The nun genuflected before the altar, then knelt to say her rosary,* bow down, worship

knife *n.* scalpel, blade, dagger, cutter

knight *n.* cavalier, champion, soldier, warrior, baronet NIGHT

knit *v.* weave, crochet, spin, twill, link, loop

knob *n.* boss, bump, handle, opener, button

knock *v.* hit, slap, punch, bang, smite, strike

knock out *v.* stun, make insensible, render unconscious

L 1

Discretion is the better part of valor.
The better part of valor is discretion.
(King Henry IV part I)

Other sources

Water, water, everywhere, and not a drop to drink
Water, water, everywhere, Nor any drop to drink
(The Rime of the Ancient Mariner)

A little knowledge is a dangerous thing
A little learning is a dang'rous thing
(Alexander Pope)

Tomorrow to fresh fields and pastures new
To-morrow to fresh woods, and pastures new
(Paradise Lost)

They shall not grow old as we that are left grow old
They shall grow not old as we that are left grow old
(Laurence Binyon)

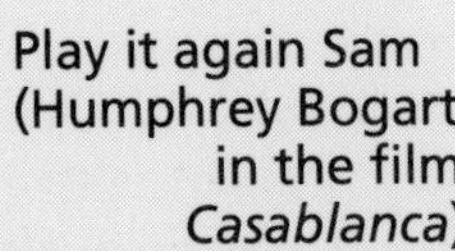

Play it again Sam
(Humphrey Bogart, in the film *Casablanca*)

Play it, Sam. Play "As Time Goes By"
(Ingrid Bergman, in the film *Casablanca*)

knoll *n.* barrow, hill, mound, hillock
knot [1] *n.* tie, bond, join, loop, kink, [2] cluster, group NOT
know *v.* perceive, discern, notice, identify, ▷*understand* NO
know-how *n.* skill, knowledge, talent
knowing *adj.* astute, knowledgeable, intelligent, perceptive ★**ignorant**
knowledge *n.* understanding, acquaintance, learning, wisdom, scholarship, information, sapience ★**ignorance**
kudos *n.* prestige, distinction, fame, glory, recognition

label *n.* badge, tag, ticket, sticker, docket, slip
labor *n.* & *v.* toil, work, drudge, strain, struggle
laborious [1] *adj.* hard-working, diligent [2] strenuous, arduous *Digging potatoes is arduous work*, hard ★**easy**
lack [1] *n.* need, want, absence, deficiency, scarcity *During the hot weather, there was a scarcity of water* [2] *v.* need, require, want, miss
laconic *adj.* terse, curt, brief, concise ★**wordy**
lad *n.* boy, fellow, kid, youth, chap
laden *adj.* loaded, burdened, hampered, weighed down ★**empty**
ladle *v.* dip, scoop, dish, shovel
lady *n.* woman, female, dame, damsel, matron, mistress
lag *v.* dawdle, loiter, tarry, saunter, ▷*linger* ★**lead**
lagoon *n.* pool, pond, lake, basin
lair *n.* den, nest, retreat, hideout, hole
lake *n.* lagoon, loch, pond, spring, reservoir
lam *v.* beat, hit, clout, knock, ▷*strike*
lame [1] *adj.* crippled, hobbled, disabled [2] weak *That's a weak excuse for forgetting my birthday!*, inadequate, unconvincing
lament *v.* deplore, mourn, grieve, sorrow, ▷*regret* ★**rejoice**
lamp *n.* lantern, light, flare, torch, flashlight
lance [1] *n.* spear, pike, javelin, shaft [2] *v.* puncture, pierce, cut
land [1] *n.* country, district, tract, area, nation, region [2] *v.* alight, arrive, carry, touch down *We had engine trouble, so the aircraft touched down in the desert*
landlord *n.* host, hotelier, innkeeper, owner
landmark *n.* milestone, milepost, beacon, monument, signpost
landscape *n.* scenery, view, prospect, countryside
lane *n.* alley, drive, passage, way LAIN
language *n.* tongue, speech, utterance, dialect, jargon

languid *adj.* leisurely, unhurried, sluggish, slow, easy **★lively**
languish *v.* decline, droop, flag, pine, suffer, yearn **★flourish**
lanky *adj.* tall, rangy, gangling, scrawny **★squat**
lantern *n.* lamp, flashlight, torch
lap [1] *v.* lick, drink, sip, sup [2] *n.* circuit, course, distance [3] thighs
lapse *v.* expire, die, pass, elapse, go by, deteriorate LAPS
larder *n.* pantry, storeroom, cellar
large *adj.* big, ample, substantial, great, broad, ▷*huge* **★small**
lark *n.* adventure, escapade, spree, joke, frolic, gambol
lash [1] *v.* beat, cane, whip, flay, flog [2] *n.* prod, goad, drive, whip
lass *n.* girl, maiden, maid, young woman
last [1] *adj.* final, concluding, latest, utmost, aftermost **★first** [2] *v.* remain, linger *The foggy weather lingered for most of the morning*, endure, stay
latch *n.* bolt, bar, padlock, fastener
late *adj.* tardy, behindhand, departed, slow **★early**
lately *adv.* recently, latterly, formerly
lather *n.* suds, foam, bubbles, froth
latter *adj.* final, last, latest, recent, closing **★former**
laud *v.* compliment, praise, applaud, glorify **★blame**
laugh *v.* chuckle, giggle, guffaw, snicker **★cry**
launch [1] *v.* start, begin, commence, establish, initiate [2] *n.* motorboat
lavish [1] *adj.* abundant, generous, liberal, extravagant [2] *v.* waste, squander *My parents left me a small fortune, but I squandered it all*, give
law *n.* rule, ordinance, regulation, edict, decree
lawful *adj.* legal, legitimate, rightful **★illegal**
lawyer *n.* attorney, counsel, jurist, barrister, solicitor, advocate
lax *adj.* careless, casual, slack, relaxed, vague **★strict** LACKS
lay [1] *v.* put, set *It's time for dinner; let's set the table*, deposit, place, spread [2] impute, charge [3] *adj.* nonprofessional, amateur *It was a very good play, performed by amateur actors*
layer *n.* seam, sheet, thickness, tier
lazy *adj.* idle, inactive, slothful, slow, sluggish **★active**
lead *v.* conduct, guide, escort, direct, command **★follow**
leader *n.* guide, pilot, conductor, chief, head, master
leaf *n.* frond, blade, sheet LIEF
league *n.* band, association, society, guild, group
leak *v.* trickle, ooze, seep, exude, flow out LEEK
lean [1] *adj.* spare, slim, thin, skinny *Lina has no flesh on her; she is very skinny*, [2] *v.* bend, curve, tilt, incline LIEN
leap *v.* spring, bound, jump, hop, skip
learn *v.* find out, ascertain, determine, acquire knowledge, understand
learned *adj.* cultured, educated, scholarly, literate **★ignorant**
learning *n.* scholarship, education, knowledge, ▷*wisdom* **★ignorance**
least *adj.* fewest, smallest, slightest, lowest, tiniest **★most** LEASED
leave [1] *v.* abandon, desert, forsake, quit, go [2] bequeath, bestow [3] *n.* vacation, furlough *Jack's on a furlough from the Army*, permission
lecture *n.* talk, speech, address, sermon
ledge *n.* shelf, ridge, step
legacy *n.* bequest, inheritance, gift
legal *adj.* legitimate, lawful, valid, sound **★illegal**
legend [1] *n.* fable, myth, tale, fiction [2] inscription *The box bore a brass plate with an inscription*, heading, caption
legible *adj.* clear, readable, understandable, distinct **★illegible**
legitimate *adj.* legal, lawful, proper, rightful, ▷*genuine* **★illegal**
leisurely *adj.* unhurried, slow, easy, carefree, tranquil **★hectic**
lend *v.* load, advance, provide, supply, grant, lease **★borrow**

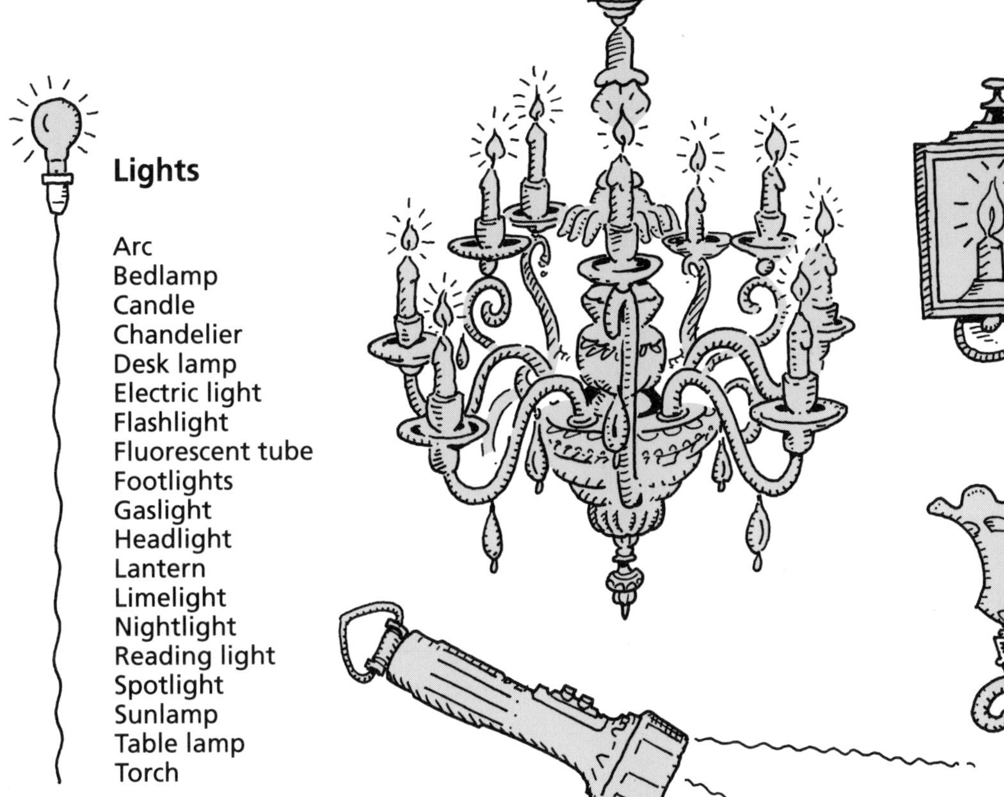

lengthen *v.* extend, elongate, stretch, draw out, prolong ★**shorten**

lengthy *adj.* long, drawn out, longwinded, ▷*tedious* ★**short**

lenient *adj.* tolerant, merciful, sparing, forbearing, indulgent ★**severe**

less *adj.* lesser, smaller, inferior, lower

lessen *v.* reduce, cut, become smaller, diminish, decrease ★**increase** LESSON

lesson *n.* instruction, lecture, information, teaching, exercise LESSEN

let [1] *v.* allow, permit, suffer, authorize *The mayor authorized our school to hold the celebrations in the main square,* grant [2] lease

let down [1] *v.* lower, take down [2] betray, abandon, disappoint ★**satisfy**

letter [1] *n.* dispatch, communication, epistle, message [2] character *The book was printed in Hebrew characters,* sign, symbol

level [1] *n.* plane, grade [2] *adj.* even, flat, smooth ★**uneven** [3] *v.* aim, direct, point [4] demolish *Many houses were demolished during the earthquake,* destroy

liable [1] *adj.* answerable, accountable, responsible [2] apt *My parents are apt to be annoyed if I play music too loud,* prone, inclined

liar *n.* deceiver, fibber, teller of tales LYRE

libel *v.* slander, malign, blacken, defame, slur ★**praise**

liberal *adj.* open-handed, generous, open-hearted, free, lavish

liberate *v.* set free, save, release, ★**restrict**

liberty *n.* freedom, independence ★**slavery**

license *v.* allow, permit, entitle ★**ban**

lie [1] *n.* untruth, falsehood [2] *v.* recline *I shall recline on the sofa for the afternoon,* lounge, repose, ▷*loll* [3] tell a lie, fib, invent LYE

life *n.* being, existence, activity, energy, ★**death**

lift *v.* raise, erect, hoist, elevate, hold up ★**lower**

light [1] *n.* radiance, glow, shine, glare, brightness [2] lamp, beacon, flame [2] *v.* ignite, illuminate, kindle *The scouts kindled a fire to cook our food* [3] *adj.* fair, light-colored, sunny ★**dark** [4] lightweight, buoyant, airy ★**heavy**

like [1] *adj.* similar, resembling, akin ★**unlike** [2] *v.* admire, love, adore, cherish, prize ★**dislike**
likely *adj.* probable, expected, possible
likeness [1] *n.* resemblance, appearance [2] photograph *That's a wonderful photograph of my grandmother,* portrait
likewise *adv.* also, too, furthermore, further
limb *n.* leg, arm, extension, branch, shoot, bough
limit [1] *n.* barrier, boundary, border, edge, end, restraint [2] *v.* reduce, restrict *The heavy rain was restricted to the hilly country,* confine ★**free**
limited *adj.* restricted, reduced, narrow, confined ★**unrestricted**
limp [1] *adj.* flabby, flimsy, flexible [2] *v.* hobble, falter, shuffle
line [1] *n.* stripe, streak, dash, bar [2] cord, thread [3] row, queue, file [4] calling *Being an opera singer is a noble calling but a difficult one,* occupation
linger *v.* loiter, lag, dally, tarry, delay, ▷*dawdle* ★**speed**
link [1] *n.* bond, tie, connection, joint [2] *v.* unite, join, couple, bracket ★**separate**
liquefy *v.* liquidize, melt
liquid *n.* fluid, liquor, solution
list [1] *n.* schedule, table, catalog, register [2] *v.* tilt, lean, heel *The yacht heeled over as it turned into the wind,* careen, slope
listen *v.* hear, hearken, hark, heed
listless *adj.* languid, dull, lethargic, lifeless, ▷*sluggish* ★**lively**
literally *adv.* actually, faithfully, precisely, really ★**loosely**
literate *adj.* educated, well-educated, learned, lettered ★**illiterate**
lithe *adj.* agile, nimble, flexible, supple ★**stiff**
litter *n.* clutter, jumble, rubbish, mess, refuse
little [1] *adj.* small, tiny, short, slight, trivial, petty, ▷*small* ★**large** [2] *adv.* hardly, rarely, seldom
live [1] *adj.* alive, living, existing, active, alert ★**dead** [2] *v.* be, subsist, breathe, exist
lively *adj.* active, brisk, vivacious, animated, agile ★ **listless**
livid [1] *adj.* angry, enraged, furious, mad [2] ashen *We were really scared, and Bob's face was ashen,* grayish, pale, leaden
living [1] *adj.* alive, existing [2] *n.* job, occupation, work
load [1] *n.* freight, cargo, goods, burden [2] *v.* fill, pack, burden, pile up, stack LODE, LOWED
loaf [1] *v.* waste time, idle, dally, dawdle [2] *n.* block, cube, lump, cake
loan [1] *n.* credit, advance, allowance [2] *v.* allow, lend, advance *The bank advanced me the money to pay the mortgage* LONE
loath or **loth** *adj.* reluctant, disinclined, opposed
loathe *v.* abhor, detest, despise, dislike, ▷*hate* ★**like**
lobby *n.* hallway, entrance, vestibule, foyer
local *adj.* regional, district, provincial
locate *v.* find, discover, detect, unearth
lock [1] *n.* bolt, fastener, latch, clasp [2] *v.* bolt, fasten, secure [3] *n.* floodgate, weir [4] curl, braid, tress *I kept a tress of her hair in a locket*
lodge [1] *v.* stay at, put up, shelter, get stuck *A fishbone got stuck in his throat,* remain [2] *n.* inn, hotel
lofty [1] *adj.* tall, high, noble, great [2] proud, exalted, arrogant ★**modest**
logical *adj.* fair, justifiable, reasonable, sound ★**illogical**
loiter *v.* lag, trail, linger, dally, dawdle, hang around
loll *v.* recline, sprawl, lounge, lie, rest, flop
lone *adj.* single, sole, lonely, separate, unaccompanied LOAN
lonely *adj.* alone, forsaken, friendless, remote, forlorn, lonesome
long [1] *adj.* lengthy, extended, expanded ★**short** [2] *v.* crave, hanker, yearn, desire
look [1] *v.* appear, seem [2] peer, glance, watch, behold [3] *n.* appearance, glance, gaze *Her gaze fell upon me, and I had to answer the next question*
loom *v.* menace, portend, rise, emerge, appear
loop *n.* bend, circle, coil, noose, twist

loophole *n.* escape, way out, excuse, get-out
loose [1] *adj.* slack, separate, apart, flimsy, flabby, baggy [2] free, relaxed, [3] vague, indefinite
loosely *adv.* freely, separately, vaguely
loosen *v.* slacken, relax, undo, detach, release, unfasten ★**tighten**
loot *n.* booty, haul, sway, spoils, plunder LUTE

lord *n.* noble, ruler, duke, marquess, earl, viscount, baron
lose [1] *v.* mislay, misplace, miss ★**find** [2] be defeated, suffer defeat *The rebels suffered defeat at the hands of the army,* fail ★**win**
loser *n.* failure, dud, flop ★**winner**
loss *n.* damage, harm, forfeit, ruin, misfortune ★**gain**
lost *adj.* mislaid, missing, gone, vanished, strayed, ruined ★**found**
lot [1] *n.* group, batch, assortment [2] fate, portion, fortune [3] plot, patch, land
lotion *n.* balm, salve, ointment, cream, liniment
loud [1] *adj.* noisy, blatant, shrill, blaring, deafening [2] gaudy, vulgar, tasteless ★**quiet**
lounge [1] *v.* recline, lie, loll, sprawl, laze [2] *n.* lobby *Tea was served in the hotel's charming lobby,* reception room, waiting room
lout *n.* oaf, clod, boor, lummox
lovable *adj.* winsome, charming, attractive, fascinating ★**hateful**
love [1] *v.* adore, idolize, worship, dote on, cherish, treasure [2] *n.* affection, passion, devotion, ardor ★**hate**
lovely *adj.* charming, delightful, beautiful, adorable ★**hideous**
low [1] *adj.* base, vulgar, crude, improper [2] not high, flat, level [3] soft, faint, muffled, deep [4] humble, modest, lowly [5] cheap, inexpensive ★**high** LO
lower [1] *v.* let down, fall, descend [2] debase, disgrace, degrade [3] *adj.* inferior, lesser, smaller, minor
loyal *adj.* constant, staunch *Bill was Kathy's staunch friend for years,* true, ▷*faithful* ★**disloyal**
lucid *adj.* clear, obvious, intelligible, bright, ▷*transparent* ★**murky**
luck *n.* chance, fortune, success, windfall ★**misfortune**
lucky *adj.* fortunate, successful, blessed, charmed, favored ★**unlucky**
ludicrous *adj.* absurd, foolish, silly, outlandish, ▷*ridiculous*
lug *v.* pull, draw, drag, haul, tow, heave
luggage *n.* baggage, cases, trunks, boxes
lull [1] *v.* calm, dwindle, cease, slacken, subside [2] *n.* calm, hush, respite
lumber [1] *n.* clutter, jumble, junk, rubbish, trash [2] timber
luminous *adj.* shining, radiant, bright
lump *n.* bit, piece, chunk, block, knob, swelling *I noticed a rather mysterious swelling on my arm*
lunatic *n.* insane person, maniac, psychopath
lunge *v.* push, thrust, plunge, charge, pounce
lurch *v.* lean, list, reel, rock, stagger, stumble
lure *v.* attract, draw, decoy, ensnare, invite, ▷*tempt* ★**repulse**
lurid *adj.* ghastly, disgusting, grim, grisly, melodramatic, sensational
lurk *v.* slink, skulk, crouch, hide, prowl, snoop
luscious *adj.* juicy, succulent, mellow, delicious, scrumptious ★**nauseous**
lush *adj.* wild, luxuriant, green, rich, abundant
lust *n.* desire, passion, craving, greed
luster *n.* brightness, brilliance, gleam, sheen
lusty *adj.* hale, hearty, vigorous, energetic, rugged, tough ★**weak**
luxury *n.* affluence, wealth, richness, comfort, bliss
lyre *n.* harp, lute, zither LIAR

M m

macabre *adj.* ghastly, grisly, hideous, horrible, ▷*ghostly*

machine *n.* engine, contrivance, device

mad [1] *adj.* angry, furious [2] lunatic, crazy, ▷*insane* ★**sane**

madcap *adj.* flighty, reckless, thoughtless, impulsive

magazine [1] *n.* periodical, publication [2] storehouse, depot, arsenal

magic [1] *n.* wizardry, witchcraft, sorcery, conjuring [2] *adj.* bewitching *She greeted me with a bewitching smile*, fascinating, miraculous

magician *n.* conjuror, wizard, witch, sorcerer, juggler

magistrate *n.* judge, justice, bailiff

magnanimous *adj.* forgiving, generous, charitable, liberal ★**paltry**

magnate *n.* industrialist, merchant, tycoon, VIP, leader MAGNET

magnet *n.* lodestone, attraction, bait, draw MAGNATE

magnetic *adj.* attracting, attractive, absorbing, entrancing, ▷*charming* ★**repulsive**

magnificent *adj.* majestic, noble, grand, brilliant, superb, ▷*splendid* ★**modest**

magnify *v.* enlarge, increase, exaggerate, ▷*enhance* ★**diminish**

maid [1] *n.* maiden, virgin, miss, damsel [2] maidservant, domestic help, waitress MADE

mail [1] *n.* letters, post, correspondence, epistles [2] armor *The knight's armor was of breastplates and chain mail*, shield MALE

maim *v.* mutilate, injure, mangle, crush, ▷*disable* ★**heal**

main [1] *adj.* leading, principal, head *Such important matters are dealt with at our head office*, chief, central [2] *n.* channel, duct, line, pipe

mainly *adv.* chiefly, generally, mostly, on the whole, usually

maintain [1] *v.* sustain, keep, support, provide for [2] affirm, advocate *The chairman advocated an increase in charges*, assert

Mail

majestic *adj.* dignified, grand, noble, august, elevated, ▷*magnificent* ★**unimportant**

major [1] *adj.* senior, chief, leading, more important, greater ★**minor** [2] *n.* officer, soldier

majority *n.* greater number, most part, bulk, mass ★**minority**

make [1] *v.* build, construct, fabricate, fashion [2] compel, drive, coerce [3] designate *Liz was designated as next head of the department*, appoint

make up [1] *v.* invent, fabricate, create [2] forgive and forget, bury the hatchet *At last, my brother and sister stopped arguing and decided to bury the hatchet*

makeshift *adj.* improvised, temporary, stopgap *I fixed the car engine, but it was only a stopgap repair* ★**permanent**

malady *n.* illness, sickness, ailment, affliction, disease

malevolent *adj.* malign, baleful, venomous, malicious, ▷*hostile* ★**benevolent**

malice *n.* bitterness, rancor, spite, enmity, ▷*hatred* ★**kindness**

malicious *adj.* malignant, spiteful, resentful, bitter, ▷*hateful* ★**kind**

maltreat *v.* bully, harm, abuse, injure, ▷*hurt* ★**assist**

mammoth *adj.* giant, colossal, enormous, ▷*huge* ★**small**

man [1] *n.* male, sir, mankind, gentleman [2] valet, manservant [3] *v.* equip, fit out, arm, crew

manage [1] *v.* direct, control, administer [2] get along *I get along quite well on my own*, fare, cope with ★**fail**

manager *n.* director, superintendent, overseer, foreman, boss

mandate *n.* authority, command, instruction, warrant

maneuver *v.* direct, drive, guide, handle, ▷*manipulate*

mangle *v.* crush, deform, destroy, maul, ▷*maim*

mania *n.* madness, delirium, craze, fad, enthusiasm, passion

manifest *v.* signify, suggest, demonstrate, display, ▷*show* ★**hide**

manipulate *v.* work, handle, wield, conduct, ▷*operate*

manly *adj.* male, masculine, brave, bold, strong, ▷*fearless*

manner *n.* fashion, style, form, mode, demeanor, bearing, way MANOR

manor *n.* estate, country house, château, hall MANNER

mansion *n.* house, castle, residence, ▷*manor*

mantle *n.* canopy, cape, covering, hood, shroud MANTEL

mantel *n.* fireplace shelf, mantelpiece MANTLE

manual [1] *adj.* hand-operated, physical [2] *n.* guide, guidebook, handbook *We found the electric typewriter easier to use than the manual typewriter*

manufacture *v.* make, build, fabricate, ▷*construct*

manuscript [1] *n.* script, article, essay, theme [2] handwriting, autograph

many *adj.* numerous, varied, various, frequent, countless ★**few**

map *n.* chart, plan, diagram, outline

mar *v.* deface, disfigure, injure, blemish, damage, ▷*spoil* ★**enhance**

march *v.* stride, walk, pace, step, file, trek

margin *n.* edge, border, rim, side, boundary, brim, brink ★**center**

mariner *n.* seaman, sailor, seafarer, deckhand, tar, seadog

mark [1] *n.* feature, emblem, impression *The letter had a hand-stamped impression on it*, blemish [2] *v.* scratch, blemish, stain [3] take notice of, observe

marked *adj.* noticeable, conspicuous, apparent, clear, striking ★**slight**

market *n.* bazaar, marketplace, mart, fair

maroon *v.* desert, beach, strand, abandon, cast away ★**rescue**

marry *v.* wed, get married, espouse, mate, unite ★**separate**

marsh *n.* swamp, mire, moor, morass, bog

marshal *v.* gather, group, deploy, assemble MARTIAL

martial *adj.* military, militant, hostile, warlike ★**peaceful** MARSHAL

marvel *n.* miracle, wonder, spectacle, sensation

marvelous *adj.* wonderful, wondrous, fabulous, spectacular, ▷*remarkable* ★**ordinary**

masculine *adj.* manlike, manly, strong, robust, strapping, ▷*male* ★**feminine**

mash *v.* crush, squash, pulverize, grind

mask [1] *n.* camouflage, veil, domino [2] *v.* conceal, disguise *Aladdin went to the market-place disguised as a beggar*, shield ★**uncover**

mass *n.* batch, combination, hunk, load, quantity, lump

massacre *v.* exterminate, butcher, murder, slaughter, kill

massive *adj.* big, large, bulky, enormous, ▷*huge* ★**small**

master [1] *n.* controller, director, leader, captain, champion [2] *v.* tame *Our job on the ranch was to tame the wild horses*, control, defeat, subdue

match [1] *n.* light, fuse, taper, lucifer [2] *v.* copy, pair, equal, tone with

mate [1] *n.* spouse, husband, wife, companion, chum, comrade [2] *v.* breed, join, wed, yoke

material [1] *n.* fabric, textile, cloth, stuff, matter [2] *adj.* actual, real, concrete *There was concrete evidence of the prisoner's innocence*

maternal *adj.* motherly, parental, kind, affectionate, protective

matter [1] *n.* affair, concern, subject, topic [2] stuff, material, substance *This rock contains some sort of mineral substance* [3] trouble, distress [4] *v.* signify, count, affect

mature *adj.* ripe, mellowed, seasoned, developed, grown-up, adult ★**immature**

maul *v.* batter, beat, molest, paw, ▷*mangle*

maxim *n.* saying, motto, axiom, proverb

maximum *adj.* supreme, highest, most, greatest, top, largest ★**minimum**

maybe *adv.* possibly, perhaps, perchance

maze *n.* labyrinth, puzzle, tangle, confusion, ▷*muddle* MAIZE

meadow *n.* grassland, field, mead, pasture

meager *adj.* thin, spare, slight, flimsy, sparse, ▷*scanty* ★**substantial**

meal *n.* repast, dinner, lunch, breakfast, supper, ▷*feast*

mean [1] *v.* signify, denote, express, suggest [2] *adj.* cruel, base, low, paltry, miserly ★**generous** [3] average, medium MIEN

meaning *n.* significance, explanation, sense

means [1] *n.* resources, money, wealth [2] technique, ability *She has the ability to become a professional player,* method

measure [1] *n.* meter, gauge, rule [2] limit, extent, amount [3] *v.* estimate, value, quantify *It is hard to quantify how much damage has been done*

meat *n.* flesh, viands, victuals, food MEET METE

mechanical [1] *adj.* automatic, machine-driven [2] routine, unthinking

medal *n.* award, decoration, ribbon, prize, trophy MEDDLE

meddle *v.* interfere, intervene, intrude, tamper MEDAL

medicine *n.* remedy, cure, physic, medicament, nostrum, drug

mediocre *adj.* average, common, inferior, middling, ▷*ordinary* ★**excellent**

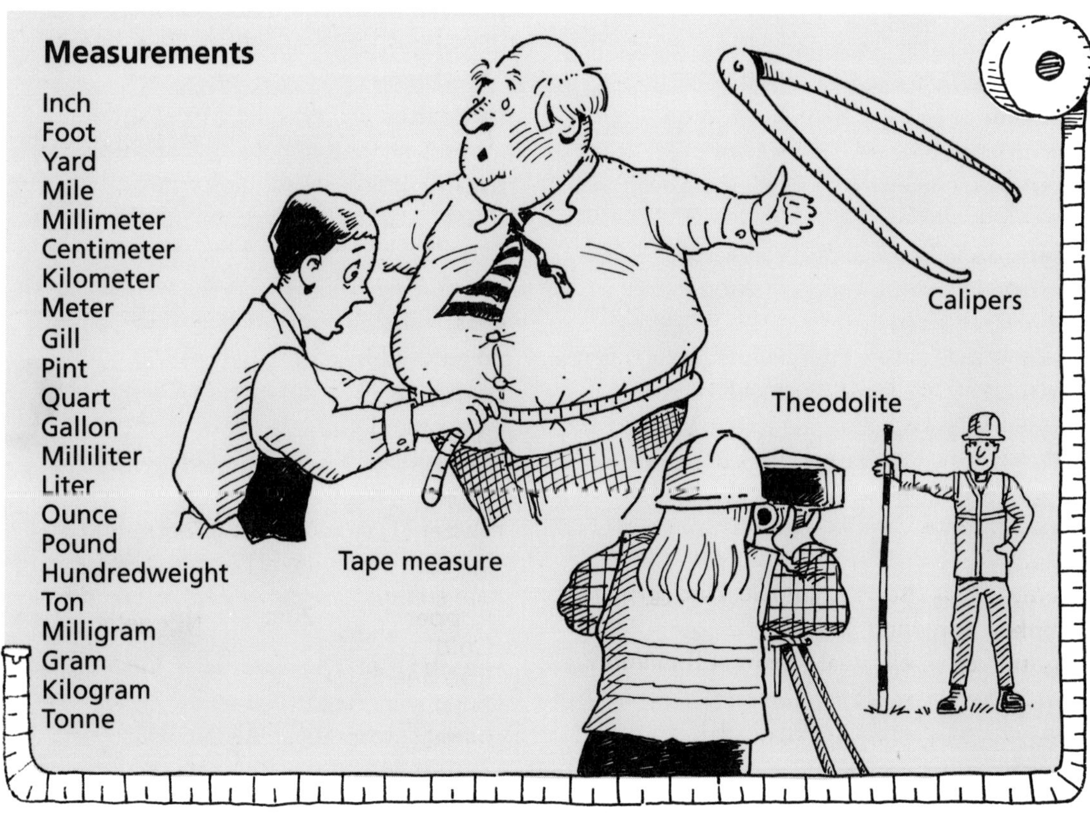

meditate *v.* ponder, puzzle over, think, reflect, contemplate
medium [1] *n.* means, agency, center [2] conditions, setting, atmosphere *I like school because it has such a wonderful atmosphere of learning* [3] *adj.* average, fair, ▷*mediocre*
medley *n.* assortment, jumble, collection, hotchpotch
meek *adj.* docile, humble, quiet, patient, uncomplaining, ▷*mild* ★**arrogant**
meet *v.* come together, converge, join, flock, assemble, encounter MEAT METE
meeting *n.* gathering, assembly, convention
melancholy *adj.* glum, gloomy, unhappy, sad, ▷*miserable* ★**cheerful**
mellow [1] *adj.* ripe, rich, full-flavored ★**unripe** [2] jovial, cheerful [3] smooth, soothing, delicate *The wine had a smooth, delicate flavor*
melodious *adj.* sweet, mellow, silver-toned, rich, resonant ★**harsh**
melody *n.* tune, air, lay, song, chant, theme
melt *v.* dissolve, liquefy, soften, thaw ★**solidify**
member [1] *n.* fellow, associate, representative [2] limb, part, portion, leg, arm
memorable *adj.* unforgettable, fresh, indelible, noticeable, striking, ▷*conspicuous*
memorial *n.* monument, memento, relic, mausoleum *The old emperor was buried in the state mausoleum*
memorize *v.* learn, commit to memory, remember
memory *n.* recall, recapture, recollection, renown, ▷*fame*
menace *v.* threaten, intimidate, frighten, alarm, ▷*bully*
mend *v.* restore, correct, promote, improve, rectify, heal, ▷*repair* ★**damage**
menial [1] *adj.* servile, ignoble, base [2] *n.* flunkey, underling, lackey
mental *adj.* intellectual, theoretical *Edward's knowledge of music is purely theoretical; he can't play or sing*, abstract ★**physical**
mention *v.* declare, announce, observe, disclose, speak of, say
mercenary [1] *adj.* acquisitive, grasping, greedy, ▷*selfish* [2] *n.* soldier of fortune *The men who were killed were not Austrians, but soldiers of fortune*, freelance, hireling
merchandise *n.* wares, goods, commodities, cargo, freight, stock
merchant *n.* dealer, trader, marketeer, vender, retailer, tradesman
merciful *adj.* humane, clement, lenient, compassionate, sparing, forgiving ★**merciless**
merciless *adj.* callous, cruel, pitiless, unrelenting, inhuman ★**merciful**
mercy *n.* compassion, clemency, forgiveness, forbearance, grace, ▷*pity* ★**cruelty**
mere *adj.* pure, unmixed, absolute, unaffected, simple, paltry
merge *v.* mix, mingle, combine, fuse, blend, weld, ▷*unite*
merit [1] *n.* excellence, quality, virtue, worth, caliber, ▷*talent* ★**failing** [2] *v.* deserve, be worthy of
merry *adj.* jolly, gleeful, cheerful, mirthful, sunny, ▷*happy* ★**melancholy**
mesh *n.* net, lattice, snare, netting, tangle, trap
mess [1] *n.* muddle, confusion, clutter, jumble, chaos, ▷*plight* ★**order** [2] dining hall, eating place
message *n.* communication, letter, missive, notice, note, dispatch *The reporter sent a dispatch to her paper in Lisbon*
messenger *n.* courier, runner, agent, bearer, carrier, herald

Metals

Aluminum
Brass
Bronze
Chromium
Copper
Gold
Iron and Steel
Lead
Manganese
Mercury
Nickel
Platinum
Silver
Tin
Zinc

Nuggets
Girder

mete *v.* measure, apportion, distribute, divide, deal MEAT MEET

meter [1] *n.* measure, gauge, rule [2] cadence *He recited some of his poems, which had a peculiar cadence to them*, rhythm, lilt, swing

method *n.* routine, usage, way, means, system, rule, manner, ▷*mode*

mettle *n.* spirit, life, fire, animation, ardor, boldness, ▷*courage*

middle [1] *n.* center, heart, midst [2] *adj.* medium, average, normal

midget [1] *n.* dwarf, gnome, pygmy [2] *adj.* little, miniature, small, ▷*tiny* ★**giant**

mien *n.* appearance, air, look, manner, expression MEAN

miffed *adj.* annoyed, nettled, offended, hurt, ▷*upset* ★**delighted**

might [1] *n.* strength, ability, power, force, energy [2] *v. past tense of* **may** *She might not have gone had she known it would snow* MITE

mighty *adj.* strong, powerful, potent, stupendous, ▷*hefty* ★**weak**

mild *adj.* moderate, calm, gentle, genial, docile, ▷*meek* ★**harsh**

military *adj.* martial, soldierly, warlike

mill [1] *n.* grinder, works, factory, plant [2] *v.* crush, grind, pulverize *The rock was pulverized and used for making roads*, grate

mimic *v.* impersonate, copy, simulate, imitate

mince *v.* shred, chop, crumble, grind, hash MINTS

mind [1] *n.* brain, intellect, soul, spirit [2] *v.* listen to, obey, follow orders [3] take care of, look after [4] be careful, watch out for

mine [1] *n.* quarry, colliery, shaft, deposit, tunnel [2] bomb, explosive [3] *v.* excavate, dig out [4] *pron.* belonging to me *This store is mine*

mingle *v.* mix, blend, combine, ▷*merge*

miniature [1] *adj.* tiny, small, dwarf, midget, minute [2] *n.* small portrait

mimimum *adj.* least, smallest, lowest, slightest ★**maximum**

minister [1] *n.* clergyman, vicar, priest [2] ambassador, diplomat *My aunt was a diplomat and was a minister in the embassy* [3] government official, secretary

minor *adj.* lesser, smaller, lower, junior, trivial, trifling ★**major** MINER

mint [1] *v.* stamp, forge, cast [2] *adj.* new, perfect, untarnished [3] *n.* peppermint, plant

minute [1] *n.* (*min*-it) flash, instant, moment [2] *adj.* (my-*nyute*) slight, tiny, small, ▷*miniature* ★**huge**

miracle *n.* marvel, wonder, phenomenon

miraculous *adj.* supernatural, amazing, wondrous, prodigious ★**ordinary**

mire *n.* slime, muck, ooze, mud

mirror [1] *n.* looking glass, reflector [2] *v.* imitate, simulate, reflect *The essay reflected my feelings about my old home*, copy

mirth *n.* hilarity, laughter, jocularity, fun, frolic, jollity ★**melancholy**

misbehave *v.* do wrong, disobey, offend, be naughty ★**behave**

miscellaneous *adj.* various, varied, divers, sundry, mixed, jumbled

mischief *n.* roguery, pranks, damage, hurt, annoyance, harm

mischievous *adj.* rascally, villainous, naughty, destructive, spiteful ★**good**

misconduct *n.* misbehavior, wrongdoing, naughtiness, rudeness

miser *n.* niggard, skinflint, scrooge, penny-pincher, tightwad ★**spendthrift**

miserable *adj.* forlorn, wretched, pitiable, desolate, suffering ★**cheerful**

misery *n.* sorrow, woe, grief, anguish, distress, ▷*unhappiness* ★**happiness**

misfit *n.* eccentric *Professor Jones is something of an eccentric and comes to college in her slippers*, drop-out, oddball, nonconformist

misfortune *n.* adversity, bad luck, hardship, evil, calamity, ▷*disaster* ★**luck**

misgiving *n.* distrust, mistrust, doubt, apprehension, anxiety, ▷*qualm* ★**confidence**

mishap *n.* misadventure, blow, accident, ▷*misfortune*

misjudge *v.* underestimate, overestimate, overrate, underrate, ▷*mistake*

mislay *v.* lose, misplace, miss

mislead *v.* deceive, lead astray, hoodwink, take in, outwit, ▷*bluff*

miss [1] *v.* fail, fall short of, skip, pass over, mistake [2] grieve over, yearn for, lament [3] *n.* girl, young woman, damsel
missile *n.* projectile, arrow, dart, pellet, shot, rocket
mission *n.* errand, task, assignment, object, objective, end, aim, ▷*quest*
mist *n.* moisture, dew, vapor, fog, cloud MISSED
mistake [1] *n.* error, fault, lapse, blunder, oversight [2] *v.* slip up, misunderstand, confuse
mistaken *adj.* erroneous, untrue, false, fallacious, ▷*wrong* ★**correct**
mistrust *v.* disbelieve, distrust, doubt, fear, ▷*suspect* ★**trust**
misunderstand *v.* mistake, misinterpret, take wrongly ★**grasp**
misuse *v.* exploit, abuse, corrupt
mite [1] *n.* grain, atom, morsel, particle [2] spiderlike creature *The plants were infested with mites* MIGHT
mitigate *v.* allay, ease, abate, moderate, justify ★**aggravate**
mix *v.* blend, whip, mingle, combine, ▷*stir*
mix up *v.* confuse, confound, muddle, jumble, ▷*bewilder*
mixture *n.* miscellany, medley, jumble, blend
moan *v.* wail, groan, grouse, grumble, grieve
mob *n.* crowd, mass, gang, flock, rabble, company, throng
mobile *adj.* active, portable, wandering, movable ★**immobile**
mock [1] *v.* mimic, imitate, jeer at, laugh at, ridicule, ▷*flatter* [2] *adj.* pretended, artificial
mode *n.* fashion, style, vogue, manner, way, form, ▷*method* MOWED
model [1] *n.* pattern, original, prototype *This car is a prototype, and we will produce many like it* [2] mannequin [3] replica, representation
moderate *adj.* reasonable, medium, gentle, mild, quiet, modest, ▷*fair*
modern *adj.* new, up-to-date, modish, stylish, recent
modest *adj.* bashful, demure, diffident, unassuming, humble ★**vain**
modesty *n.* humility, diffidence, reserve, shyness, decency ★**vanity**
modify *v.* transform, convert, change, alter, revise, redesign
moist *adj.* damp, humid, watery, clammy, dank, ▷*wet* ★**dry**
moisture *n.* damp, dampness, liquid, wetness
mold [1] *v.* form, shape, fashion, cast, create [2] *n.* pattern, matrix [3] earth, loam
moldy *adj.* mildewed, putrid, bad
molest *v.* annoy, bother, pursue, attack, torment, ▷*harry*
moment [1] *n.* second, instant, twinkling [2] importance, worth, weight *I think your argument has some weight, and I agree with you*
momentous *adj.* notable, outstanding, decisive, important ★**insignificant**
monarch *n.* king, sovereign, ruler, emperor, prince *The head of state in Monaco is a prince*

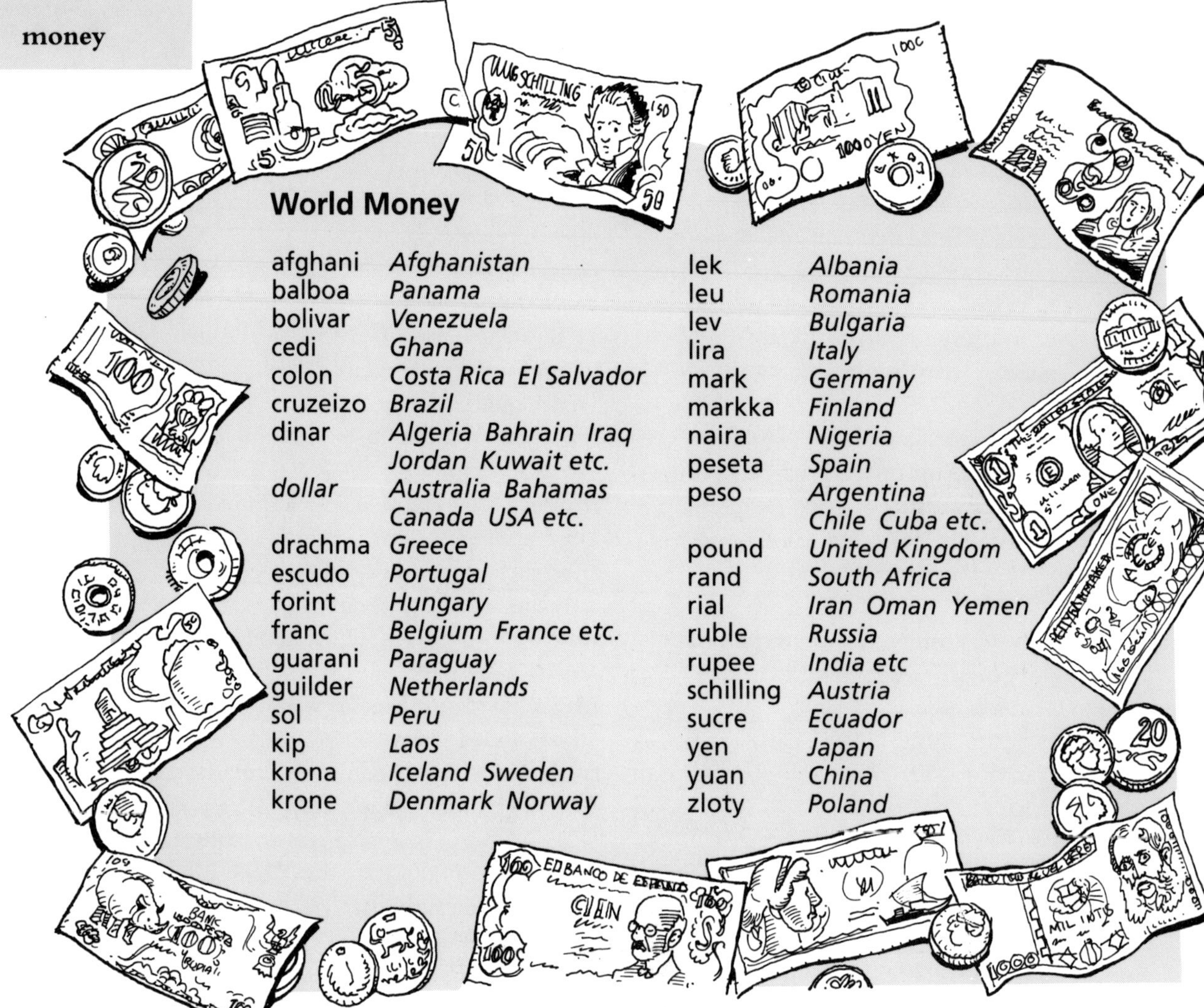

World Money

afghani	*Afghanistan*
balboa	*Panama*
bolivar	*Venezuela*
cedi	*Ghana*
colon	*Costa Rica El Salvador*
cruzeizo	*Brazil*
dinar	*Algeria Bahrain Iraq Jordan Kuwait etc.*
dollar	*Australia Bahamas Canada USA etc.*
drachma	*Greece*
escudo	*Portugal*
forint	*Hungary*
franc	*Belgium France etc.*
guarani	*Paraguay*
guilder	*Netherlands*
sol	*Peru*
kip	*Laos*
krona	*Iceland Sweden*
krone	*Denmark Norway*
lek	*Albania*
leu	*Romania*
lev	*Bulgaria*
lira	*Italy*
mark	*Germany*
markka	*Finland*
naira	*Nigeria*
peseta	*Spain*
peso	*Argentina Chile Cuba etc.*
pound	*United Kingdom*
rand	*South Africa*
rial	*Iran Oman Yemen*
ruble	*Russia*
rupee	*India etc*
schilling	*Austria*
sucre	*Ecuador*
yen	*Japan*
yuan	*China*
zloty	*Poland*

money *n.* wealth, cash, coin, legal tender

mongrel *n.* hybrid, mixed, crossbreed, dog

monitor [1] *n.* listener, auditor, watchdog, prefect [2] *v.* check, supervise, oversee

monologue *n.* lecture, oration, speech, recitation, sermon

monopolize *v.* control, take over, appropriate, ▷*dominate* ★**share**

monotonous *adj.* tedious, uninteresting, dull, prosaic *His speech was so prosaic that I almost dropped off to sleep!*, repetitive, ▷*tiresome*

monster *n.* beast, fiend, wretch, villain, brute

monstrous *adj.* hideous, frightful, dreadful, terrible, criminal, ▷*wicked*

mood *n.* state of mind, humor, temper, disposition *My grandmother's gentle disposition won her many friends*

moody *adj.* morose, sulky, sullen, peevish, cantankerous *I didn't like Uncle Harry; he was a cantankerous old man* ★**cheerful**

moor [1] *v.* tether, picket, tie, chain, anchor, secure [2] *n.* heath, moorland

mop [1] *n.* sponge, swab, towel [2] hair, tresses, locks, mane

mope *v.* be dejected, grieve, moon, pine, sulk

moral *adj.* virtuous, good, honest, honorable, ▷*upright* ★**immoral**

morbid *adj.* gruesome, macabre, melancholy

more [1] *adj.* in addition, also, beyond, extra, further [2] *adv.* better, again, longer

morning *n.* dawn, daybreak, daylight, cockcrow *I rose at cockcrow, saddled my horse, and was off to Richmond*, sunrise ★**evening** MOURNING

morose *adj.* glum, sullen, sulky, broody, taciturn, ▷*moody* ★**cheerful**

morsel *n.* bit, bite, piece, scrap, nibble

mortal [1] *adj.* human, feeble, ephemeral [2] fatal, final, deadly, severe

most [1] *adj.* greatest [2] *adv.* mostly, chiefly, mainly, utmost
mostly *adv.* as a rule, principally, usually, normally
mother [1] *n.* female parent, mom, mommy, mama [2] *v.* nurse, protect, rear, care for
motherly *adj.* caring, comforting, loving, maternal, gentle
motion [1] *n.* movement, locomotion, action, passage [2] proposal *I vote that we accept the proposal,* suggestion
motionless *adj.* stationary, still, transfixed, stable, inert ★**moving**
motive *n.* reason, purpose, occasion, impulse, cause, ▷*spur*
mottled *adj.* speckled, spotted, pied, piebald
motto *n.* saying, slogan, watchword, maxim *My mother's maxim was "Always look on the bright side,"* proverb
mound *n.* hillock, pile, knoll, rise, mount
mount *v.* ascend, climb, rise, vault
mourn *v.* lament, deplore, sorrow, regret, weep, ▷*grieve* ★**rejoice**
mournful *adj.* doleful, somber, cheerless, sorrowful, ▷*melancholy* ★**joyful**
mouth *n.* aperture, opening, entrance, orifice, inlet, jaws
mouthful *n.* bite, morsel, sample, taste, tidbit
move [1] *v.* march, proceed, walk, go [2] propose, suggest, recommend [3] propel, drive, impel
moving *adj.* touching, affecting, stirring *The band played a stirring rendition of "Dixie,"* emotional
much [1] *adj.* abundant, considerable, ample [2] *adv.* considerably, greatly, often [3] *n.* lots, loads, heaps, plenty
muck *n.* dirt, filth, mire, ooze, mud, scum
muddle [1] *n.* confusion, clutter, jumble, mix-up [2] *v.* bungle, tangle, confound, ▷*bewilder*
muff *v.* botch, mismanage, miss, spoil, ▷*muddle*
muffle [1] *v.* deaden, mute, muzzle, silence [2] wrap, envelop, wind, swaddle
mug [1] *n.* innocent, fool, simpleton [2] cup, beaker, tankard [3] *v.* attack, beat up, rob
muggy *adj.* clammy, dank, damp, humid, close ★**dry**
mull *v.* meditate *I meditated over the weekend before deciding what to do,* consider, study, think about
multiply *v.* increase, spread, grow, extend, intensify ★**decrease**
multitude *n.* crowd, legion, throng, swarm, horde ★**handful**
mum *adj.* dumb, silent, quiet, mute
munch *v.* crunch, chew, bit, nibble, ▷*eat*
murder *v.* slay, assassinate, butcher, destroy, slaughter, ▷*kill*
murky *adj.* foggy, cloudy, dark, gloomy, dull, misty ★**bright**
murmur *n.* & *v.* whisper, mutter, mumble, drone
muscular *adj.* brawny, athletic, burly, beefy, powerful, ▷*robust* ★**puny**
muse *v.* meditate, ponder, puzzle over, brood, deliberate
must [1] *v.* ought to, should, be obliged to [2] *n.* duty, necessity, requirement
muster *v.* marshal, collect, assemble, rally *The troops rallied and prepared to attack again,* enroll
musty *adj.* moldy, rank, mildewy, decayed
mute *adj.* silent, speechless, voiceless, soundless ★**loud**
mutilate *v.* injure, hurt, cut, damage, hack, ▷*maim*
mutiny *n.* & *v.* protest, revolt, strike, riot
mutter *v.* mumble, grouse, grumble, ▷*murmur* ★**exclaim**
mutual *adj.* common, reciprocal, interchangeable, ▷*joint* ★**one-sided**
mysterious *adj.* obscure, unrevealed, unexplained, secret, ▷*hidden* ★**clear**
mystery *n.* puzzle, enigma, secrecy, riddle, problem
mystify *v.* confuse, bamboozle, hoodwink, puzzle, mislead, ▷*baffle* ★**enlighten**
myth *n.* fable, legend, supposition, fabrication, tradition, fantasy ★**fact**
mythical *adj.* fabulous, fabled, legendary, traditional, imaginary ★**true**

N n

nab *v.* arrest, apprehend, seize, catch, capture, grab

nag [1] *v.* pester, hector, heckle, badger, annoy, henpeck, scold *My parents scolded me for coming home late* [2] *n.* horse, hack, pony

nail [1] *n.* brad, peg, pin, spike, tack [2] *v.* hammer, fix, tack, peg [3] capture, catch, seize

naïve *adj.* innocent, unworldly, unsophisticated, simple, trusting ★**cunning, sophisticated**

naked *adj.* nude, bare, unclothed, undressed ★**clothed**

name [1] *n.* title, description, designation [2] character, reputation *A good reputation is very important to me,* distinction [3] *v.* christen, style, term, entitle

nap [1] *v.* sleep, doze, drowse, rest [2] *n.* down, fiber, fuzz *Velvet is a cloth with a kind of fuzz on the surface*

narrate *v.* describe, tell, recite, yarn

narrow *adj.* slender, fine, small, ▷*thin* ★**wide**

nasty *adj.* dirty, mucky, foul, offensive, unpleasant, ▷*squalid* ★**nice**

national *adj.* civil, governmental, public, general

native *adj.* natural, inborn, aboriginal, domestic, local

natural *adj.* frank, genuine, innate, instinctive, ordinary, usual

naturally *adj.* absolutely, certainly, frankly, normally

nature [1] *n.* temper, personality, disposition

naughty *adj.* mischievous, rascally, wicked, disobedient, ▷*bad* ★**well-behaved**

nauseous *adj.* disgusting, sickening, repulsive, revolting ★**pleasant**

nautical *adj.* maritime *Ancient Greece was a great maritime nation,* seamanlike, naval, sailing

navigate *v.* voyage, cruise, sail, guide, pilot

navy *n.* ships, fleet, armada, flotilla

near *adj.* close, nearby, adjacent, bordering, beside, ▷*nigh* ★**remote**

nearly *adv.* about, almost, all but, thereabouts, roughly

neat [1] *adj.* tidy, spruce, smart, stylish ★**untidy** [2] accurate, adept *Jim wants to be a juggler: he's already very adept,* agile, clever

necessary *adj.* needed, essential, basic, required, compulsory ★**optional**

need [1] *v.* require, want, crave, ▷*demand* ★**have** [2] *n.* distress, want, necessity, deprivation *After the long war, the people suffered many deprivations* KNEAD

needed *adj.* wanted, desired, lacking, ▷*necessary* ★**unnecessary**

needless *adj.* pointless, unnecessary, superfluous, useless ★**necessary**

needy *adj.* destitute, down-and-out, deprived, ▷*poor* ★**well-off**

neglect *v.* overlook, ignore, scorn, slight, disregard, ▷*spurn* ★**cherish**

neglected *adj.* unkempt, abandoned, dilapidated, uncared for ★**cherished**

negligent *adj.* neglectful, forgetful, slack, indifferent, ▷*careless* ★**careful**

negotiate *v.* bargain, deal, treat, haggle, mediate

neighborhood *n.* vicinity, surroundings, district, area, locality *There are many fine houses in this locality*

neighborly *adj.* hospitable, friendly, kind, obliging, ▷*helpful*

nerve [1] *n.* mettle, guts, pluck, audacity [2] cheek, sauce, impudence *Mr. Thompson already owes us money and has the impudence to ask for more!*

nervous *adj.* tense, taut, jumpy, flustered, anxious, timid ★**confident**

nest *n.* den, burrow, haunt, refuge, resort

nestle *adj.* cuddle, snuggle, huddle, nuzzle

net [1] *v.* catch, trap, lasso, capture [2] *n.* mesh, lattice, trap, web, lace *I have some new lace curtains* [3] *adj.* clear *I made a clear $15,000 after taxes,* final, lowest

National and Religious Holidays

Advent All Saints' Day
Anzac Day Ascension Day
Ash Wednesday Australia Day
Bastille Day Boxing Day
Canada Day Candlemas
Carnival Christmas
Commonwealth Day
Diwali Day of the Dead
Easter
Father's Day Fourth of July
Gandhi's Birthday Good Friday Guy Fawkes Day
Halloween Hanukkah
Kenyatta Day Kwanza
Labor Day Lent
Mardi Gras May Day
Memorial Day Midsummer Day Mother's Day
Muhammad's Birthday New Year's Day
Palm Sunday Passover
Pentecost Purim
Ramadan Rosh Hashanah
Saint Patrick's Day
Saint Valentine's Day
Shavuot Sukkot
Thanksgiving Day
Yom Kippur

A puppet from Mexican Day of the Dead Festival

nettle *v.* exasperate, annoy, ruffle, pique, ▷*vex*

neutral *adj.* impartial, unbiased, fair-minded, unprejudiced ★**biased**

never *adv.* at no time, not at all, under no circumstances ★**always**

new *adj.* recent, just out, current, latest, fresh, unused, ▷*novel* ★**old** GNU KNEW

news *n.* information, intelligence, tidings, account

next [1] *adj.* following, succeeding, after, later [2] adjacent, adjoining *I live on Park Street and my friend lives on the adjoining street*, beside

nibble *v.* bite, peck, gnaw, munch, ▷*eat*

nice [1] *adj.* pleasant, agreeable, amiable, charming, delightful ★**nasty** [2] precise, accurate, fine, subtle

niche *n.* compartment, hole, corner, recess, place

nick *v.* dent, score, mill, cut, scratch

nigh *adj.* next, close, adjacent, adjoining, ▷*near* ★**distant**

night *n.* dark, darkness, dusk, evening ★**day** KNIGHT

nimble *adj.* active, agile, spry, lithe, skillfull, ▷*deft* ★**clumsy**

nip *v.* cut, snip, pinch, twinge, bite

no [1] *adj.* not any, not one, none [2] *adv.* nay, not at all KNOW

noble *adj.* dignified, lofty *My aunt is very important and has a lofty position on the council*, generous, grand, stately, elevated ★**base**

nod [1] *v.* beckon, signal, indicate, salute [2] sleep, doze, nap

noise *n.* din, discord, clamor, clatter, hubbub, tumult, uproar ★**silence**

noisy *adj.* loud, boisterous, turbulent, rowdy, clamorous ★**quiet**

nominate *v.* appoint, assign, elect, choose, propose, suggest

nonchalant *adj.* casual, unperturbed, calm, blasé. *We enjoyed the new musical but Sue has been to many shows and is very blasé about it*, cool, detached ★**anxious**

nondescript *adj.* commonplace, colorless, dull, ordinary, ▷*plain* ★**unusual**

none *pron.* not one, not any, not a part, nil, nobody NUN

nonsense *n.* absurdity, balderdash, drivel, rot, garbage, twaddle ★**sense**
nook *n.* compartment, hole, corner, alcove, crevice, ▷*niche*
noose *n.* loop, bight, snare, rope, lasso
normal *adj.* usual, general, average, sane, lucid, rational, standard ★**abnormal**
nose [1] *n.* beak, bill, neb, snout [2] prow, stem, bow, front
nosy *adj.* inquisitive, curious, prying, snooping, intrusive
nostalgia *n.* homesickness, longing, pining, regret, remembrance
notable *adj.* eventful, momentous, outstanding, great, ▷*famous* ★**commonplace**
notch *n.* dent, nick, score, cut, cleft, indentation
note [1] *n.* letter, message, communication [2] remark, record, report [3] fame, renown, distinction [4] banknote, bill
noted *adj.* eminent, renowned, celebrated, great, ▷*famous* ★**obscure**
nothing *n.* zero, naught, null, nil, zip ★**something**
notice [1] *n.* announcement, advice, sign, poster [2] *v.* note *After noting the darkening sky, we decided it would rain*, remark, observe, perceive, make out, see ★**ignore**

After noting the darkening sky, we decided it would rain.

notify *v.* inform, tell, intimate, announce, declare ★**withhold**
notion *n.* idea, conception, opinion, belief, judgment
notorious *adj.* infamous, questionable, scandalous, blatant
notwithstanding *adv.* nevertheless, nonetheless, however, despite
nourish *v.* feed, sustain, nurture, comfort, support ★**starve**
nourishing *adj.* beneficial, healthful, nutritious, wholesome
novel [1] *adj.* fresh, unusual, original, unique, rare, uncommon [2] *n.* fiction, story, book, romance, tale
novice *n.* beginner, learner, apprentice, tyro, pupil ★**expert**
now *adv.* at this moment, at present, at once, instantly, right away
now and then *adv.* from time to time, sometimes, occasionally
nude *adj.* bare, naked, unclothed, stripped, undressed
nudge *v.* poke, push, prod, jog, shove, dig
nuisance [1] *n.* offense, annoyance, plague, trouble, bore, pest, irritation
nullify *v.* annul, invalidate, cancel, quash, ▷*abolish* ★**establish**
numb *adj.* deadened, insensible, dazed, stunned, unfeeling ★**sensitive**
number [1] *n.* figure, amount, volume, quantity, sum [2] crowd, throng, multitude *The country's president was visiting the town, watched by a multitude of people* [3] figure, symbol, ▷*numeral* [4] *v.* count, reckon, tally
numeral *n.* symbol, figure, character, cipher
numerous *adj.* many, divers, several, plentiful, ▷*abundant* ★**few**
nun *n.* sister, religious, abbess, prioress NONE
nurse [1] *v.* attend, care for, foster, support, sustain [2] *n.* hospital attendant, caretaker
nursery [1] *n.* children's room [2] greenhouse, hothouse, garden
nurture *v.* feed, nourish, cherish, foster, ▷*nurse*
nutritious *adj.* healthful, substantial, health-giving, ▷*nourishing* ★**bad**

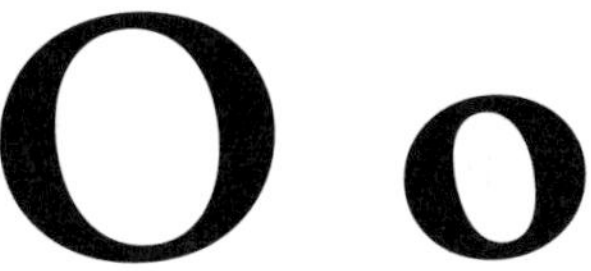

oaf *n.* brute, lout, blockhead, dolt, ruffian, lummox

obedient *adj.* respectful, obliging, law-abiding, servile, dutiful ★**rebellious**

obey *v.* comply, conform, submit, heed, mind, behave ★**disobey**

object [1] *v.* (ob-*ject*) protest, complain, argue, oppose, refuse ★**agree** [2] *n.* (*ob*-ject) thing, article, commodity, item [3] mission, purpose *The purpose of my visit is to end this conflict*, end, objective

objection *n.* dislike, exception, opposition, protest, ▷*complaint* ★**assent**

objectionable *adj.* displeasing, distasteful, disagreeable, repugnant ★**pleasant**

obligation *n.* responsibility, liability, commitment ★**choice**

oblige [1] *v.* require, compel, force, make [2] gratify, please, help, ▷*assist* ★**displease**

obliging *adj.* helpful, polite, agreeable, courteous, ▷*willing* ★**unkind**

obliterate *v.* blot out, efface, erase, wipe out, destroy

oblivious *adj.* unmindful, absentminded, heedless, unaware ★**aware**

obnoxious *adj.* repulsive, revolting, offensive, ▷*unpleasant* ★**pleasant**

obscene *adj.* dirty, unclean, vile, filthy, nasty, immoral, indecent ★**decent**

obscure [1] *adj.* indistinct, dim, vague, hidden, confusing *Chaucer wrote in Middle English, which I find confusing,* ▷*doubtful* ★**clear** [2] *v.* conceal, hide, cloud, darken, cover, ▷*hide* ★**clarify**

observant *adj.* attentive, watchful, heedful, ▷*alert* ★**inattentive**

observation [1] *n.* attention, study, supervision [2] utterance, comment, remark, statement *The police issued a statement*

observe [1] *v.* abide by *I intend to abide by the laws of the country,* adhere to, carry out, keep up [2] note, notice, perceive, watch, ▷*see* [3] utter, remark, mention

obsolete *adj.* dated, outmoded, unfashionable, out of date ★**current**

obstacle *n.* obstruction, barrier, bar, hindrance, ▷*drawback* ★**advantage**

obstinate *adj.* determined, dogged, unyielding, perverse *As a child I upset my parents by my perverse behavior,* ▷*stubborn* ★**docile**

obstruct *v.* hinder, impede, block, bar, choke, ▷*restrain* ★**help**

obstruction *n.* hindrance, restraint, impediment, snag

obtain *v.* acquire, achieve, gain, procure, attain, ▷*get* ★**lose**

obtuse *adj.* dull, stupid, unintelligent, stolid, thick, blunt ★**bright**

obvious *adj.* plain, evident, self-evident, explicit, apparent, ▷*clear* ★**obscure**

occasion [1] *n.* affair, episode, occurrence, circumstance [2] reason, purpose, motive

occasional *adj.* casual, rare, infrequent, periodic ★**frequent**

occult *adj.* hidden, unrevealed, secret, mysterious, supernatural *Edgar Allan Poe wrote tales of the supernatural* ★**open**

occupant *n.* owner, resident, proprietor, tenant

occupation [1] *n.* activity, employment, calling, job [2] possession, tenancy, residence

occupied [1] *adj.* busy, employed, active [2] settled, populated, peopled ★**unoccupied**

occupy [1] *v.* inhabit, live in, reside, dwell in, own, possess, hold

occur *v.* take place, befall, turn out, come to pass, result, ▷*happen*

occurrence *n.* happening, affair, circumstance, incident, occasion, ▷*event*

ocean *n.* sea, main *The pirates of the Spanish Main were the curse of shipping,* deep, tide

Oceans and Seas

Antarctic	Bay	Sound
Arctic	Fjord	Straits
Atlantic	Gulf	
Indian	Lagoon	
Pacific	Loch	

odd [1] *adj.* single, unmatched [2] singular, peculiar, quaint, queer ★**ordinary** [3] surplus, left over, remaining
odds and ends *n.* leavings, debris *The police found the debris of the crashed aircraft*, leftovers, oddments, remains
odious *adj.* hateful, offensive, detestable, ▷*abominable* ★**pleasant**
odor [1] *n.* scent, aroma, ▷*fragrance* [2] stink, stench, reek, ▷*smell*
odorous *adj.* fragrant, perfumed, aromatic, sweet-smelling
off [1] *adv.* away from, over, done [2] *prep.* along, against, opposite, distant ★**on** [3] *adj.* bad, moldy, rotten
offend [1] *v.* insult, hurt, wound, outrage, displease [2] transgress, sin ★**please**
offense *n.* insult, outrage, attack, crime, hurt
offensive *adj.* insulting, offending, rude, repugnant, hurtful, distasteful
offer [1] *v.* propose, proffer, present, tender, attempt [2] *n.* bid, endeavor, proposal
offering *n.* sacrifice, donation, gift, present
offhand [1] *adj.* brusque, casual, curt, informal, abrupt [2] informal, improvised, impromptu *My sister, who is a singer, gave an impromptu performance* ★**planned**
office [1] *n.* bureau, department, room [2] position, appointment, post
officer [1] *n.* official, administrator, functionary, executive [2] military rank, policeman, minister *A minister from the French Embassy called*
official [1] *adj.* authorized, authentic, proper, formal ★**unofficial** [2] *n.* executive, office-holder, bureaucrat *The city bureaucrats take months to get a job done*
officious *adj.* interfering, meddlesome, self-important
offspring *n.* child, children, descendant, heir, family
often *adv.* frequently, regularly, recurrently, time after time, repeatedly ★**seldom**
ointment *n.* salve, cream, balm, embrocation, liniment, lotion
old [1] *adj.* ancient, antique, aged, antiquated [2] crumbling, decayed *Beneath the ivy were the decayed remains of the castle wall*, decrepit ★**new** [3] out-of-date, old-fashioned, passé [4] aged, mature, elderly ★**young**
ominous *adj.* menacing, threatening, foreboding, sinister
omit *v.* leave out, neglect, let go, overlook, skip ★**include**
once *adv.* formerly, at one time, previously
one [1] *adj.* sole, alone, lone, whole [2] *n.* unit, single thing
one-sided *adj.* unequal, unfair, unjust, biased
only [1] *adj.* exclusive, single, sole, lone, solitary [2] *adv.* solely, barely, exclusively
onset *n.* start, outbreak, assault, attack, onslaught
onslaught *n.* charge, attack, bombardment
ooze [1] *n.* mire, muck, slime [2] *v.* bleed, discharge, emit, exude, leak
open [1] *v.* uncover, unlock, unfasten [2] start, commence, begin [3] *adj.* uncovered, clear, evident, apparent ★**closed** [4] frank, honest, candid, fair
opening [1] *n.* aperture, mouth, crevice, recess, hole [2] commencement, beginning
openly *adv.* candidly, frankly, plainly, sincerely ★**secretly**
operate *v.* function *Despite its age, the old millwheel continued to function*, work, manipulate, drive, ▷*perform*
operation *n.* performance, movement, action, motion, proceeding
opinion *n.* view, concept, judgment, belief, point of view
opponent *n.* antagonist, rival, competitor, contestant, foe, ▷*enemy* ★**ally**
opportune *adj.* timely *Since it had started to rain, the timely arrival of the bus was welcome*, convenient, fortunate, suitable ★**untimely**
opportunity *n.* occasion, chance, opening, scope, moment
oppose *v.* withstand, resist, obstruct, confront, hinder, ▷*defy* ★**support**
opposite [1] *adj.* facing, fronting [2] conflicting, opposing, contrary, adverse ★**same**
opposition *n.* antagonism, defiance, hostility, difference, ▷*resistance* ★**cooperation**

oppress *v.* crush, depress, harass, overpower, overwhelm
optimist *n.* hopeful person, perfectionist ★**pessimist**
optimistic *adj.* hopeful, cheerful, confident, positive ★**pessimistic**
option *n.* preference, choice, alternative
optional *adj.* possible, voluntary, unforced, open ★**compulsory**
opulent *adj.* rich, affluent, prosperous, well-to-do, ▷*wealthy* ★**poor**
oration *n.* sermon, lecture, speech, discourse
orb *n.* globe, ball, sphere
orbit [1] *n.* path, passage, trajectory [2] province, realm, domain *The river, the forest, and the castle were within her domain*
ordeal *n.* trial, nightmare, torment, agony
order [1] *n.* arrangement, pattern, grouping, organization [2] command, law, rule, decree *A decree was issued forbidding the killing of deer* [3] shipment, consignment [4] *v.* direct, instruct, command [5] arrange, control, conduct
orderly *adj.* regular, methodical, trim, neat, well-mannered ★**messy**
ordinary *adj.* common, usual, commonplace, general, customary ★**extraordinary**
organization [1] *n.* association, group, institute, establishment [2] structure, arrangement, system
organize *v.* arrange, form, structure, establish, classify ★**disorganize**
origin *n.* beginning, start, basis, foundation, root, source ★**end**
original [1] *adj.* first, aboriginal, ancient, former, primary [2] fresh, new, novel *Traveling in a horse-drawn carriage was a novel experience*
originate [1] *v.* create, conceive, compose [2] arise, begin, ▷*start* ★**end**
ornament [1] *n.* decoration, adornment, tracery, pattern [2] trinket, curio, knick-knack
ornate *adj.* decorated, adorned, flowery, embellished, showy, garish ★**plain**
oust *v.* expel, eject, evict, dismiss, propel, ▷*overthrow*

Original

Traveling in a horse-drawn carriage was a novel experience.

out [1] *adj.* away, outside, absent ★**in** [2] open, revealed, uncovered [3] *adv.* loudly, aloud, audibly
out of order *adj.* broken, not working
out of sorts *adj.* sick, ill, poorly, gloomy, fed up
outbreak *n.* epidemic *An epidemic of cholera had hit the village*, rebellion, eruption, explosion, flare-up
outburst *n.* eruption, explosion, ▷*outbreak*
outcast *n.* exile *Robinson Crusoe was an exile on a desert island*, castaway, derelict, refugee
outcome *n.* effect, consequence, conclusion, result
outcry *n.* commotion, row, uproar, tumult, shouting, hue and cry, ▷*clamor*
outdated *adj.* old, antique, old-fashioned, unfashionable, obsolete ★**modern**
outdo *v.* surpass, excel, beat, outclass, surpass, eclipse
outfit *n.* ensemble, set *My mother bought a new set of dishes in the sale for half price*, rig, rig-out, equipment, gear
outing *n.* excursion, picnic, expedition, trip, ramble

outlandish *adj.* strange, erratic, odd, queer, quaint, bizarre **★ordinary**

outlaw *n.* bandit, highwayman, hoodlum, desperado *Billy the Kid was a desperado of the Wild West,* robber

outlet *n.* exit, egress, way out, vent, spout, nozzle, opening **★inlet**

outline [1] *n.* diagram, plan, blueprint, sketch, framework, summary [2] *v.* draw, sketch, describe

outlook *n.* view, prospect, forecast, attitude, aspect

output *n.* yield, product, produce, achievement, manufacture

outrage [1] *n.* disgrace, injury, offense, affront [2] *v.* offend, insult, shock, violate

outrageous *adj.* insulting, offensive, exorbitant, monstrous **★acceptable**

outright [1] *adj.* complete, thorough, absolute, wholesale [2] *adv.* at once, completely, entirely, altogether

outset *n.* first, opening, beginning, ▷*start* **★finish**

outside [1] *n.* exterior, surface, front [2] *adj.* exterior, external, outward, surface

outsider *n.* stranger, foreigner, alien, misfit *Gulliver was something of a misfit in the land of the tiny Lilliputians*

outskirts *n.* limits, bounds, boundary, outpost, suburb

outspoken *adj.* frank, open, straightforward, blunt, direct, ▷*candid* **★tactful**

outstanding *adj.* striking, pronounced, conspicuous, notable ▷*exceptional* **★ordinary**

outward *adj.* exterior, outside, outer, superficial *At a distance, my father and Bill Jones look alike, but it's really just superficial*

outwit *v.* get the better of, swindle, defraud, dupe, ▷*cheat*

over [1] *adj.* concluded, ended, done with, settled [2] *prep.* above, more than, exceeding [3] *adv.* aloft, above, beyond, extra

overall [1] *adj.* complete, inclusive, total, broad [2] *adv.* by and large, on the whole

overbearing *adj.* domineering, dictatorial, haughty, pompous, ▷*arrogant* **★modest**

overcast *adj.* cloudy, heavy, dark, murky, dull **★bright**

overcome *adj.* overwhelm, conquer, crush, defeat, vanquish, ▷*subdue*

overdo *v.* overwork, exaggerate, go too far *I didn't mind your eating one of my apples, but taking all four was going too far!*

overdue *adj.* delayed, belated, late, behindhand **★early**

overflow *v.* swamp, deluge, inundate, submerge, soak, spill

overhaul [1] *v.* repair, mend, fix, inspect, examine [2] overtake, pass, gain on

overhead *adv.* above, upward, aloft, on high **★below**

overhear *v.* listen, eavesdrop, snoop, spy

overjoyed *adj.* elated, jubilant, rapturous, ▷*delighted* **★disappointed**

overlap *v.* overrun, go beyond, coincide, overlay

overlook [1] *v.* disregard, pardon, condone, ignore [2] neglect, miss, pass over [3] inspect, check, examine

overpower *v.* conquer, crush, master, subdue, vanquish, ▷*defeat*

overseas *adj.* abroad, foreign **★domestic**

overseer *n.* inspector, foreman, boss, manager, master, mistress

oversight *n.* omission, blunder, error, fault, lapse, ▷*mistake*

overtake *v.* catch up, pass, outdo, outstrip, pass, ▷*overhaul*

overthrow *v.* defeat, beat, topple, ▷*overpower*

overture [1] *n.* (in music) prelude, opening, introduction [2] offer, proposal, invitation

overwhelm *v.* overcome, stun, shock, overpower, deluge, inundate *The reply to our advertisement was huge: we were inundated with letters*

overwhelming *adj.* all-powerful, formidable, breathtaking, shattering **★insignificant**

owe *v.* be in debt, incur, be due

own [1] *v.* possess, occupy, hold [2] admit, confess, grant [3] *adj.* individual, personal, private

owner *n.* proprietor, possessor, landlord, master

P p

pace [1] *n.* & *v.* step, tread, stride [2] *n.* speed, rate, velocity, tempo

pacify *v.* appease, calm, moderate, tranquilize, ▷*soothe* ★**aggravate**

pack [1] *n.* bundle, bunch, swarm, crowd, group [2] *v.* cram, load, fill, throng

package *n.* parcel, packet, bundle, box, carton

packet *n.* bag, pack, container, parcel, ▷*package*

pact *n.* contract, treaty, agreement, arrangement PACKED

pad [1] *n.* tablet, notepad, jotter [2] foot, paw [3] *v.* fill, pack, shape, stuff, cushion

paddle [1] *n.* oar, sweep, scull [2] *v.* row, steer, propel [3] wade, splash, swim

pagan *n.* heathen, idol-worshiper, infidel

page [1] *n.* sheet, leaf, paper [2] boy, attendant, bellhop, messenger

pageant *n.* fair, parade, procession, exhibition, masque, ▷*show*

pail *n.* bucket, churn, tub, container PALE

pain [1] *n.* ache, pang, throb, twinge, spasm, cramp [2] *v.* hurt, sting, ache, ▷*ail* PANE

painful *adj.* aching, throbbing, sore, agonizing ★**painless**

painstaking *adj.* scrupulous *Carly kept a scrupulous record of all she spent*, careful, diligent, particular ★**negligent**

paint *v.* color, draw, daub, varnish, stain

painting *n.* drawing, illustration, picture, mural, design

pair *n.* couple, brace, two, twins, twosome PARE PEAR

pal *n.* chum, friend, buddy, crony, ▷*comrade* ★**enemy**

palace *n.* castle, château, stately home *In England you can visit stately homes belonging to the aristocracy*, mansion

pale *adj.* pallid, ashen, pasty, colorless, faint, feeble, white ★**ruddy** PAIL

pallid *adj.* ashen, colorless, livid *The man had a livid scar across his forehead*, waxen, ▷*pale*

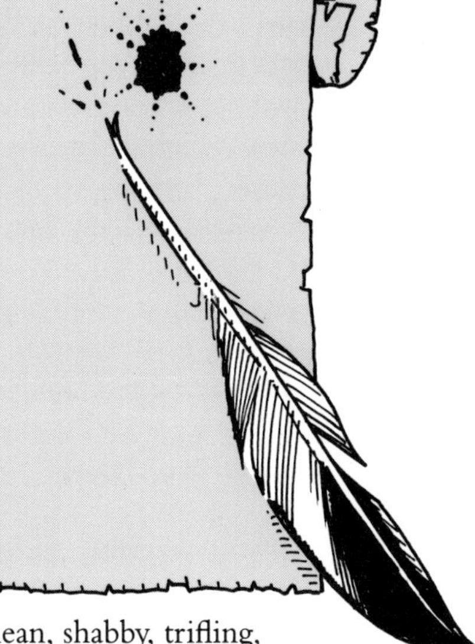

paltry *adj.* petty, mean, shabby, trifling, pitiable, trashy ★**significant**

pamper *v.* humor, indulge, coddle, fondle, ▷*spoil* ★**neglect**

pan *n.* container, ▷*pot*

pandemonium *n.* uproar, clatter, row, rumpus, din, chaos *You haven't straightened up your room: it's in chaos!*, ▷*noise* ★**calm**

pander *v.* indulge, pamper, please, give in to

pane *n.* panel, glass, window PAIN

panel [1] *n.* pane, rectangle, insert [2] jury, group, committee, forum *There will be a forum of all parties before the election*

pang *n.* ache, throe, twinge, throb, ▷*pain*

panic [1] *n.* fright, alarm, fear, terror [2] *v.* scare, frighten, startle, stampede ★**relax**

pant *v.* puff, snort, blow, gasp, heave

pantry *n.* larder, buttery, storeroom, cupboard

paper *n.* stationery, document, deed, article, dossier *The police have a dossier on all known criminals in this town*

parade [1] *n.* procession, march, display, ▷*pageant* [2] *v.* display, exhibit, flaunt, show off

paralyze *v.* cripple, disable, incapacitate, deaden, stun

paramount *adj.* leading, chief, supreme, outstanding, ▷*foremost* ★**minor**

paraphernalia *n.* baggage, equipment, gear
parasite *n.* sponger, hanger-on, leech, scrounger
parcel *n.* batch, bundle, lot, ▷*package*
parched *v.* arid, scorched, withered, dry, thirsty
pardon *v.* excuse, forgive, acquit, condone, absolve ★**condemn**
pare *v.* skin, peel, uncover, strip, scrape, shave PAIR PEAR
parent *n.* father, mother, guardian, originator
park [1] *n.* garden, green, grounds, pleasure garden, woodland [2] *v.* leave *You can leave your car outside our house,* position, station
parlor *n.* drawing room, living room, sitting room
parody *n.* caricature, burlesque, satire, imitation
parry *v.* avoid, avert, fend off, rebuff, repel
parsimonious *adj.* niggardly *The fruit pickers received a niggardly sum for their work,* sparing, miserly, stingy, ▷*frugal* ★**generous**
part [1] *n.* piece, fragment, portion, scrap [2] character, role *My sister has a leading role in the play,* duty [3] *v.* separate, divide, detach [4] depart, quit, leave
partial [1] *adj.* imperfect, limited, part, unfinished [2] biased, favorable to, inclined
partially *adv.* incompletely, somewhat, in part
participate *v.* take part, share, cooperate
particle *n.* morsel, atom, bit, seed, crumb, grain, scrap
particular [1] *adj.* choosy, fastidious, scrupulous [2] strange, odd, peculiar [3] special, distinct, notable *Old John Cotton was one of the notable citizens of our city*
partly *adv.* in part, incompletely, to some degree, up to a point ★**totally**
partner *n.* colleague, associate, ally, helper
party [1] *n.* function, celebration, festivity, social [2] group, faction *A small faction on the committee wanted the park to be closed,* body
pass [1] *v.* exceed, overstep, outstrip [2] experience *He experienced little pain after the operation,* suffer, undergo [3] neglect, ignore [4] *n.* permit, ticket, passport [5] gorge, passage, canyon
passage [1] *n.* corridor, pathway, alley [2] journey, cruise, voyage [3] sentence, paragraph, clause
passenger *n.* traveler, commuter, wayfarer
passing *adj.* casual, fleeting, hasty, temporary, brief ★**permanent**
passion *n.* desire, ardor, warmth, excitement, zeal, ▷*emotion* ★**calm**
passionate *adj.* ardent, impetuous, fiery, earnest, enthusiastic ★**indifferent**
past [1] *adj.* finished, ended, former, gone ★**present** [2] *prep.* after, exceeding, beyond [3] *n.* history, yesterday ★**future** PASSED
paste *n.* glue, cement, gum, adhesive
pastime *n.* recreation, sport, fun, hobby, amusement
pasture *n.* grass, field, meadow, mead
pat [1] *v.* tap, caress, fondle, stroke, touch [2] *adv.* timely, exactly *Celia arrived at exactly the right moment,* precisely
patch *v.* mend, patch up, sew, darn, cobble
path *n.* way, track, road, route, course, footway

Paths and Passageways

Alley	Highway	Path
Autobahn	Lane	Road
Avenue	Mountain pass	Sidewalk
Boulevard	Passage	Street
Drive		Thoroughfare

pathetic *adj.* pitiable, sad, wretched, miserable, poor, puny *Our dog Sally had puppies, but they were small and puny*
patience *n.* endurance, perseverance, composure, calmness ★**impatience** PATIENTS
patient *adj.* forbearing, long-suffering, persevering, understanding ★**impatient**
patriotic *adj.* loyal, nationalistic, public-spirited
patrol *v.* police, watch, guard, protect, tour
patronize [1] *v.* assist, encourage, foster, buy from [2] talk down to, condescend
pattern [1] *n.* model, standard, prototype [2] arrangement, decoration, ornament
pause [1] *v.* halt, cease, suspend, stop, delay [2] *n.* lull, intermission, break, interruption PAWS
pay [1] *v.* reward, award, support, compensate, discharge [2] *n.* payment, salary, wages, compensation
peace *n.* harmony, calm, concord, serenity, quiet, tranquility *We spent the day in total tranquility down by the lake* ★**tumult** PIECE
peaceful *adj.* serene, quiet, restful, harmonious, ▷*tranquil* ★**disturbed**
peak *n.* summit, apex, top, crown, pinnacle
peal *v.* ring, strike, clamor, chime, resound PEEL
peasant *n.* farmer, rustic, sharecropper, countryman, yokel
peculiar [1] *adj.* singular, odd, curious, unusual, uncommon, strange [2] unique, private, special
peddle *v.* sell, hawk, canvas, trade, vend, retail
peddler *n.* hawker, street-trader, trader
pedestal *n.* base, stand, plinth, support
peel [1] *v.* skin, strip, pare, scale [2] *n.* skin, covering, rind, coat PEAL
peep *n.* & *v.* glimpse, blink, look, ▷*peer*
peer [1] *v.* peep, stare, look, gaze [2] *n.* aristocrat, lord, noble [3] equal, fellow, counterpart PIER
peerless *adj.* unequaled, unique, beyond compare, unbeatable
peevish *adj.* cross, childish, grumpy, crusty, irritable, ▷*testy* ★**good-tempered**
peg *n.* hook, knob, pin, post, hanger, fastener
pelt [1] *v.* beat, bombard, thrash, throw [2] rain cats and dogs, teem, pour [3] *n.* skin, hide, fleece, fur
pen [1] *n.* quill, ballpoint [2] cage, coop, hutch, stall [3] *v.* write, autograph, scribble
penalty *n.* fine, forfeit, punishment, price ★**reward**
pending *adj.* awaiting, unfinished, doubtful, uncertain
penetrate [1] *v.* pierce, perforate, stab, permeate *The aroma of the sweet peas permeated the house* [2] discern, see through, comprehend
penetrating [1] *adj.* sharp, perceptive, understanding [2] shrill, stinging
pennant *n.* flag, streamer, bunting, banner
penniless *adj.* destitute, needy, poverty-striken, ▷*poor* ★**wealthy**
pensive *adj.* thoughtful, reflective, wistful, preoccupied
people [1] *n.* folk, society, the public, populace, inhabitants [2] *v.* populate, inhabit, settle
pep *n.* punch, energy, high spirits, vigor, ▷*vitality*
peppery [1] *adj.* biting, caustic *I'm afraid your essay wasn't very good; the teacher made some very caustic comments!* hot-tempered, angry [2] hot, pungent, sharp
perceive *v.* feel, sense, observe, notice, make out, understand, ▷*see*
perch [1] *v.* alight, light, sit, squat [2] *n.* rod, pole, staff, roost [3] fish
perfect [1] *adj.* absolute, ideal, sublime, excellent, splendid, faultless ★**imperfect** [2] *v.* complete, finish, fulfill, refine
perforate *v.* puncture, drill, punch, penetrate
perform [1] *v.* carry out, do, fulfill, accomplish [2] play, act, stage, present *The local drama group is to present a new play next week*
performer *n.* actor, player, singer, entertainer, artist
perfume *n.* scent, essence, aroma, odor
perhaps *adv.* possibly, perchance, maybe, conceivably

peril *n.* hazard, jeopardy, menace, risk, insecurity, ▷*danger* ★**safety**

period *n.* spell, time, duration, term, interval, course, span, age

periodical [1] *n.* magazine, publication, journal, gazette, review [2] *adj.* regular, routine, recurring, repeated

perish *v.* die, pass away, wither, disintegrate, expire, shrivel

perky *adj.* bouncy, bright, cheerful, lively, ▷*sprightly* ★**dull**

permanent *adj.* endless, ageless, timeless, constant, ▷*durable* ★**fleeting**

permission *n.* authorization, sanction, privilege, warrant *The police have a warrant for your arrest!* ★**prohibition**

permit [1] *v.* (per-*mit*) allow, grant, agree, empower [2] *n.* (*per*-mit) warrant, license, pass

perpendicular *adj.* upright, erect, sheer, steep, vertical ★**horizontal**

perpetrate *v.* commit, do, inflict, perform, practice

perpetual *adj.* everlasting, ceaseless, eternal, never-ending, ▷*endless* ★**fleeting**

perplex *v.* mystify, baffle, bewilder, confound, ▷*puzzle* ★**enlighten**

persecute *v.* harass, molest, plague, badger, ▷*bother* ★**pamper**

persevere *v.* persist, hold out, hang on, endure, continue ★**give up**

persist *v.* remain, stand fast, abide, carry on, ▷*persevere* ★**stop**

persistent *adj.* tenacious, relentless, stubborn, obstinate ★**weak**

person *n.* individual, human, being, somebody, personage

personal *adj.* individual, intimate, private, special, peculiar

personality *n.* individuality, character, disposition, nature

perspective *n.* outlook, aspect, proportion

perspire *v.* sweat, exude, ooze

persuade *v.* convince, wheedle, blandish, entice, cajole *I cajoled my mother into buying me a new swimsuit*, induce, ▷*coax* ★**discourage**

pert *adj.* saucy, flippant, jaunty, cheeky, brash ★**shy**

perturb *v.* upset, disturb, trouble, distress, fluster, ▷*bother* ★**reassure**

peruse *v.* read, study, pore over, browse, inspect

pervade *v.* penetrate, permeate, spread, saturate

perverse *adj.* contrary, wayward, opposite, disobedient, ▷*stubborn* ★**reasonable**

pessimist *n.* defeatist, killjoy, wet blanket, cynic *Uncle Bert is a real cynic: he thinks the prize draws are fixed!* ★**optimist**

pessimistic *adj.* cynical, dismal, fatalistic, defeatist, downhearted ★**optimistic**

pest *n.* nuisance, plague, blight, curse, vexation, bug

pester *v.* nag, hector, badger, annoy, disturb, harass, ▷*bother*

pet [1] *v.* fondle, caress, baby, cosset, cuddle [2] *n.* favorite, beloved, dear [3] *adj.* endearing, cherished, dearest

petition *n.* plea, appeal, entreaty, round robin, request

petrified *adj.* spellbound, frightened, scared, terrified

petty [1] *adj.* paltry, cheap, inferior, trifling, ▷*trivial* ★**important** [2] mean, measly, stingy

petulant *adj.* fretful, displeased, querulous, irritable, ▷*peevish*

phantom [1] *n.* apparition, specter, spook, ghost [2] *adj.* spooky, ghostly, imaginary

phase *n.* aspect, appearance, angle, view, period, point FAZE

phenomenal *adj.* remarkable, outstanding, marvelous, miraculous

phenomenon *n.* marvel, rarity, curiosity, sensation, spectacle

philanthropic *adj.* charitable, kind, generous, humane, benevolent, bountiful, public-spirited ★**selfish**

philosophical *adj.* calm, cool, logical, thoughtful, impassive, unruffled

phobia *n.* dread, fear, awe, neurosis, hang-up *My father has a hang-up about bats; he can't stand them!*, horror

phrase *n.* expression, idiom, saying, utterance, sentence FRAYS

physical [1] *adj.* material, substantial, solid, concrete [2] bodily, personal, sensible

pick [1] *v.* select, choose, single out, gather [2] *n.* pike, pickaxe

picket [1] *n.* patrol, scout, sentinel, lookout, guard [2] post, rail, panel, fence [3] *v.* strike

pickle [1] *n.* preserve [2] difficulty, predicament [3] *v.* cure, salt, preserve, souse

picture [1] *n.* painting, tableau, portrait, illustration, drawing [2] movie, film [3] *v.* illustrate, imagine, fancy

picturesque *adj.* attractive, artistic, pictorial, scenic

piece *n.* portion, fragment, lump, morsel, bit, ▷*scrap* PEACE

pier *n.* wharf, dock, quay, jetty PEER

pierce *v.* perforate, drill, bore, ▷*penetrate*

piercing [1] *adj.* loud, deafening, shrill, penetrating [2] keen, sharp, cutting

pigment *n.* color, dye, hue, paint, stain

pile *n.* & *v.* heap, mass, stack, load, store

pilfer *v.* purloin, rifle, rob, filch, ▷*steal*

pilgrim *n.* traveler, wanderer, wayfarer

pilgrimage *n.* excursion, journey, mission, tour, trip

pillage *v.* plunder, ravage, loot, ransack *Thieves broke into the museum and ransacked all the cases,* rifle

pillar *n.* column, shaft, tower, obelisk, monument

pillow *n.* cushion, bolster, support

pilot [1] *n.* guide, steersman, coxswain, helmsman [2] aviator, flyer, airman

pimple *n.* spot, blemish, swelling, boil

pin [1] *n.* fastener, clip, spike, peg [2] *v.* fix, fasten, attach, join, tack

pinch [1] *v.* nip, squeeze, crush, tweak [2] pilfer, steal [3] *n.* dash, drop, splash [4] crisis, difficulty, jam

pine *v.* hanker, yearn, long for, languish *The flowers in the garden are languishing from lack of water,* sicken

pinnacle *n.* summit, top, crest, peak, apex

pioneer *n.* founder, leader, trailblazer, explorer, innovator

pious *adj.* devout, godly, holy, moral, religious

pipe [1] *n.* tube, duct, passage, hose, conduit [2] whistle, flute

piquant *adj.* appetizing, spicy, tangy, savory, pungent

pique *v.* annoy, displease, irritate, affront, vex PEAK

pirate [1] *n.* corsair *In days of old the ships in the Mediterranean were often raided by corsairs,* buccaneer, privateer, sea-rover [2] *v.* copy, plagiarize, steal

pistol *n.* gun, revolver, automatic PISTIL

pit [1] *n.* hole, hollow, crater, trench, mine [2] dent, dimple, depression

pitch [1] *v.* fling, throw, cast, sling, toss [2] fall, drop, descend [3] raise, set up, erect [4] *n.* angle, slope, degree [5] sales message

pitcher *n.* jar, beaker, crock, jug, ewer, vessel

piteous *adj.* pitiful, heartbreaking, mournful, ▷*pathetic*

pitiless *adj.* merciless, unmerciful, cruel, unrelenting ★**merciful**

pity [1] *n.* mercy, compassion, charity, tenderness [2] *v.* spare, forgive, grieve for, sympathize with

pivot [1] *n.* axle, axis, hinge, turning point, spindle, swivel [2] *v.* revolve, rotate, turn, spin

Planets

The nine planets of our solar system travel around a star we call the Sun.

Earth
Jupiter
Mars
Mercury
Neptune
Pluto
Saturn
Uranus
Venus

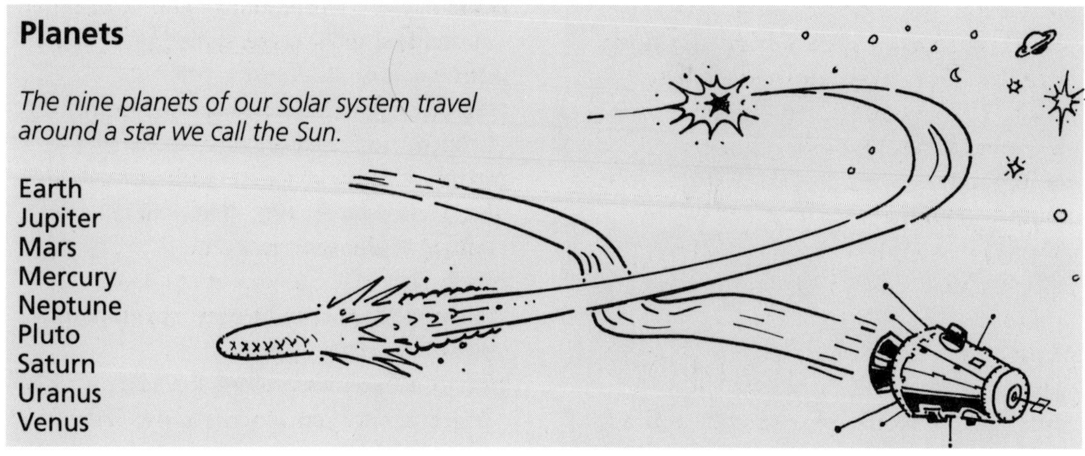

placate *v.* appease, pacify, soothe, satisfy, ▷*humor* ★**infuriate**

place [1] *n.* spot, locality, site, situation, position [2] house, flat, residence [3] *v.* put, deposit, establish, allocate, arrange

placid *adj.* peaceful, quiet, serene, mild, ▷*restful* ★**ruffled**

plague [1] *n.* epidemic, disease, contagion, pest, blight [2] *v.* persecute, pester *Our picnic was pestered by flies*, infest, annoy, ▷*badger*

plain [1] *adj.* unadorned, simple [2] obvious, clear, apparent [3] blunt, direct, candid [4] smooth, level, flat [5] *n.* prairie, plateau, tableland PLANE

plan [1] *n.* design, chart, diagram, drawing [2] project, proposal, arrangement, scheme [3] *v.* design, prepare, arrange, invent

plane [1] *adj.* level, even, flat, smooth [2] *n.* aircraft [3] smoothing tool PLAIN

planned *adj.* prepared, ready, arranged

plant [1] *v.* sow, scatter, implant [2] place, set, establish [3] *n.* herb, shrub, vegetable [4] equipment, machinery, factory

plaster [1] *n.* cement, mortar, paste [2] *n.* bandage, dressing [3] *v.* spread, smear, daub

plastic [1] *adj.* moldable, pliable, malleable, soft, supple [2] *n.* thermoplastic

plate [1] *n.* dish, platter, palette [2] sheet, panel [3] *v.* laminate, cover, gild, anodize

platform *n.* rostrum *I was called up to the rostrum to receive my prize*, stage, stand, dais

plausible *adj.* believable, credible, convincing, glib, persuasive ★**unlikely**

play [1] *v.* sport, gambol, frisk, romp, frolic [2] perform, act, represent [3] *n.* drama, performance [4] sport, amusement, recreation

player *n.* actor, sportsman, artist, musician, performer, contestant

playful *adj.* frisky, frolicsome, larky, lively, sportive ★**serious**

plead *v.* appeal, argue, ask, implore, request, beseech

pleasant *adj.* affable, agreeable, cheerful, nice, ▷*charming* ★**unpleasant**

please [1] *v.* gratify, enchant, amuse, entertain, ▷*delight* [2] like, choose, wish, prefer

pleased *adj.* delighted, gratified, satisfied, ▷*contented* ★**annoyed**

pleasing *adj.* agreeable, enchanting, entertaining, ▷*satisfying* ★**unpleasant**

pleasure *n.* delight, joy, amusement, entertainment, enjoyment, ▷*fun* ★**trouble**

pledge [1] *n.* promise, vow, undertaking, warrant, oath [2] *v.* bind, contract, promise, undertake

plentiful *adj.* lavish, ample, profuse, bountiful, ▷*abundant* ★**scanty**

plenty *n.* enough, profusion, affluence, ▷*abundance* ★**scarcity**

pliable *adj.* supple, flexible, pliant, malleable, moldable, bendy ★**rigid**

plight *n.* predicament, difficulty, condition, dilemma *We made it to the train station on time, but when we realized we had forgotten our tickets we were in a dilemma*, jam

plod *v.* toil, labor, drudge, slog, grind

plot [1] *n.* scheme, plan, intrigue [2] story, narrative [3] *v.* hatch, intrigue, scheme

pluck [1] *v.* gather, pick, pull, yank, catch [2] *n.* courage, determination, bravery

plucky *adj.* courageous, daring, heroic, hardy, ▷*brave* ★**feeble**

plug [1] *n.* stopper, cork, bung [2] *v.* stop, block, choke, cork [3] publicize, boost, promote

plum [1] *n.* prize, bonus, treasure [2] *adj.* best, choice, first-class

plump *adj.* buxom, stout, chubby, rotund, pudgy ★**skinny**

plunder [1] *n.* booty, loot, swag, spoils [2] *v.* fleece, rob, ransack, pillage, loot

plunge *v.* dive, pitch, submerge, duck, immerse, swoop, hurtle

poach [1] *v.* pilfer, steal, filch, purloin [2] cook

pocket [1] *n.* compartment, pouch, sack, bag [2] *v.* filch, pinch, steal

poem *n.* ode, verse, rhyme, ballad, lyric

poetic *adj.* artistic, elegant, graceful, flowing, lyrical

poignant *adj.* moving, touching, pathetic, biting, penetrating

point [1] *n.* spike, barb, pike, prong, end, tip [2] locality, place, spot [3] aspect, object, aim, purpose [4] headland, cape [5] *v.* aim, direct, level, train

pointless *adj.* meaningless, senseless, silly, vague, feeble, ▷*absurd* ★**significant**

poise [1] *n.* confidence, assurance, dignity, self-possession, balance [2] *v.* stand, hover, brood over

poison [1] *n.* venom, virus, toxin [2] *v.* taint, fester, corrupt, infect

poisonous *adj.* deadly, evil, lethal *Don't even touch those red berries: they're lethal!*, noxious, toxic, venomous

poke *v.* jab, push, nudge, jostle, ram, thrust, ▷*shove*

pole *n.* stick, stave, stake, rod, post, bar, mast, shaft, spar

policy *n.* discretion, course, action, practice, rule, procedure

polish [1] *v.* burnish, buff, smooth, brighten, clean [2] *n.* gloss, glaze, shine [3] refinement, grace, culture

polished [1] *adj.* glossy, burnished, shiny [2] refined, cultivated, cultured

polite *adj.* courteous, attentive, civil, well-bred, elegant, discreet ★**impolite**

poll [1] *n.* election, vote, count, census [2] *v.* clip, shear, trim

pollute *v.* adulterate, debase, befoul, taint, poison, corrupt ★**purify**

pomp *n.* ceremony, show, splendor, pageantry, magnificence ★**simplicity**

pompous *adj.* showy, self-important, bombastic, ▷*pretentious* ★**modest**

ponder *v.* meditate, consider, reflect, deliberate, think about

pool [1] *n.* lagoon, pond, lake [2] accumulation, funds, reserve, kitty [3] *v.* combine, contribute, share

poor [1] *adj.* destitute, penniless, miserable ★**rich** [2] low quality, faulty, feeble, shoddy *The goods in the market may be cheap, but they're just shoddy garbage* ★**superior** PORE POUR

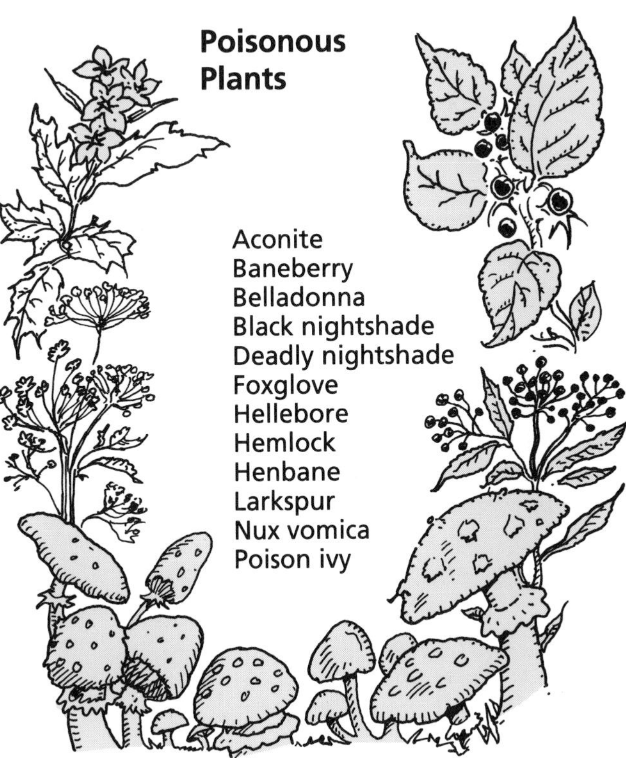

poorly [1] *adj.* ailing, ill, sick, seedy [2] *adv.* badly, inexpertly, crudely ***well**
pop [1] *v.* bang, burst, crack, explode [2] slide, slip, insert
popular [1] *adj.* well-liked, favorite, in favor, fashionable [2] current, common, vulgar, prevailing
pore *v.* scan, examine, peruse, scrutinize POOR POUR
portable *adj.* lightweight, convenient, transportable, ▷*handy* ***awkward**
portion *n.* piece, fragment, share, fraction, ▷*part*
portly *adj.* plump, stout, fat, burly, bulky
portrait *n.* likeness, painting, picture, profile
portray *v.* describe, depict, represent, picture, illustrate, impersonate
pose [1] *v.* stand, poise, posture, position [2] *n.* position, stand, guise, stance *I think you will learn to play golf well; you have a good stance*
position [1] *n.* spot, situation, location, place, site [2] job, post, situation [3] posture, attitude [4] rank, standing, status
positive [1] *adj.* certain, sure, confident ***doubtful** [2] real, true, absolute ***negative** [3] precise, definite, unmistakable
possess *v.* have, own, hold, occupy ***lose**
possessions *n.* wealth, assets, property, goods
possible *adj.* conceivable, imaginable, likely, feasible, attainable ***impossible**
possibly *adv.* perhaps, maybe, perchance conceivably
post [1] *n.* rail, pole, beam, banister, stake [2] position, employment, job [3] mail
poster *n.* placard, bill, advertisement, sign
posterior *adj.* hind, behind, after, rear ***front**
postpone *v.* put off, defer, shelve, adjourn, ▷*delay* ***advance**
posture *n.* bearing, stance, attitude, carriage
pot *n.* basin, bowl, pan, vessel, container, jar
potential [1] *adj.* possible, probable, latent *The professor discovered that I had a latent talent for languages*, dormant, budding [2] *n.* ability, talent, capacity, ▷*flair*
potion *n.* beverage, medicine, mixture, tonic, brew
pouch *n.* bag, poke, sack, purse, pocket, wallet
pounce *v.* strike, lunge, spring, swoop, fall upon, ▷*attack*
pound [1] *v.* beat, batter, crush, hammer [2] *n.* enclosure, compound, pen [3] weight [4] currency *In Britain, the currency is based on the pound sterling*
pour *v.* spout, jet, gush, spill, cascade, rain PORE POUR
pout *v.* grimace, glower, sulk, scowl, mope ***smile**
poverty [1] *n.* distress, need, bankruptcy, privation, ▷*want* [2] scarcity, shortage ***plenty**
powder [1] *n.* dust, sand, ash, grit, bran [2] *v.* pulverize, crunch, grind
power [1] *n.* authority, command, control, ability [2] energy, force, strength
powerful *adj.* mighty, vigorous, forceful, ▷*strong* ***weak**
practical [1] *adj.* useful, effective, workable [2] experienced, qualified, trained, ▷*skilled* ***impractical**
practice [1] *n.* custom, habit, usage [2] work, conduct, performance, action ***theory** [2] *v.* carry out, apply, do, execute, ▷*perform*
praise [1] *v.* acclaim, applaud, glorify, exalt ***criticize** [2] *n.* applause, flattery, compliment, approval ***criticism** PRAYS PREYS
prance *v.* gambol *I love to watch the lambs gambol in the spring*, frolic, romp, caper, swagger
prank *n.* trick, joke, antic, lark, jape, stunt
prattle *n.* & *v.* chatter, jabber, gossip, drivel, babble
pray *v.* beg, beseech, entreat, implore, request PREY
prayer *n.* petition, entreaty, worship, devotion, supplication
preach *v.* lecture, moralize, advocate *The president advocated a return to "traditional values,"* urge, proclaim
precarious *adj.* perilous, hazardous, insecure, dangerous, ▷*risky* ***safe**

precaution *n.* forethought, provision, anticipation, care, providence, ▷*prudence*

precede *v.* lead, head, usher, go before, preface ★**follow**

precious *adj.* valuable, costly, cherished, treasured, dear, beloved, ▷*costly* ★**worthless**

precise [1] *adj.* definite, exact, pointed, accurate [2] formal, particular, strict ★**vague**

precisely *adv.* absolutely, just so, exactly, correctly

precision *n.* exactitude, accuracy, care, detail

precocious *adj.* over-forward, fast, smart, clever ★**backward**

predicament *n.* situation, state, condition, embarrassment, fix, ▷*plight*

predict *v.* foresee, foretell, prophesy, presage, divine

predominant *adj.* leading, main, powerful, superior, ruling, controlling ★**minor**

preen *v.* prance, swagger, strut, spruce up, doll up, groom

preface *n.* introduction, prelude, prologue, preamble, foreword

prefer *v.* choose, select, desire, like better, fancy, ▷*favor* ★**reject**

prejudice [1] *n.* bigotry, intolerance, bias, discrimination [2] *v.* influence, warp, twist, distort, undermine ★**benefit**

prejudiced *adj.* biased, bigoted *The people in this town are very bigoted against strangers*, one-sided, unfair, intolerant ★**fair**

preliminary *adj.* introductory, preparatory, opening, initial ★**final**

premature *adj.* untimely, previous, early, immature ★**late**

premeditated *adj.* calculated, planned, prearranged, intentional ★**spontaneous**

premier [1] *n.* prime minister, first minister, head of government [2] *adj.* chief, first, head, leading, principal

premises *n.* grounds, house, building, lands

prepare *v.* arrange, adapt provide, get ready, concoct, plan ★**demolish**

preposterous *adj.* absurd, ridiculous, laughable, ▷*unreasonable* ★**reasonable**

prescribe *v.* indicate, order, propose, recommend, specify

presence [1] *n.* existence, appearance, aspect [2] nearness, neighborhood, proximity

PRESENTS

present [1] *n.* (*pres*-ent) gift, donation, bounty, favor [2] *adj.* here, on the spot, ready, current [3] *v.* (pre-*sent*) offer, tender, bestow, award, exhibit

presently *adv.* soon, shortly, before long, immediately

preserve [1] *v.* protect, safeguard, conserve, shield, ▷*keep* [2] *n.* jam, jelly, relish

press [1] *v.* bear down, depress, clamp, jam, compress, flatten [2] *n.* printing machine [3] newspapers, reporters, journalism

pressure [1] *n.* strain, tension, stress, urgency [2] weight, compression, force

prestige *n.* repute, authority, weight, power

presume *v.* infer *I infer from your smile that you have passed your exam*, suppose, grant, take for granted, assume

presumptuous *adj.* arrogant, bold, audacious, insolent, ▷*forward* ★**modest**

pretend [1] *v.* make believe, simulate, sham, feign, masquerade [2] aspire, claim, strive for

pretext *n.* excuse, pretense, guise, device

pretty *adj.* attractive, beautiful, comely, dainty, bonny, ▷*lovely* ★**ugly**
prevail *v.* obtain, overcome, predominate, ▷*triumph* ★**lose**
prevalent *adj.* current, common, popular, in use, accepted ★**uncommon**
prevent *v.* avert, forestall, ward off, discourage, stop, ▷*hinder* ★**help**
previous *adj.* former, prior, earlier, premature, untimely ★**later**
prey *n.* quarry, chase, booty, victim PRAY
prey on *v.* plunder, fleece, oppress, terrorize
price *n.* cost, amount, expense, payment, value, worth
priceless [1] *adj.* invaluable, precious, cherished, costly [2] amusing, comic, humorous, hilarious *The clown's antics were hilarious*
prick *v.* jab, jag, puncture, stab, pierce
pride *n.* conceit, vanity, egotism, self-importance, honor, exaltation, pleasure PRIED
prim *adj.* puritanical, demure, starchy, priggish ★**informal**
primary *adj.* first, original, chief, essential, fundamental
prime [1] *adj.* principal, chief, basic, original [2] best, finest, choice
primitive [1] *adj.* simple, austere, crude [2] uncivilized, savage, barbarous
principal [1] *adj.* main, chief, head, leading, foremost [2] *n.* head, leader, boss, director PRINCIPLE
principle [1] *n.* law, regulation, rule, doctrine [2] virtue, worth, integrity, rectitude *The president of the club was given the keys to the city as a "person of high moral rectitude"* ★**wickedness** PRINCIPAL
print [1] *v.* impress, stamp, brand, publish [2] *n.* impression, printing, imprint
prior [1] *adj.* previous, former, earlier [2] *n.* abbot, monk
prison *n.* jail, penitentiary, dungeon, lock-up
private [1] *adj.* particular, personal, special, own [2] solitary, remote *He spent his vacations in a remote cabin*, quiet ★**public**
privilege [1] *n.* advantage, benefit, exemption [2] right, authority, entitlement, prerogative *It was the emperor's prerogative to pardon offenders*

Printing

Collotype
Computer-setting
Cylinder press
Flatbed press
Intaglio
Letterpress
Linotype
Lithography
Monotype
Photogravure
Rotary press
Silk screen
Type
Web offset

prize [1] *n.* reward, premium, trophy, honor [2] booty, spoils, plunder [3] *adj.* best, champion, winning [4] *v.* value, appreciate, cherish [5] force, lever, pry, lift, raise PRIES
probable *adj.* likely, presumable, reasonable, possible ★**improbable**
probe [1] *v.* poke, prod [2] examine, investigate, scrutinize
problem [1] *n.* puzzle, question, riddle, poser, quandary [2] difficulty, dilemma, predicament
proceed [1] *v.* advance, continue, go on, progress ★**recede** [2] arise, flow, spring, emanate *A strong sulfurous odor emanated from the crater of the volcano*
process [1] *n.* procedure, operation, movement, system, method [2] *v.* convert, alter, handle, refine
procession *n.* parade, pageant, march, cavalcade
proclaim *v.* declare, announce, advertise, publish, expound
procure *v.* secure, acquire, win, gain, attain, get ★**lose**
prod *v.* goad, poke, nudge, incite, urge, shove
prodigal *adj.* extravagant, reckless, lavish, ▷*spendthrift* ★**thrifty**
prodigious [1] *adj.* miraculous, abnormal,

amazing, remarkable, ▷*extraordinary* ★**ordinary** [2] huge, mighty, ▷*enormous* ★**tiny**

produce [1] *n.* (*pro*-duce) product, output, yield, crop, harvest [2] *v.* (pro-*duce*) provide, yield, create, deliver, put forward

product *n.* output, crop, harvest, merchandise, commodity

profane *adj.* impious, blasphemous, unholy, worldly, sinful ★**sacred**

profess *v.* declare, avow, acknowledge, own

profession [1] *n.* occupation, career, job, calling, employment [2] avowal, admission

professional *adj.* skilled, efficient, experienced, ▷*expert* ★**amateur**

proffer *v.* present, offer, tender, submit

proficient *adj.* competent, able, skilled, ▷*expert* ★**clumsy**

profit [1] *n.* benefit, gain, advantage, acquisition ★**loss** [2] *v.* improve, gain, reap, acquire ★**lose** PROPHET

profound [1] *adj.* deep, penetrating, fathomless [2] wise, shrewd, learned, sagacious *The leader of the tribe was old, wise, and sagacious* ★**shallow**

profuse *adj.* bountiful, extravagant, exuberant, prolific, sumptuous, ▷*lavish* ★**sparse**

progress [1] *n.* (*prog*-ress) advancement, growth, development ★**decline** [2] *v.* (pro-*gress*) advance, proceed, go, forge ahead, travel

prohibit *v.* forbid, bar, deny, ban, obstruct, hinder, ▷*prevent* ★**permit**

project [1] *n.* (*pro*-ject) work, affair, plan, scheme, undertaking [2] *v.* (pro-*ject*) propel, hurl, jut, protrude [3] contrive, scheme, plan

prolific *adj.* fruitful, creative, productive, fertile ★**scarce**

prolong *v.* lengthen, stretch, draw out, spin out, ▷*extend* ★**shorten**

prominent [1] *adj.* famous, notable, distinguished ★**minor** [2] projecting, standing out, bulging, jutting

promise [1] *n.* commitment, undertaking, warrant, pledge [2] *v.* agree, guarantee, vow

promote [1] *adj.* cultivate, advance, assist, ▷*encourage* [2] dignify, elevate, upgrade, honor ★**degrade**

prompt [1] *adj.* punctual, timely, quick, smart, ready ★**tardy** [2] *v.* hint, remind, urge, ▷*encourage* ★**deter**

prone [1] *adj.* inclined, apt, liable, disposed ★**unlikely** [2] prostrate *The poor fellow lay prostrate on the ship's deck*, face down, recumbent ★**upright**

pronounce [1] *v.* speak, utter, say, articulate [2] declare, decree, proclaim

pronounced *adj.* outstanding, striking, noticeable, ▷*distinct* ★**vague**

proof *n.* evidence, testimony, confirmation, criterion, scrutiny ★**failure**

prop *n.* & *v.* stay, brace, truss, support

propel *v.* start, push, force, impel, send, ▷*drive* ★**stop**

proper [1] *adj.* correct, without error, right, accurate, exact [2] respectable, decent, becoming, seemly ★**improper** [3] personal, own, special ★**common**

property [1] *n.* possessions, wealth, chattels, buildings, wealth [2] quality, virtue, characteristic, peculiarity

prophecy (*prof*-essee) *n.* forecast, divination, prediction

prophesy (*prof*-esseye) *v.* predict, foretell, foresee

proportion [1] *n.* ratio, percentage, part, fraction [2] adjustment, arrangement

proposal *n.* proposition, offer, outline

propose [1] *v.* put forward, offer, suggest [2] ask for the hand of *Sir, I have the honor to ask you for the hand of your daughter in marriage*, pop the question

proprietor *n.* owner, possessor, landlady, landlord

prosaic *adj.* tedious, uninteresting, boring, dull, mundane, ordinary ★**interesting**

prosecute [1] *v.* indict, put on trial, summon, sue [2] continue, pursue, carry on, conduct ★**abandon**

prospect [1] *n.* outlook, forecast, promise, expectation [2] view, landscape, vista, aspect

prosper *v.* succeed, flourish, grow ★**fail**

prosperous *adj.* affluent, wealthy, rich,

successful, thriving ★**unsuccessful**
protect *v.* defend, preserve, guard, secure, shelter, support ★**endanger**
protest [1] *v.* (pro-*test*) complain, object, dispute, challenge ★**accept** [2] *n.* (*pro*-test) objection, complaint, dissent
protracted *adj.* extended, drawn out, lengthy, prolonged ★**shortened**
protrude *v.* project, bulge, jut ★**recede**
proud [1] *adj.* arrogant, haughty, supercilious, boastful ★**humble** [2] lofty, majestic, noble, splendid ★**mean**
prove *v.* show, demonstrate, authenticate, confirm, verify ★**disprove**
provide *v.* supply, furnish, equip, contribute, afford ★**withhold**
province [1] *n.* realm, sphere, orbit, place, department [2] region, state, county
provoke *v.* prompt, incite, excite, enrage, inflame, ▷*aggravate* ★**appease**
prowess *n.* ability, strength, might, bravery, ▷*valor* ★**clumsiness**
prowl *v.* stalk *Somewhere in the darkness a large gray animal stalked its prey,* roam, slink
prudent *adj.* careful, cautious, discreet, shrewd, ▷*thrifty* ★**rash**
prudish *adj.* straitlaced, narrow-minded, demure, priggish, ▷*prim*
prune [1] *v.* cut, shorten, trim, crop [2] *n.* dried plum
pry *v.* snoop, peep, meddle, intrude
public [1] *adj.* communal, civil, popular, social, national [2] *n.* the people, the populace, society
publish *v.* broadcast, distribute, circulate, communicate, bring out
pucker *v.* fold, crease, cockle, furrow, wrinkle ★**straighten**
puerile *adj.* callow, immature, juvenile
puff *v.* inflate, swell, blow, pant, distend
pull [1] *v.* haul, drag, tow, heave ★**push** [2] gather, pluck, detach, pick
pump [1] *v.* inflate, expand, swell [2] interrogate, question, grill
punch [1] *v.* strike, beat, hit, cuff [2] puncture, pierce, perforate, bore
punctual *adj.* prompt, on time, precise, timely ★**tardy**
puncture *n.* perforation, hole, leak, wound
pungent *adj.* sharp, bitter, poignant, biting, ▷*acrid* ★**mild**
punish *v.* chastise, correct, discipline, chasten, reprove, scold
puny *adj.* feeble, weak, frail, small, petty, stunted, insignificant ★**large**
pupil *n.* student, scholar, schoolchild, learner
puppet [1] *n.* doll, marionette [2] catspaw *The prisoner was not the true culprit, but only a catspaw,* figurehead, pawn
purchase [1] *v.* buy, procure, secure, obtain, get, ▷*buy* ★**sell** [2] *n.* bargain, investment
pure [1] *adj.* immaculate, spotless, stainless, clear, ▷*clean* ★**impure** [2] virtuous, chaste, honest, blameless
purely *adv.* simply, barely, merely, only
purge [1] *v.* purify, clean, cleanse [2] liquidate, exterminate, kill
purify *v.* clean, clarify, wash, purge
purloin *v.* rob, thieve, take, filch, pilfer, ▷*steal*
purpose *n.* intent, design, will, goal, target
purse [1] *n.* handbag, wallet, pouch, reticule, [2] *v.* pucker, crease, compress, wrinkle
pursue [1] *v.* follow, track, trace, ▷*chase* [2] *v.* practice, maintain, work for
pursuit [1] *n.* hunt, chase, hue and cry [2] occupation, hobby, interest *Stamp collecting has always been one of my main interests*
push [1] *v.* shove, thrust, press, drive, propel [2] *n.* advance, assault, drive
put [1] *v.* set, place, deposit, repose, lay [2] express, propose, state
put down [1] *v.* write, jot down, record, note [2] crush, humiliate, subdue [3] kill
put off [1] *v.* postpone, defer, delay, adjourn [2] dishearten, unsettle, perturb
putrid *adj.* decomposed, rotten, rancid, rank, stinking ★**wholesome**
putter *v.* dabble, fiddle, tinker, mess around
puzzle [1] *v.* baffle, confuse, mystify, perplex, ▷*bewilder* [2] *n.* conundrum, brainteaser, problem, dilemma
puzzling *adj.* baffling, curious, strange, bewildering, ▷*peculiar*

Q q

quack *n.* impostor, charlatan *She pretended to tell fortunes by cards, but she was nothing but a charlatan*, mountebank, humbug, fake

quaff *v.* imbibe, swallow, ▷*drink*

quagmire *n.* bog, mire, marsh, ▷*swamp*

quail *v.* tremble, flinch, shrink, cower, succumb ★**withstand**

quaint *adj.* curious, whimsical, fanciful, singular, old-fashioned, droll

quake [1] *v.* tremble, quaver, shiver, quiver, shudder [2] *n.* shock, convulsion *The convulsions from the earthquake were felt hundreds of miles away*

qualification [1] *n.* fitness, capacity, ability, accomplishment [2] restriction, limitation, modification *The engineer's design was accepted with certain modifications*

qualify [1] *v.* empower, enable, fit, suit [2] moderate, limit, restrict

quality [1] *n.* characteristic, condition, power [2] excellence, worth, goodness

qualm *n.* doubt, misgiving, hesitation

quandary *n.* difficulty, doubt, ▷*dilemma*

quantity *n.* amount, number, volume, sum

quarrel [1] *n.* dispute, squabble, wrangle, disagreement ★**harmony** [2] *v.* argue, bicker, brawl, squabble ★**agree**

quarry [1] *n.* game, prey, object, victim, target [2] mine, excavation, pit

quarter [1] *n.* area, territory, place, district [2] one-fourth [3] mercy *The commander of the invading army showed no mercy to the local defenders*, grace, lenience

quarters *n.* lodgings, dwelling, billet, rooms

quash *v.* abolish, nullify, suppress, overthrow, subdue

quaver *v.* shake, tremble, shiver, shudder, vibrate

quay *n.* pier, dock, wharf, landing, jetty KEY

queasy *adj.* bilious, squeamish, sick, faint

queer *adj.* strange, odd, whimsical, peculiar

quell *v.* crush, stifle, extinguish, defeat

quench [1] *v.* douse *We carefully doused our campfire before leaving the site*, put out, cool, check [2] slake *The cattle rushed to the river and slaked their thirst*, cool, allay

query [1] *n.* question, doubt, objection [2] *v.* ask, inquire, question, doubt ★**accept**

quest *n.* chase, hunt, search, pursuit, venture

question [1] *n.* query, inquiry, interrogation, [2] topic, problem, issue [3] *v.* ask, inquire, interrogate ★**answer**

questionable *adj.* doubtful, uncertain, undecided, unbelievable ★**certain**

queue [1] *n.* row, line, procession, line-up [2] pigtail, coil, braid CUE

quibble *v.* argue, trifle, split hairs, carp *If you like our plan, don't carp about the details*

quick [1] *adj.* speedy, rapid, express, swift, ▷*fast* [2] alert, active, agile, lively ★**slow** [3] clever, intelligent, acute ★**dull** [4] hasty, sharp, touchy ★**mild**

quicken *v.* accelerate, ▷*hasten* ★**delay**

quiet [1] *adj.* silent, soundless, noiseless, hushed ★**noisy** [2] placid, smooth, undisturbed ★**busy** [3] *n.* peace, rest, tranquillity, silence ★**tumult**

quilt *n.* blanket, cover, comforter, eiderdown

quip *n.* joke, gag, gipe, jest, wisecrack, retort

quirk *n.* pecularity, curiosity, foible *Despite his age and one or two foibles, old Uncle Fred was very agile*, mannerism, ▷*habit*

quit [1] *v.* cease, desist, stop [2] leave, depart, relinquish [3] give up, surrender

quite *adv.* absolutely, altogether, wholly

quits *adj.* even *If I pay what I owe, it makes us even*, all square, level, equal

quiver [1] *v.* tremble, quake, shiver, shudder [2] *n.* holster, scabbard, sheath

quiz [1] *v.* question, ask, examine, grill [2] *n.* test, examination, contest *Barbara was the winner in the radio spelling contest*

quizzical [1] *adj.* incredulous, skeptical, suspicious [2] whimsical, teasing, amused

quota *n.* allowance, allocation, ration

quotation [1] *n.* extract, selection, passage [2] cost, estimate, price

quote *v.* recite, recollect, tell, mention ★**contradict**

R r

rabble *n.* crowd, mob, scum, riffraff
race [1] *n.* competition, contest, chase, dash [2] people, nation, folk, stock, breed, tribe [3] *v.* run, speed, hurry, scamper, gallop, sprint
rack [1] *n.* shelf, stand, frame, framework [2] *v.* distress, strain, torment, pain WRACK
racket [1] *n.* uproar, noise, hubbub, tumult, ▷*din* [2] fraud, deception, swindle
racy [1] *adj.* pungent, piquant, zestful [2] spirited, smart, lively
radiant [1] *adj.* brilliant, bright, luminous, shining [2] splendid, glorious, happy ★**dull**
radiate [1] *v.* gleam, sparkle, beam, shine [2] emit, spread, diffuse
radical [1] *adj.* extreme, fanatical, deep-seated [2] original, fundamental *The new teacher made some fundamental changes in our lessons*, natural ★**superficial**
raffle *n.* draw, sweepstake, lottery
rafter *n.* joist, girder, beam, support
ragamuffin *n.* scarecrow, urchin, ▷*waif*
rage [1] *n.* wrath, fury, ferocity, passion, madness, ▷*anger* [2] *v.* rave, fret, fume *The mad bull was fuming with rage as we leaped over the fence*, storm, flare up
ragged *adj.* shabby, seedy, shaggy, rough, torn ★**smart**
raid [1] *n.* invasion, attack, strike, sortie [2] *v.* attack, invade, ransack, plunder *The ship was attacked and plundered by pirates* RAYED
rail [1] *n.* post, picket, fence, railing [2] *v.* scold, rant, blast, reproach
rain *n.* & *v.* deluge, drizzle, flood, shower, torrent REIGN REIN
raise [1] *v.* elevate, lift, erect, hoist *The flag was hoisted as the ship came into port* ★**lower** [2] excite, awaken, rouse [3] promote, increase, advance [4] cultivate, grow, breed RAZE
rake *v.* grope, scrape, collect, gather, assemble
rally [1] *v.* meet, assemble, convene *The members of the club will convene next month* ★**disperse** [2] encourage, restore, reunite
ram [1] *v.* cram, crowd, push, pack, stuff, poke, wedge [2] charge, beat, crash, drive
ramble [1] *v.* stroll, meander, saunter, roam, rove [2] chatter, digress *Joe's speech was very long, as he kept digressing from the point*, dodder
ramp *n.* gradient, slope, incline, grade
rampage [1] *n.* storm, rage, riot, uproar, tumult [2] rave, rush, run wild *Someone left the gate open, and the pigs ran wild in the cabbage patch*
ramshackle *adj.* unstable, shaky, unsteady, flimsy, rickety, ▷*decrepit* ★**stable**
rancid *adj.* sour, curdled, rank, putrid, musty
rancor *n.* spite, grudge, animosity, hatred, ▷*malice* RANKER
random *adj.* haphazard, vague, casual, accidental, ▷*chance* ★**deliberate**
range [1] *n.* extent, length, span, magnitude, area [2] kind, sort, class, order [3] *v.* wander, rove, roam, stray
rank [1] *n.* grade, class, position, level [2] *adj.* foul, musty, offensive, coarse [3] luxuriant, fertile, dense *The whole county was covered with dense forest*
rankle *v.* burn, smolder, fester, be embittered
ransack *v.* plunder, pillage, search, scour
ransom [1] *n.* release, deliverance, payoff, price [2] *v.* rescue, redeem *Jill was lazy at school to begin with, but redeemed herself with hard work*, liberate
rant *v.* rave, declaim, bluster, roar, shout
rap *v.* tap, pat, strike, knock
rape *v.* violate, abuse, assault, attack
rapid *adj.* speedy, quick, swift, ▷*fast* ★**slow**
rapt *adj.* engrossed, intent, captivated, fascinated, delighted RAPPED WRAPPED
rapture *n.* bliss, ecstasy, delight, ▷*joy* ★**sorrow**
rare [1] *adj.* unusual, uncommon, scarce, occasional [2] valuable, fine, precious ★**common** [3] underdone *I would like my steak to be underdone and rather rare*, lightly cooked
rascal *n.* rogue, knave, villain, scamp, scoundrel, blackguard ★**gentleman**
rash [1] *adj.* headstrong, audacious, hasty,

foolhardy, ▷*reckless* ★**cautious** [2] *n.* eruption, outbreak, epidemic *There has been an epidemic of break-ins in our town*
rashness *n.* audacity, carelessness, hastiness, recklessness ★**carefulness**
rasp [1] *v.* file, grate, grind [2] irk, irritate, vex [3] *n.* file, tool
rate [1] *n.* pace, tempo *It took us some time to get used to the tempo of life in the city,* velocity, speed [2] tax, charge, cost [3] *v.* appraise, assess, estimate, merit, value
rather [1] *adv.* somewhat, to some extent, sort of [2] first, preferably, sooner
ration [1] *n.* portion, share, allotment, helping [2] *v.* allocate, allot, restrict, control
rational [1] *adj.* sensible, sound, wise, intelligent, sane ★**crazy** [2] reasonable, fair, proper ★**absurd**
rattle [1] *v.* jangle, jingle, vibrate [2] muddle, confuse, daze, ▷*bewilder*
raucous *adj.* harsh, hoarse, rough, strident, gutteral
ravage *v.* devastate, destroy, pillage, ransack, desolate, wreck
rave [1] *v.* rant, ramble *The old man rambled on for hours about his heroic deeds in the war,* roar, rage, storm [2] favor, be ecstatic about
ravenous *adj.* hungry, starving, famished, voracious, ▷*greedy*
ravishing *adj.* beautiful, bewitching, delightful, charming, ▷*enchanting*
raw [1] *adj.* uncooked [2] unripe, green *I was pretty green during the first six months in the job,* inexperienced [3] sensitive, painful, tender [4] cold, exposed, chilly
ray *n.* beam, gleam, glimmer, shaft, stream, spark
raze *v.* demolish, destroy, flatten, obliterate, ruin RAISE RAYS
reach [1] *v.* arrive at, gain, get to, attain, grasp [2] stretch, extend [3] *n.* extent, length, grasp, distance, scope
react *v.* respond, reverberate *The sound of the church bell reverberated through the village,* behave, respond
read *v.* peruse, pore over, study, browse, understand REED

readily *adv.* easily, eagerly, freely, gladly, promptly ★**reluctantly**
ready [1] *adj.* prepared, alert, prompt, willing ★**reluctant** [2] convenient, handy ★**remote** [3] skillful, facile, expert ★**clumsy**
real [1] *adj.* genuine, authentic, factual ★**false** [2] substantial, existent, actual ★**imaginary** REEL
realistic [1] *adj.* authentic, lifelike [2] practical, down-to-earth *Sue is a real romantic type, but her boyfriend is much more down-to-earth,* unromantic ★**fanciful**
realize [1] *v.* understand, comprehend, feel [2] earn, gain, obtain, acquire
really *adv.* truly, indeed, actually, absolutely
realm *n.* domain, province, sphere *My mother has taken up writing and is much involved in the sphere of books,* region, territory
reap *v.* harvest, gather, obtain, realize, derive, gain ★**squander**
rear [1] *n.* back, end, tail, behind, posterior [2] *adj.* hind, after, following [3] *v.* foster, breed, educate [4] lift, raise, elevate
reason [1] *n.* purpose, motive, basis, cause, explanation [2] wisdom, sense, intellect [3] *v.* consider, think, argue
reasonable [1] *adj.* sensible, valid, rational ★**absurd** [2] moderate, fair, just [3] inexpensive, low-priced *Everything in our new supermarket is very low-priced* ★**excessive**
reassure *v.* inspire, hearten, convince, ▷*encourage* ★**discourage**

rebate *n.* refund, repayment, discount, allowance
rebel [1] *v.* (re-*bel*) revolt, mutiny, disobey, resist [2] *n.* (*reb*-el) revolutionary, mutineer *Fletcher Christian was the leader of the mutineers on the* Bounty, traitor
rebellious *adj.* defiant, disobedient, mutinous, resistant ★**obedient**
rebuke *v.* reprimand, reproach, scold, tell off ★**praise**
recall [1] *v.* recollect, remember [2] cancel, overrule, countermand *We were just about to pull down the building when our orders were countermanded*, call back
recede *v.* ebb, retreat, flow back, decline, shrink, withdraw, return ★**proceed**
receipt *n.* acknowledgment, voucher
recent *adj.* late, new, fresh, novel, modern ★**out-of-date**
recently *adv.* lately, currently, latterly
receptacle *n.* container, holder, vessel, bowl
reception [1] *n.* entertainment, function, party [2] acceptance, acknowledgment
recess [1] *n.* alcove, corner, socket, niche, slot, nook [2] intermission, interlude, pause
recession *n.* slump, stagnation, depression ★**boom**
recipe *n.* formula, method *I'll show you my mother's method of making angel food cake; it never fails*, prescription
recite *v.* recount, chant, speak, declaim, relate, describe
reckless *adj.* unwary, incautious, daring, brash, heedless, ▷*rash* ★**cautious**
reckon [1] *v.* calculate, figure, count, tally *I have checked the accounts, and my figures tally with yours*, account [2] judge, expect, believe
reclaim *v.* recover, redeem, reform, retrieve, restore, salvage
recline *v.* lounge, sprawl, lie, rest, loll, repose
recognize [1] *v.* recall, recollect, remember, identify, know [2] see *I will explain my idea slowly, and you will see what I mean*, comprehend, understand
recoil [1] *v.* rebound, backfire, boomerang [2] falter, flinch, shrink, quail *My little brother quailed at the sound of the thunder*
recollect *v.* recall, recognize, place, ▷*remember* ★**forget**
recommend *v.* suggest, advise, propose, commend, approve ★**veto**
recompense [1] *n.* payment, compensation, remuneration [2] *v.* reimburse, repay, ▷*reward*
reconcile [1] *v.* accept, harmonize, pacify, placate ★**estrange** [2] adjust, settle, square
record [1] *v.* (re-*cord*) note, register, enter, inscribe, list [2] *n.* (*rec*-ord) album, disk, platter, CD, LP [3] chronicle, archive, almanac *We'll get hold of the almanac and check the time of high tide*, register [4] performance, championship
recount [1] *v.* (re-*count*) relate, tell, recite, describe [2] *n.* (*re*-count) count again
recover [1] *v.* reclaim, retrieve, redeem, regain [2] get better, recuperate, revive ★**worsen**
recreation *n.* pastime, sport, amusement, games, fun
recruit [1] *n.* trainee, beginner, apprentice [2] *v.* enlist, enroll, draft, mobilize
rectify *v.* correct, put right, repair, remedy, restore
recuperate *v.* get better, rally, improve, mend, ▷*recover* ★**worsen**
recur *v.* return, reappear, come back, repeat, revert
redden *v.* crimson, color, flush, ▷*blush*
redeem [1] *v.* buy back, compensate for, exchange [2] save, liberate, free
reduce [1] *v.* lessen, diminish, curtail, contract [2] overcome, defeat, humiliate
reek *v.* smell, stink, fume, exhale, smoke
reel [1] *v.* roll, rock, shake, stagger, falter, totter [2] *n.* bobbin, spool, spindle REAL
refer *v.* relate, connect, associate, assign, belong
referee *n.* umpire, arbitrator, judge
reference [1] *n.* allusion, insinuation, innuendo *From your innuendo, it seems that you think I'm joking!*, ▷*hint* [2] recommendation, testimonial, credentials
refine *v.* clarify, purify, filter, process, cultivate
refined [1] *adj.* civilized, cultivated, cultured, ▷*polite* [2] purified, pure, clarified ★**coarse**

reflect [1] *v.* think, contemplate, deliberate, consider [2] mirror, copy, imitate, image
reform [1] *v.* improve, correct, ▷*rectify* [2] remodel, reorganize ★**worsen**
refrain [1] *v.* avoid, abstain, forbear, resist, keep from [2] *n.* chorus, melody, tune
refresh *v.* rejuvenate, renew, restore, cheer, enliven ★**exhaust**
refrigerate *v.* chill, cool, freeze
refuge *n.* haven, harbor, asylum, sanctuary, ▷*shelter*
refugee *n.* exile, fugitive, emigrant
refund *v.* repay, rebate, reimburse *I must reimburse you for all you spent on my behalf*, pay back, return
refuse [1] *v.* (re-*fuze*) decline, say no, demur, repudiate [2] *n.* (*ref*-use) trash, garbage, rubbish, waste
refute *v.* deny, dispute, disprove, discredit ★**prove**
regain *v.* recover, get back, retrieve, redeem
regal *adj.* royal, princely, majestic, noble, stately
regard [1] *v.* esteem, revere, honor, respect ★**dislike** [2] notice, observe, see, gaze [3] *n.* affection, esteem, fondness, repute ★**contempt**
regardless [1] *adj.* heedless, neglectful, indifferent ★**careful** [2] *adv.* anyhow, anyway, in any case
region *n.* area, zone, territory, locality, province, country
register [1] *n.* roll, roster, record, archives *We can trace the town's history from the ancient archives* [2] *v.* enter, record, inscribe, enroll, sign on
regret [1] *v.* repent, rue, deplore, lament, mourn, apologize ★**welcome** [2] *n.* remorse, sorrow, apology, grief
regular [1] *adj.* normal, customary, periodical, formal ★**unusual** [2] orderly, steady, unchanging ★**variable**
regulate [1] *v.* control, manage, govern, determine [2] adjust, measure, time, correct
regulation [1] *n.* rule, law, command, bylaw *There is a local bylaw forbidding football on Sunday* [2] order, control, government

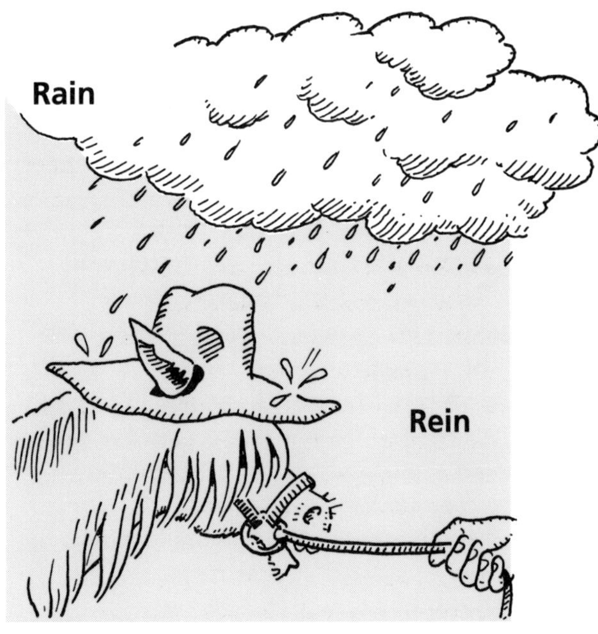

rehearse *v.* repeat, practice, drill, prepare, run through
reign [1] *n.* rule, sway, power, control [2] *v.* govern, rule, dominate, command RAIN REIN
rein *v.* & *n.* bridle, hold, check, harness RAIN REIGN
reinforce *v.* support, strengthen, toughen, stiffen ★**weaken**
reject [1] *v.* (re-*ject*) discard, get rid of, refuse, repel, deny [2] *n.* (*re*-ject) cast-off, scrap, throw-out
rejoice *v.* glory, exult, cheer, please, ▷*delight* ★**lament**
relapse [1] *v.* revert, backslide, turn back, recede [2] *n.* repetition, recurrence, setback
relate *v.* describe, recount, tell, mention, detail
related *adj.* associated, allied, connected, linked, akin ★**different**
relative [1] *n.* kinsman, kinswoman, cousin, relation, sibling *I have four siblings—three sisters and one brother* [2] *adj.* comparative, approximate, relevant
relax *v.* diminish, loosen, ease, reduce, relieve, unwind ★**tighten**
relaxed *adj.* composed, cool, easygoing, mellow, ▷*casual* ★**tense**
release *v.* let go, loose, liberate, acquit,

discharge, ▷*free* ★**detain**
relent *v.* relax, soften, yield, ease, give in, unbend ★**harden**
relentless *adj.* unmerciful, remorseless, grim, pitiless, ▷*cruel* ★**humane**
relevant *adj.* applicable, pertinent, appropriate, apt, ▷*suitable* ★**irrelevant**
reliable *adj.* dependable, trustworthy, responsible, honest, ▷*sound* ★**unreliable**
relic *n.* fragment, vestige, antique, keepsake, memento *This brooch is a memento of my great-grandmother: she wore it on her wedding day*
relief *n.* aid, assistance, respite, support, succor, ▷*help* ★**aggravation**
relieve *v.* release, support, comfort, lighten, relax, console ★**aggravate**
religious *adj.* pious, devout, orthodox, devoted, God-fearing, faithful
relinquish *v.* renounce, let go, waive, disclaim, give up, ▷*abandon* ★**retain**
relish [1] *v.* enjoy, like, approve, ▷*appreciate* ★**loathe** [2] *n.* savor, flavor, tang, gusto *The fried chicken was a great success; everyone ate with enormous gusto!*, zest, sauce
reluctant *adj.* hesitant, averse, loth, disinclined, squeamish ★**willing**
rely on *v.* depend on, count on, believe in
remain [1] *v.* stay, tarry, dwell, wait, rest ★**depart** [2] persist, last, endure
remainder *n.* remnant, residue, leavings
remark [1] *v.* utter, observe, state, mention, ▷*say* [2] notice, perceive, note, ▷*see*
remarkable *adj.* unusual, surprising, curious, prominent, ▷*outstanding* ★**ordinary**
remedy [1] *n.* cure, restorative, medicine [2] relief, solution, treatment, corrective [3] *v.* relieve, heal, cure, put right
remember *v.* recollect, recognize, think back, ▷*recall* ★**forget**
remind *v.* suggest, hint, cue, prompt
remit [1] *v.* relax, desist, slacken, modify, excuse, forgive [2] pay, square, settle up
remnant *n.* residue, remains, rest ▷*remainder*
remorse *n.* regrets, contrition, pity
remote [1] *adj.* distant, far, isolated ★**near** [2] unrelated, alien, foreign ★**significant**
remove *v.* dislocate, take away, transfer, withdraw, carry off
rend *v.* split, fracture, tear apart, sever, break
render [1] *v.* give, present, surrender, deliver [2] play, execute, perform
renew [1] *v.* modernize, mend, prolong, renovate [2] reissue *Next week we start to reissue some of the old silent movies*, revive
renounce *v.* disown, disclaim, give up, repudiate, forsake ★**retain**
renowned *adj.* eminent, noted, famed, notable, ▷*celebrated* ★**obscure**
rent [1] *v.* hire, lease, let, charter [2] *n.* tear, rip, break, crack, fissure
repair [1] *v.* fix, mend, correct, remedy, rectify *We are sorry there was an error in your account; we will rectify it right away* [2] *n.* restoration, adjustment
repast *n.* meal, food, snack, spread
repay [1] *v.* refund, reimburse, pay [2] avenge, retaliate, revenge, punish
repeal *v.* revoke, annul, abolish, quash *The man's innocence was proved and his sentence was quashed*, ▷*cancel* ★**establish**
repeat *v.* duplicate, renew, reiterate, do again
repel [1] *v.* repulse, deter, reject, push back [2] revolt, disgust, nauseate ★**attract**
repellent *adj.* distasteful, hateful, discouraging, ▷*repulsive* ★**attractive**
repent *v.* sorrow, deplore, grieve, ▷*regret*
replace [1] *v.* supersede, succeed, follow, substitute [2] put back, reinstate, restore
replenish *v.* fill, refill, restock, furnish, provide, top up ★**empty**
replica *n.* facsimile, copy, likeness, duplicate
reply [1] *v.* answer, respond, rejoin, retort, acknowledge [2] *n.* answer, response, acknowledgment, riposte
report [1] *n.* statement, account, message, communication, tidings [2] noise, explosion, bang [3] *v.* tell, disclose, reveal, expose
repose [1] *v.* rest, settle, lie down, sleep, recline [2] *n.* ease, peace, quiet, tranquillity ★**tumult**
represent [1] *v.* depict, picture, portray, illustrate [2] stand for, mean, denote
representative [1] *n.* agent, delegate, envoy,

deputy [2] *adj.* typical, figurative
repress *v.* restrain, suppress, bottle up, smother, stifle
reprimand [1] *v.* admonish, blame, rebuke, ▷*chide* [2] *n.* reproach *The service in the hotel was excellent, beyond reproach*, talking-to, scolding **★praise**
reproach *v.* scold, reprove, reprimand, blame, ▷*rebuke* **★approve**
reproduce [1] *v.* copy, duplicate, imitate, simulate [2] breed, multiply, generate
reprove *v.* reproach, reprimand, ▷*rebuke* **★approve**
repudiate *v.* renounce, disown, disavow, disclaim **★acknowledge**
repugnant *adj.* unattractive, disagreeable, offensive, ▷*repulsive*, **★pleasant**
repulse *v.* repel, rebuff, drive back, reject, ▷*spurn* **★attract**
repulsive *adj.* obnoxious, disgusting, loathsome, ▷*repugnant* **★attractive**
reputation *n.* standing, position, esteem, honor, good name
request [1] *v.* demand, beg, entreat, beseech, ▷*ask* [2] *n.* petition, entreaty, invitation
require [1] *v.* need, want, demand, crave [2] expect, cause, instruct
rescue [1] *v.* save, set free, liberate, recover, release [2] *n.* liberation, deliverance, salvation *Salvation for the starving islanders came when the plane dropped food and supplies* **★capture**
research *v.* examine, explore, investigate, inquire, ▷*study*
resemble *v.* look like, mirror, take after, be like **★differ**
resent *v.* resist, begrudge, dislike, take exception to **★like**
resentful *adj.* offended, bitter, piqued, huffy, ▷*indignant* **★contented**
reserve [1] *v.* hoard, retain, withhold, ▷*keep* [2] *n.* modesty, shyness, restraint [3] supply, backlog, stock
reservoir *n.* lake, spring, pool, container
reside *v.* live, occupy, inhabit, lodge, ▷*dwell*
residence *n.* house, home, habitation, dwelling, mansion RESIDENTS
resign *v.* retire, abdicate, step down, give notice, abandon, ▷*quit* **★join**
resign oneself to *v.* accept, comply, reconcile *Robinson Crusoe became reconciled to loneliness on his island*, yield, give in, ▷*submit* **★resist**
resist *v.* withstand, oppose, defy, refrain, hinder, ▷*thwart* **★submit**

Resign oneself to

Robinson Crusoe became reconciled to loneliness on his island.

resistance *n.* defiance, obstruction, opposition, hindrance **★acceptance**
resolute *adj.* determined, resolved, obstinate, stubborn, dogged *Despite the bad weather, the climbers were dogged in their will to reach the peak* **★weak**
resolve [1] *v.* determine, intend, decide [2] decipher, unravel, disentangle [3] *n.* resolution, purpose, will
resort [1] *v.* frequent, haunt, visit [2] *n.* alternative, chance, course [3] spa, watering place, hotel, vacation spot
resourceful *adj.* clever, ingenious, bright
respect [1] *n.* esteem, honor, regard, repute, dignity [2] *v.* esteem, honor, revere, venerate *The names of the pioneers and explorers will always be venerated*
respectable *adj.* decent, admirable, honest, honorable, proper **★disreputable**
respectful *adj.* deferential, courteous, polite,

dutiful ★**disrespectful**

respite *n.* break, halt, interval, lull, recess, let-up

respond *v.* answer, reply, retort, tally, accord, agree ★**differ**

responsible [1] *adj.* accountable, dependable, sensible, ▷*reliable* ★**unreliable** [2] liable, guilty

rest [1] *n.* repose, relaxation, peace, tranquillity [2] break, pause, respite, spell [3] remainder, residue, balance [4] *v.* repose, settle, sleep, relax WREST

restful *adj.* peaceful, quiet, calm, placid ★**disturbing**

restless *adj.* uneasy, fitful, agitated, nervous, fretful ★**calm**

restore [1] *v.* replace, reinstate, return [2] refurbish, recondition, renovate *We renovated this old sofa which we found in a junk shop*

restrain *v.* stop, prevent, hold back, subdue, ▷*check* ★**encourage**

restrict *v.* confine, limit, cramp, handicap, ▷*regulate* ★**free**

result [1] *n.* effect, consequence, outcome, end ★**cause** [2] *v.* ensue, happen, turn out, follow ★**begin**

resume *v.* renew, recommence, start again, go back to, ▷*continue* ★**interrupt**

retain *v.* hold, restrain, withhold, detain, ▷*keep* ★**relinquish**

retaliate *v.* avenge, reciprocate, fight back, repay, retort ★**submit**

retire [1] *v.* retreat, go back, ▷*withdraw* ★**advance** [2] abdicate, resign, relinquish

retort [1] *n.* riposte, reply, rejoinder [2] *v.* return, answer, reply

retract *v.* recant, deny, disavow, take back ★**maintain**

retreat [1] *v.* retire, depart, shrink, ▷*withdraw* ★**advance** [2] *n.* sanctuary *This section of the park is being made into a bird santuary*, shelter, den, haven

retrieve *v.* redeem, recover, regain, rescue, ▷*salvage* ★**lose**

return [1] *v.* rejoin, come back, reappear [2] restore, give back, repay, refund [3] *n.* form, document, list

reveal *v.* disclose, expose, show, display, uncover, divulge ★**hide**

revel [1] *v.* make merry, celebrate, have fun [2] *n.* celebration, gala, party, spree

revenge [1] *n.* vengeance, reprisal, retaliation [2] *v.* avenge, get one's own back

revenue *n.* income, receipts, earnings

revere *v.* honor, esteem, regard, adore, venerate, respect ★**despise**

reverse [1] *v.* cancel, change, overrule, repeal, revoke [2] *n.* adversity, disaster, bad luck, misfortune [3] *adj.* backward, contrary, opposite *We turned our car around and went back in the opposite direction*

review [1] *v.* reconsider, examine, survey [2] *n.* inspection, examination [3] synopsis, journal, magazine REVUE

revise *v.* edit, amend, improve, rewrite, alter

revive *v.* awaken, rally, recover, refresh, ▷*rouse*

revoke *v.* repeal, abolish *Many British people want to abolish fox-hunting*, cancel, quash, reverse, withdraw

revolt [1] *v.* rebel, mutiny, riot [2] nauseate, sicken, disgust [3] *n.* rebellion, uprising, revolution

revolting *adj.* obnoxious *The chemical factory's chimney was giving off obnoxious fumes*, repulsive, offensive, ▷*repugnant* ★**pleasant**

revolve *v.* rotate, spin, gyrate, turn

reward [1] *n.* award, payment, benefit, bonus, profit ★**punishment** [2] *v.* compensate, repay, remunerate ★**punish**

rhyme *n.* verse, poem, ditty, ode RIME

rhythm *n.* beat, pulse, throb, stroke, timing

ribald *adj.* smutty, vulgar, coarse, gross

rich [1] *adj.* wealthy, prosperous, affluent, opulent ★**poor** [2] fertile, loamy, fruitful, abundant ★**barren** [3] delicious, sweet, luscious, delicate

rid *v.* get rid of, unburden, expel, free

riddle [1] *n.* puzzle, cryptogram, enigma [2] *v.* puncture, bore, perforate, pierce

ride [1] *v.* sit, travel, drive, journey [2] *n.* journey, jaunt, lift, trip

ridge [1] *n.* groove, furrow, fold [2] highland, chain, range *A range of hills could be seen in the distance*

Rivers and Waterways

Arroyo
Brook
Canal
Channel
Creek
Lake
Loch
Pool
Pond
River
Spring
Strait
Stream
Surf
Tide
Waterfall

ridicule [1] *n.* scorn, derision, travesty, sarcasm, mockery [2] *v.* deride, mock, jeer, banter *His banter can be amusing, but he doesn't know when to stop and sometimes offends people*

ridiculous *adj.* laughable, absurd, foolish, preposterous, ▷*silly* ★**sensible**

rife *adj.* common, current, frequent, prevalent, ▷*widespread* ★**scarce**

rifle [1] *v.* loot, rob, plunder, ▷*ransack* [2] *n.* gun, musket, firearm

rift [1] *n.* fissure, breach, crack [2] disagreement, clash, break

right [1] *adj.* correct, proper, true ★**incorrect** [2] honest, upright, fair [3] seemly, fit, suitable, becoming ★**improper** [4] *n.* truth, justice, honesty ★**wrong** RITE WRITE

righteous *adj.* honorable, upright, moral

rigid [1] *adj.* stiff, firm, inflexible [2] stern, austere, harsh ★**flexible**

rigorous *adj.* stern, severe, strict, rigid

rim *n.* border, margin, edge, verge *We knew we were on the verge of disaster,* brink

ring [1] *n.* circle, band, collar [2] bell, chime, tinkle [3] *v.* chime, strike, jingle, sound WRING

riot [1] *n.* uproar, tumult, brawl, broil ★**calm** [2] *v.* revolt, rampage, rebel

ripe [1] *adj.* mellow, mature, seasoned [2] developed, adult, full-grown

rise [1] *v.* ascend, mount, soar, arise, grow ★**fall** [2] appear, occur, happen ★**vanish** [3] *n.* ascent, advance, increase ★**fall**

risk [1] *v.* chance, dare, hazard, gamble [2] *n.* adventure, peril, danger, jeopardy ★**safety**

risky *adj.* perilous, chancy, dangerous, tricky, uncertain ★**safe**

rite *n.* custom, ritual, practice RIGHT

rival [1] *adj.* opposing, competing, conflicting [2] *n.* opponent, adversary ★**associate**

river *n.* stream, waterway, brook, torrent *Before the rains came, this torrent was only a small stream*

road *n.* street, avenue, drive, lane, highway, freeway, route, way RODE ROWED

roam *v.* rove, ramble, range, stroll, wander

roar *v.* bellow, bawl, yell, blare, cry

rob *v.* cheat, defraud, loot, plunder, ▷*steal*

robber *n.* bandit, brigand, thief, crook

robe *n.* costume, dress, gown, habit

robust *adj.* strong, healthy, lusty, sturdy, ▷*vigorous* ★**delicate**

rock [1] *n.* stone, boulder, cobble, pebble, crag, reef [2] *v.* totter, reel, sway, falter [3] quiet, still, tranquilize, soothe

rod *n.* baton, stick, stave, pole, perch, cane

rogue *n.* rascal, blackguard, scamp, knave, ▷*scoundrel* ★**gentleman**

role *n.* character, post, duty, function *At the end of the party, my function will be to clear up*

roll [1] *n.* record, register, list [2] spool, scroll, reel [3] *v.* revolve, rotate, turn [4] smooth, level, press [5] lurch, reel, pitch, ROLE

romance [1] *n.* love story, novel, love affair [2] adventure, excitement, fantasy, glamour

romantic [1] *adj.* amorous, passionate, loving [2] visionary, fanciful *Many people have a fanciful idea of how things were in the old days,* fantastic, extravagant ★**ordinary**

romp *v.* gambol, caper, frolic, prance, play

roof *n.* ceiling, covering, cover, canopy

room [1] *n.* apartment, chamber, area, compartment, salon [2] space, capacity

root [1] *n.* seed, source, radicle [2] basis, element, stem, origin
rope *n.* cable, cord, hawser, line, lasso
rosy [1] *adj.* cheerful, encouraging, hopeful, optimistic [2] pink, flesh-colored
rot [1] *v.* corrupt, crumble, decay, perish [2] *n.* bunkum *The last speaker at the meeting was talking a lot of bunkum!*, balderdash, bosh
rotate *v.* revolve, turn, spin, pivot, gyrate
rotten [1] *adj.* decayed, putrid, decomposed, fetid [2] deplorable, despicable, nasty, vicious *People have told some vicious lies about my dad*
rough [1] *adj.* wrinkled, craggy, coarse, shaggy, broken [2] rude, crude, imperfect [3] blunt, gruff, brusque, discourteous RUFF
round [1] *adj.* circular, rotund, spherical [2] *n.* ring, circle, loop
rouse [1] *v.* waken, arouse, excite, disturb [2] anger, inflame, incite ★**calm**
rout *v.* crush, defeat, conquer, overthrow
route *n.* road, track, way, journey, direction
routine *n.* usage, practice, formula, technique, method, habit *After being alone for so long, I have gotten into the habit of talking to myself*
rove *v.* tramp, roam, wander, stroll, drift
row [1] *n.* (*ro*) string, line, queue, rank, column [2] *v.* paddle, scull ROE [3] *n.* (as in *now*) fight, squabble, noise, quarrel ★**calm**
rowdy *adj.* rough, unruly, boisterous, noisy, wild ★**quiet**
royal *adj.* sovereign, princely, stately, majestic, ▷*regal*
rub *v.* stroke, brush, scrub, wipe, polish
rubbish *n.* debris, trash, junk, garbage
rude [1] *adj.* coarse, primitive, ill-bred, impolite, boorish, bad-mannered [2] crude, formless, shapeless ★**polished** ROOD RUED
rue *v.* be sorry for, deplore, grieve, ▷*regret*
ruffian *n.* hoodlum, hooligan, lout, scoundrel, rogue, ▷*rascal*
ruffle [1] *v.* fluster, worry, excite, agitate [2] crumple, rumple, crease, cockle
ruffled *adj.* upset, worried, flustered, harassed
rugged [1] *adj.* rough, craggy, shaggy, ragged [2] rigorous, robust, strong, strenuous
ruin [1] *v.* demolish, wreck, damage, smash [2] bankrupt, impoverish, overwhelm
rule [1] *v.* control, govern, command, manage, direct [2] decide, determine, settle, judge [3] *n.* law, regulation [4] straightedge
ruler [1] *n.* leader, director, king, queen, monarch, governor [2] rule, straightedge
rumble *v.* roar, thunder, boom, roll
rumor *n.* hearsay, report, gossip, scandal *The bribery scandal, added to high taxes, brought down the government*
rumpus *n.* uproar, racket, riot, commotion, hurly-burly ★**calm**
run [1] *v.* hurry, hasten, speed, sprint ★**saunter** [2] leak, flow, ooze [3] operate, propel, drive [4] *n.* race, course
run away *v.* escape, flee, bolt, abscond ★**stay**
rupture *v.* & *n.* break, burst, puncture, split
rural *adj.* rustic, countrified, pastoral ★**urban**
ruse *n.* dodge, hoax, scheme, trick, ploy RUES
rush *v.* & *n.* dash, speed, hurry, scramble, stampede, rampage ★**saunter**
rust *n.* corrosion, mold, blight, mildew, stain, deterioration
rustic *adj.* rural, pastoral, country, homely, simple
rustle *n.* & *v.* crackle, swish, murmur, whisper
rut *n.* furrow, channel, groove, score, track
ruthless *adj.* cruel, savage, harsh, ferocious, pitiless ★**merciful**

Rulers, Monarchs, and Leaders

Caesar
Czar
Czarina
Emperor
Empress
King
Mikado
Mogul
Pharaoh
President
Prime Minister
Prince
Princess
Queen
Rajah
Sultan

S s

sack [1] *n.* bag, pouch, pack [2] *v.* rob, plunder, pillage [3] discharge, dismiss, lay off SAC

sacred *adj.* holy, blessed, hallowed, spiritual ★**profane**

sacrifice [1] *n.* offering [2] *v.* forfeit, give up, relinquish, ▷*abandon*

sad *adj.* sorrowful, melancholy, unhappy, mournful, woeful, ▷*sorry* ★**happy**

sadden *v.* mourn, grieve, distress, lament ★**please**

safe [1] *adj.* secure, protected, sure ★**unsafe** [2] *n.* vault, coffer, cashbox, strongbox

safety *n.* shelter, security, sanctuary, protection, refuge ★**danger**

sag *v.* bend, curve, bow, decline, flag, ▷*droop* ★**bulge**

sage [1] *adj.* wise, sensible, shrewd, sagacious ★**foolish** [2] *n.* wise person, savant *We were taught by an old savant of the university, Professor Hankins*, philosopher ★**fool**

said *adj.* expressed, stated, above-mentioned

sail *v.* cruise, voyage, navigate, float, skim SALE

sailor *n.* seaman, seafarer, mariner, jack tar, seadog SAILER

sake *n.* motive, reason, purpose, object, principle

salary *n.* pay, earnings, reward, wages, income

sale *n.* auction, transaction, selling, trade, disposal SAIL

sally *n.* jest, joke, crack, riposte, ▷*quip*

salute [1] *v.* greet, accost, welcome, hail, honor [2] *n.* greetings, welcome, acknowledgment

salvage *v.* save, conserve, rescue, restore, reclaim, ▷*preserve* ★**abandon**

same [1] *adj.* identical, duplicate, alike, similar [2] aforesaid, aforementioned *I leave all my possessions to my wife, the aforementioned Angela Gomez*

sample [1] *n.* specimen, example, model, pattern, illustration [2] *v.* inspect, try, taste

sanction *v.* permit, allow, authorize, approve

sanctuary *n.* retreat, shelter, shrine, asylum, ▷*refuge*

sane *adj.* normal, rational, reasonable, lucid, ▷*sensible* ★**insane**

sap *v.* bleed, drain, exhaust, reduce, weaken ★**strengthen**

sarcastic *adj.* biting, cutting, sardonic, cynical, ironic, caustic *My cousins made some caustic comments after I played the violin*

satire *n.* invective, sarcasm, burlesque, ridicule, parody

satisfaction *n.* contentment, delight, gratification, compensation ★**grievance**

satisfy *v.* gratify, fulfill, appease, suit, please, ▷*delight* ★**disappoint**

saturate *v.* soak, steep, drench, souse, waterlog *I am afraid our old canoe is too waterlogged ever to be used again*

saucy *adj.* forward, pert, impudent, cheeky, disrespectful ★**civil**

saunter *v.* roam, loiter, wander, linger, dawdle, amble, ▷*stroll* ★**hasten**

savage [1] *adj.* barbaric, wild, uncivilized, ferocious, brutal ★**civilized** [2] *n.* brute, oaf, barbarian

Sacred Books

Apocrypha	Gospels
Bhagavad-Gita	Granth
Bible	Hebrew Bible
Book of Mormon	Koran
Book of Common Prayer	Talmud
	Torah
	Tripitaka
	Upanishad
	Veda

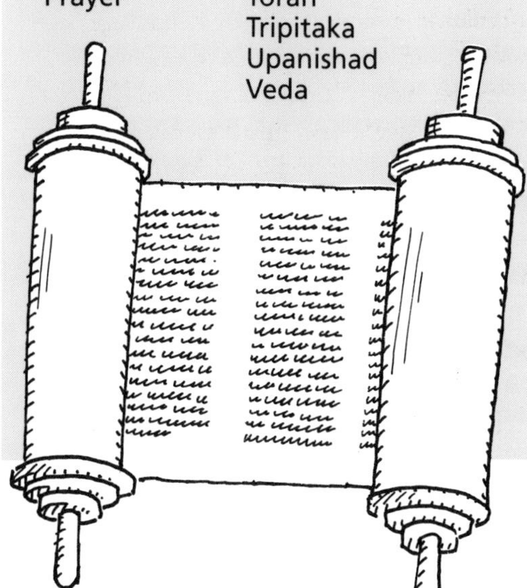

save [1] *v.* liberate, set free, rescue, protect, guard [2] keep, preserve, salvage, hoard, put aside ★**squander**

savory *adj.* appetizing, flavorful, luscious, agreeable ★**tasteless**

say *v.* speak, utter, state, pronounce, talk, tell, assert

saying *n.* proverb, statement, adage, idiom, maxim

scale [1] *n.* measure, balance, calibration [2] crust, plate, flake [3] clef, key *I will play this next piece in the key of C*, mode [4] *v.* climb, ascend, clamber up

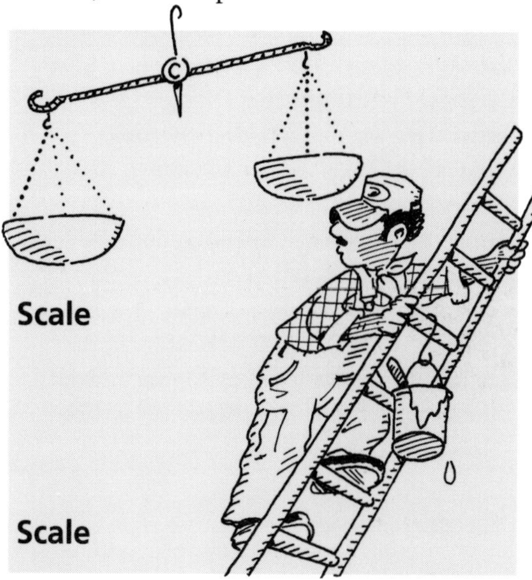

scamp *n.* knave, rogue, rascal, scoundrel, scalawag *Someone rang our doorbell, but when I opened the door, the scalawag had gone*

scamper *v.* hurry, run, scurry, hasten, sprint, ▷*rush*

scan *v.* examine, glance at, scrutinize, pore over, ▷*check*

scandal *n.* disgrace, libel, slander, offense, infamy, rumor, discredit ★**honor**

scanty *adj.* meager, insufficient, sparse, inadequate, poor, scant ★**plenty**

scar [1] *n.* blemish, mark, stigma, wound [2] *v.* brand, damage, disfigure

scarce *adj.* rare, infrequent, sparse, scanty, uncommon ★**common**

scarcity *n.* lack, deficiency, dearth, rarity, infreqency ★**abundance**

scare *v.* frighten, startle, shock, alarm, dismay ★**reassure**

scatter *v.* spread, disperse, strew, ▷*sprinkle* ★**collect**

scene *n.* sight, spectacle, vision, view, exhibition, landscape SEEN

scent [1] *n.* aroma, tang, fragrance, smell, odor [2] *v.* detect, sniff, smell CENT SENT

schedule *n.* timetable *We checked the timetable before buying our train tickets*, program, catalog, diary

scheme *n.* plot, plan, project, design, proposal, idea

scholar [1] *n.* pupil, student, schoolchild, learner [2] intellectual *That café is a favorite gathering place for intellectuals*, savant, academic

scholarly *adj.* learned, educated, literate, cultured ★**illiterate**

scoff *v.* sneer, mock, deride, jeer, ridicule ★**respect**

scold *v.* rebuke, admonish, reprove, find fault with, ▷*chide* ★**praise**

scoop *v.* bail, ladle, spoon, excavate, gouge, hollow

scope *n.* extent, margin, compass, range, latitude, field

scorch *v.* sear, burn, singe, blister, shrivel

score [1] *v.* cut, mark, scratch [2] register, record, win

scorn [1] *n.* mockery, disdain, ridicule, disregard [2] *v.* despise, mock, spurn, slight ★**respect**

scoundrel *n.* rascal, knave, thief, rogue, villain, ▷*vagabond* ★**gentleman**

scour [1] *v.* cleanse, rinse, scrub, purge [2] search, seek, ransack, rake

scourge [1] *v.* beat, whip, thrash, cane [2] *n.* curse, evil, misfortune, plague ★**blessing**

scowl *v.* & *n.* frown, glower, grimace, glare ★**smile**

scramble [1] *v.* clamber, climb [2] jostle, struggle, swarm, push [3] *n.* turmoil, bustle, confusion ★**order**

scrap [1] *n.* piece, morsel, bit, portion, fragment, grain [2] *v.* abandon, discard, junk

scrape [1] *v.* scratch, groove, abrade, file, grate, scour [2] *n.* predicament, fix, difficulty
scratch *v. & n.* wound, cut, mark, score
scream *v. & n.* screech, cry, shriek, howl, yell
screen [1] *n.* awning *Before the ceremony, an awning was erected over the entrance to the hotel,* canopy, shade, protection [2] *v.* protect, hide, conceal, veil
screw *v.* twist, turn, wrench, tighten, compress
scribble *v.* write, scrawl, scratch
scribe *n.* writer, penman, clerk, historian
script *n.* handwriting, manuscript, text, words, libretto *Sir Arthur Sullivan wrote the music for The Mikado, and W. S. Gilbert wrote the lyrics and libretto*
scrub [1] *v.* scour, brush, mop, cleanse [2] *n.* brushwood, undergrowth
scruffy *adj.* messy, dirty, frowzy, seedy, shabby, sloppy ▷*slovenly* ★**neat**
scrumptious *adj.* delightful, delicious, appetizing, exquisite
scrupulous *adj.* painstaking, particular, rigorous, strict, conscientious ★**careless**
scrutinize *v.* examine, inspect, peruse, study
scuffle *v. & n.* tussle, skirmish, fight, struggle, squabble
scum *n.* dross, foam, froth, dregs, crust
scuttle [1] *v.* scramble, scamper, scoot, hurry [2] destroy, smash, wreck
seal [1] *n.* signet, stamp [2] cork, bung, closure [3] sea mammal [4] *v.* fasten, close, shut
seam [1] *n.* ridge, scar, lode, furrow [2] hem, pleat, tuck SEEM
search [1] *v.* seek, quest, hunt, trail, track, scour, explore [2] *n.* exploration, investigation, quest, pursuit
season [1] *n.* period, time, occasion, term [2] *v.* accustom, acclimatize, mature [3] flavor, spice, salt
seat [1] *n.* bench, chair, stool, sofa, couch, throne [2] headquarters, place, site [3] *v.* accommodate, locate, place
secret *adj.* mysterious, hidden, concealed, obscure, private ★**public**
section *n.* division, group, department, segment, portion

secure [1] *adj.* safe, protected [2] confident, certain, sure, stable ★**uncertain** [3] *v.* fasten, protect, close, lock ★**unfasten** [4] acquire, procure, obtain ★**lost**
sedate *adj.* staid, sober, demure, earnest, ▷*steady* ★**flippant**
see [1] *v.* behold, witness, sight, observe [2] heed, examine, watch, note [3] understand, comprehend, know SEA
seedy *adj.* shabby, squalid, poor, grubby, unkempt, ▷*slovenly* ★**spruce**
seek *v.* look for, search, inquire, endeavor, hunt
seem *v.* appear, look like, sound like, look as if SEAM
seemly *adj.* fit, suitable, proper, decent, decorous ★**unseemly**
seethe *v.* simmer, fizz, bubble, boil, foam
seize *v.* grasp, snatch, take, clutch, arrest, ▷*grab* ★**abandon** SEAS SEES
seldom *adv.* rarely, infrequently, hardly, scarcely ★**often**
select [1] *adj.* choice, preferred, fine, prime *All the fruit on the trees in the orchard are in their prime,* first-class ★**common** [2] *v.* choose, pick out, single out, prefer
selfish *adj.* greedy, self-centered, narrow, illiberal, ▷*stingy* ★**generous**
sell *v.* vend, market, retail, trade, peddle ★**buy**
send *v.* transmit, dispatch, forward, mail, direct ★**detain**
send for *v.* command, order, summon, request ★**dismiss**
sensation [1] *n.* feeling, perception, impression, awareness [2] excitement, commotion, scandal
sensational *adj.* exceptional, scandalous, lurid, ▷*exciting* ★**ordinary**
sense [1] *n.* sensation, impression, feeling [2] understanding, mind, tact, intellect [3] wisdom, significance, meaning CENTS SCENTS
senseless *adj.* silly, stupid, absurd, ▷*foolish* ★**sensible**
sensible [1] *adj.* wise, intelligent, astute, shrewd [2] reasonable, rational [3] conscious, aware, mindful ★**senseless**

sensitive [1] *adj.* susceptible, responsive, acute [2] thin-skinned, touchy
sentence [1] *n.* phrase, clause [2] judgment, decision, condemnation, doom
sentimental *adj.* romantic, tender, emotional, impressionable *Because Rachel is at such an impressionable age, her mother does not want her to see the movie*
separate [1] *adj.* disconnected, apart, detached ★**united** [2] *v.* detach, part, divide, break, disconnect ★**unite**
sequel *n.* continuation, consequence, result, outcome
serene *adj.* tranquil, calm, peaceful, undisturbed, clear ★**tempestuous**
series *n.* sequence, progression, succession, run, string
serious *adj.* grave, earnest, solemn, thoughtful, severe, grim ★**trivial**
serve *v.* attend, assist, aid, oblige, help, officiate, act
service [1] *n.* aid, help, assistance, attendance, employment [2] ceremony, rite *Stuart is at college studying the marriage rites of the ancient Incas*
set [1] *n.* group, pack, outfit, series [2] *v.* settle, put, place, seat, locate [3] stiffen, congeal, harden [4] *adj.* decided, resolved, determined, fixed
setback *n.* defeat, delay, problem, snag, hold-up ★**advantage**
settle [1] *v.* establish, regulate, fix [2] pay, liquidate, finish [3] populate, colonize [4] live, dwell, reside
several *adj.* various, numerous, sundry, separate
severe *adj.* strict, rigid, unkind, hard, austere, ▷*stern* ★**lenient**
sew *v.* stitch, tack, baste, fasten, seam SO SOW
shabby *adj.* torn, ragged, mean, shoddy, tacky, ▷*squalid* ★**neat**
shack *n.* hut, cabin, shanty, shed, hovel
shackle *v.* & *n.* manacle, handcuff, chain, rope, fetter
shade [1] *n.* shadow, gloom, darkness, dusk [2] blind, awning, screen [3] color, tint, hue, tone [4] ghost, spirit, wraith *Out of the darkness, a wraith-like figure loomed up before us*
shadow [1] *n.* shade [2] *v.* follow, stalk, tail
shady [1] *adj.* shadowy, shaded ★**sunny** [2] crooked, infamous, disreputable ★**honest**
shaft [1] *n.* pillar, column, support [2] hilt, handle, rod [3] mine, pit, well, tunnel
shaggy *adj.* hairy, tousled, unkempt, rough ★**smooth**
shake *v.* flutter, tremble, throb, shudder, ▷*quiver* ★**still**

Ships and Boats

Gondola

Trawler

Kayak

shallow [1] *adj.* not deep [2] trivial, empty, silly, empty-headed ★**profound**
sham *adj.* false, imitation, counterfeit, forged, ▷*bogus* ★**genuine**
shame *n.* & *v.* dishonor, discredit, ▷*disgrace*
shameful *adj.* disgraceful, scandalous, outrageous, ▷*disreputable* ★**honorable**
shape [1] *n.* form, structure, outline, pattern [2] *v.* form, fashion, make, create
share [1] *v.* allot, divide, participate, co-operate [2] *n.* portion, allotment, allowance
sharp [1] *adj.* acute, keen, pointed [2] clear, distinct, clean-cut [3] painful, severe, intense [4] pungent, acrid, acid [5] alert, shrewd, acute, ▷*clever* ★**dull**
shatter *v.* smash, wreck, break, fracture, ruin, ▷*destroy*
shave *v.* shear, crop, slice, shred, graze, trim

shear *v.* fleece, strip, cut, ▷*shave* SHEER
sheath *n.* scabbard, quiver, holster, holder, case, casing
shed [1] *n.* hut, barn, lean-to, shanty [2] *v.* cast off, molt *Our dog is molting and is leaving white hairs all over the carpet*, spill [3] beam, radiate
sheepish *adj.* timid, diffident, foolish, embarrassed, shamefaced ★**unabashed**
sheer [1] *adj.* absolute, simple, pure, unmixed [2] transparent, filmy, thin [3] steep, abrupt, perpendicular *The trail ended at the foot of huge, perpendicular cliffs* SHEAR
shell *n.* pod, case, husk, hull, shuck, crust
shelter [1] *n.* roof, sanctuary, safety, home, retreat, cover [2] *v.* shield, cover, protect, screen ★**expose**
shield *n.* & *v.* guard, screen, safeguard, ▷*shelter*
shift [1] *v.* alter, move, change, displace, remove [2] *n.* turn, spell, stint
shifty *adj.* untrustworthy, devious, treacherous, ▷*wily* ★**honest**
shine *v.* & *n.* glow, gleam, glitter, sparkle, flash
ship [1] *n.* boat, barge, craft, vessel [2] *v.* export, send, transport *(see page 115)*
shirk *v.* dodge, avoid, shun, evade, slack
shiver *v.* quaver, quiver, shake, shudder, ▷*tremble*
shock [1] *n.* blow, jolt, clash, collision [2] scare, start, turn [3] *v.* stupefy, daze, stun
shocking *adj.* scandalous, awful, frightful, ▷*horrible* ★**agreeable**
shoot [1] *v.* fire, discharge, bombard, propel [2] germinate *We grew some beans in a glass jar and watched them germinate*, grow, bud, sprout [3] *n.* bud, twig, sprout CHUTE
shop [1] *n.* store, market, emporium [2] *v.* buy, market, purchase
shore [1] *n.* beach, coast, strand, seashore, seaside [2] *v.* prop, support, bolster up, brace
short [1] *adj.* brief, concise, condensed ★**long** [2] deficient, incomplete, scanty ★**full** [3] sharp, severe, bad-tempered [4] small, puny, squat, diminutive, tiny ★**tall**
shortcoming *n.* defect, fault, flaw, inadequacy, ▷*weakness*
shorten *v.* cut, crop, abbreviate, lessen, ▷*diminish* ★**lengthen**
shortened *adj.* abbreviated, abridged, condensed ★**enlarged**
shortly *adj.* presently, soon, before long, directly
shout *n.* & *v.* cry, scream, roar, shriek, cheer, whoop, bellow
shove *v.* push, jostle, prod, nudge, move, propel ★**pull**
show [1] *v.* display, parade, exhibit, flaunt, reveal ★**hide** [2] prove, testify to, demonstrate [3] explain, teach, instruct [4] *n.* exhibition, display, ceremony, play
shower [1] *v.* scatter, spray, sprinkle, rain [2] *n.* downpour, cloudburst [3] barrage, volley, discharge
shred [1] *n.* particle, piece, scrap, tatter, fragment [2] *v.* tear, rip, strip
shrewd *adj.* profound, deep, discerning, ▷*wise* ★**obtuse**
shriek *n.* & *v.* screech, ▷*shout*
shrill *adj.* treble, high-pitched, screeching, ear-piercing
shrink [1] *v.* contract, dwindle, shrivel, become smaller [2] flinch, cringe, recoil, withdraw
shrivel *v.* wither, contract, wrinkle, decrease, pucker, parch, ▷*wilt*
shudder *v.* shake, quake, tremble, ▷*quiver*
shuffle [1] *v.* mix, jumble, rearrange [2] hobble, limp
shun *v.* avoid, elude, ignore, spurn, steer clear of ★**accept**
shut *v.* fasten, close, secure, slam, bar, latch, lock ★**open**
shut up [1] *v.* imprison, cage, intern [2] be silent, hold one's tongue
shy [1] *adj.* bashful, diffident, timid, wary, shrinking ★**bold** [2] *v.* flinch, quail, recoil
sick [1] *adj.* ill, poorly, ailing, unwell, feeble [2] weary, fed up, displeased [3] nauseated
side [1] *n.* border, edge, flank, margin, half [2] party, sect, group, team SIGHED
sift *v.* strain, drain, separate, screen, sieve, riddle
sigh [1] *v.* grieve, lament, moan, complain [2] wheeze, breathe

sight [1] *n.* appearance, spectacle, scene, mirage [2] seeing, perception, visibiity [3] *v.* behold, glimpse, observe CITE SITE

sign [1] *n.* symbol, emblem, mark [2] omen, token [3] signboard, signpost, placard [4] *v.* endorse, autograph, inscribe

signal [1] *n.* beacon *As soon as the ships were sighted, beacons were lit all along the coast*, sign, flag, indicator [2] *adj.* distinguished, impressive, outstanding

significant *adj.* symbolical, meaningful, weighty, ▷*important* ★**unimportant**

signify *v.* denote, indicate, suggest, imply, ▷*mean*

silence *n.* quiet, hush, peace, tranquillity ★**noise**

silent *adj.* hushed, noiseless, soundless, still, mute, ▷*quiet* ★**noisy**

silly *adj.* absurd, senseless, stupid, fatuous, ▷*foolish* ★**wise**

similar *adj.* resembling, alike, harmonious, common, ▷*like* ★**different**

simple [1] *adj.* elementary, plain, uncomplicated, ▷*easy* [2] trusting, open, naïve ★**intricate**

simply *adv.* merely, purely, barely, solely, only

sin [1] *n.* misdeed, wrong, vice, evil, wickedness [2] *v.* err, offend, trespass, stray, do wrong

since [1] *conj.* because, as, for, considering [2] *prep.* subsequently, after

sincere *adj.* true, unaffected, frank, open, truthful, ▷*genuine* ★**insincere**

sing *v.* vocalize, warble, yodel, trill, croon, chant, carol, hum, chirp

singe *v.* scorch, burn, scald, sear, char

singer *n.* vocalist, minstrel, songster, chorister, crooner

single [1] *adj.* one, only, sole [2] solitary, alone, separate [3] unmarried, celibate *The priests of the Roman Catholic Church are celibate*

singular *adj.* odd, peculiar, curious, surprising, ▷*unusual* ★**ordinary**

sinister *adj.* menacing, threatening, unlucky, disastrous, ▷*evil* ★**harmless**

sink [1] *v.* drop, dip, descend, decline, ▷*fall* ★**rise** [2] *n.* basin, drain

Singers

Alto
Baritone
Bass
Basso profundo
Cantor
Chorister
Contrabass
Contralto
Countertenor
Mezzo-soprano
Prima donna
Soprano
Tenor
Treble
Vocalist

sit *v.* perch, seat, squat, roost, rest, settle

site *n.* spot, plot, locality, place, station, post, ▷*situation* CITE SIGHT

situation [1] *n.* position, location, place, site, whereabouts, standpoint [2] predicament, plight, state

size [1] *n.* dimensions, proportions, measurement [2] magnitude, bulk, volume, weight SIGHS

skeptical *adj.* doubtful, unbelieving, incredulous, ▷*dubious* ★**convinced**

sketch [1] *n.* drawing, picture, cartoon [2] draft, blueprint, outline [3] *v.* draw, portray, depict

skillful *adj.* adroit, able, adept, dexterous, expert, competent, ▷*clever* ★**clumsy**

skill *n.* ability, expertness, knack, facility, ▷*talent*

skim *v.* brush, touch, graze, float, glide

skimp *v.* stint, scrimp, economize, scrape

skin *n.* peel, rind, hide, husk, pelt

skinny *adj.* thin, lean, scraggy, weedy ★**fat**

skip [1] *v.* jump, hop, dance, caper [2] pass over, miss, disregard, omit

skirmish *n.* & *v.* scuffle, fight, affray, scrap, combat

skirt [1] *n.* petticoat, kilt [2] border, hem, edge, margin [3] *v.* border, flank, evade, avoid

skulk *v.* lurk, hide, cower, slink, sneak
slab *n.* board, stone, boulder, piece, chunk
slack [1] *adj.* limp, flabby, loose, relaxed ★**tight** [2] lazy, sluggish, ▷*idle* ★**busy**
slander *v.* libel, malign, accuse, abuse, ▷*defame* ★**praise**
slant [1] *v.* & *n.* incline, angle, cant, ▷*slope*
slap *v.* smack, whack, strike, hit, spank
slash *v.* & *n.* cut, slit, gash, hack, rip
slaughter *v.* slay, butcher, massacre, ▷*kill*
slave [1] *n.* bondsman, bondswoman, serf, vassal, drudge, captive [2] *v.* drudge, toil, labor, grind
slavery *n.* bondage, enslavement, serfdom, servility, drudgery, captivity ★**freedom**
slay *v.* murder, massacre, ▷*kill* SLEIGH
sleek *adj.* shiny, smooth, glossy, slick
sleep *v.* & *n.* snooze, nap, doze, drowse, repose, slumber
slender [1] *adj.* narrow, thin, fine, slight, ▷*slim* ★**thick** [2] trivial, inadequate, meager
slice [1] *v.* shred, shave, cut, strip, segment [2] *n.* segment, piece, cut, slab
slick [1] *adj.* shiny, smooth, ▷*sleek* [2] glib, suave, plausible
slide *v.* slip, slither, glide, skim, skate
slight [1] *adj.* delicate, tender, ▷*slender* [2] small, little, meager, trifling, trivial ★**significant** [3] *n.* & *v.* snub, insult, disdain
slim *adj.* fine, slight, ▷*slender* ★**fat**
slime *n.* mire, ooze, mud, filth
sling [1] *v.* hurl, toss, throw [2] *n.* loop, bandage, strap, support
slink *v.* prowl, creep, sidle, sneak, ▷*skulk*
slip [1] *v.* slide, slither, glide [2] fall, lurch, drop, slip over [3] *v.* & *n.* blunder, slip up
slippery [1] *adj.* smooth, glassy [2] untrustworthy, tricky, ▷*shifty* ★**trustworthy**
slit *v.* gash, cut, ▷*slash*
slogan *n.* motto, catchword, war cry, saying
slope [1] *n.* slant, grade, gradient, incline, ascent, descent, rise [2] *v.* lean, incline, descend, ascend
sloppy [1] *adj.* careless, slipshod, inattentive, ▷*slovenly* [2] dowdy, messy, tacky [3] dingy, dirty
slot *n.* recess, opening, hole, groove
slovenly *adj.* slipshod, careless, negligent, disorderly, sloppy, untidy, dowdy
slow [1] *adj.* inactive, tardy, late, slack, leisurely, ▷*sluggish* ★**fast** [2] *v.* slow down, slacken, lose speed, relax ★**accelerate** SLOE
sluggish *adj.* slothful, lazy, inactive, languid, indolent, ▷*idle* ★**brisk**
slumber *v.* snooze, doze, ▷*sleep* ★**awaken**
sly *adj.* cunning, tricky, furtive, sneaky, artful, ▷*wily* ★**frank**
smack *v.* slap, strike, ▷*hit*
small [1] *adj.* minute, tiny, slight, diminutive, ▷*little* ★**large** [2] trivial, petty, feeble, paltry inferior
smart [1] *adj.* alert, bright, ▷*intelligent* [2] elegant, neat, spruce, dressy ★**dull** [3] *v.* sting, burn, throb ▷*ache*
smash *v.* break, hit, destroy, wreck, demolish
smear *v.* plaster, daub, coat, varnish, cover, spread
smell *n.* aroma, fragrance, scent, perfume, stink, stench, odor, tang
smile *v.* grin, simper, smirk, beam, ▷*laugh*
smoke [1] *n.* vapor, mist, gas [2] *v.* fume, reek, whiff, smolder, vent
smooth [1] *adj.* level, even, flat, plain, sleek ★**rough** [2] *v.* flatten, level, press
smother *v.* choke, throttle, stifle, restrain
smudge *n.* & *v.* mark, smear, blur, stain, blight
smug *adj.* self-satisfied, content, complacent, conceited
smut *n.* dirt, smudge, blot, spot, smear
snack *n.* lunch, repast, morsel, bite
snag *n.* catch, complication, drawback, hitch
snap [1] *v.* break, crack, snip [2] snarl, growl
snare [1] *v.* trap, catch, seize, net [2] *n.* trap, noose, pitfall
snatch *v.* seize, grab, clutch, grip, take, pluck, grasp
sneak [1] *v.* slink, prowl, crouch, ▷*skulk* [2] *n.* wretch, coward, informer
sneer *v.* jeer, scoff, gibe, scorn, ridicule, taunt
sniff *v.* smell, breathe in, inhale, scent
snivel *v.* weep, cry, blub, sniffle
snobbish *adj.* condescending, snooty, lofty, patronizing, stuck-up

snoop *v.* pry, eavesdrop, peep, peek, sneak
snooze *v.* doze, sleep, slumber, ▷*sleep*
snub *v.* slight, slur, spurn, cut, ▷*humiliate*
snug *adj.* cozy, sheltered, secure, safe, restful, ▷*comfortable*
so *adv.* accordingly, thus, therefore, likewise SEW SOW
soak *v.* moisten, wet, douse, saturate, steep
soar *v.* glide, fly, rise, hover, tower SORE
sob *v.* lament, cry, sigh, ▷*weep*
sober *adj.* temperate, abstemious *Uncle Arthur was very abstemious, and never drank anything alcoholic,* calm, composed, serious, somber ★**excited**
sociable *adj.* companionable, affable, friendly, genial ★**withdrawn**
social [1] *adj.* neighborly, civic, public [2] convivial, ▷*sociable*
soft [1] *adj.* pliable, plastic, flexible, supple ★**hard** [2] kind, gentle, mild, ▷*tender* ★**harsh** [3] low, faint, quiet ★**loud**
soften [1] *v.* melt, dissolve, mellow ★**solidify** [2] moderate, diminish, quell
soil [1] *n.* earth, dirt, mold [2] *v.* foul, dirty, sully, taint
sole *adj.* only, single, lone, one SOUL
solemn [1] *adj.* grim, serious, ▷*somber* [2] impressive, stately, sedate ★**frivolous**
solid [1] *adj.* steady, firm, stable, sturdy [2] dense, compact, hard ★**soft**
solidify *v.* congeal, harden, clot, cake, set ★**soften**
solitary *adj.* alone, lonely, remote, separate, only
solution [1] *n.* blend, mixture, brew, fluid [2] answer, explanation
solve *v.* unravel, untangle, elucidate, ▷*explain* ★**complicate**
somber *adj.* dark, serious, solemn, grim, gloomy, funereal ★**bright**
some *adj.* any, more or less, about, several SUM
sometimes *adv.* at times, from time to time, occasionally ★**always**
somewhat *adv.* in part, a little, not much
song *n.* air, tune, carol, ballad, ode, ditty *The new pop song was based on an old sailors' ditty*

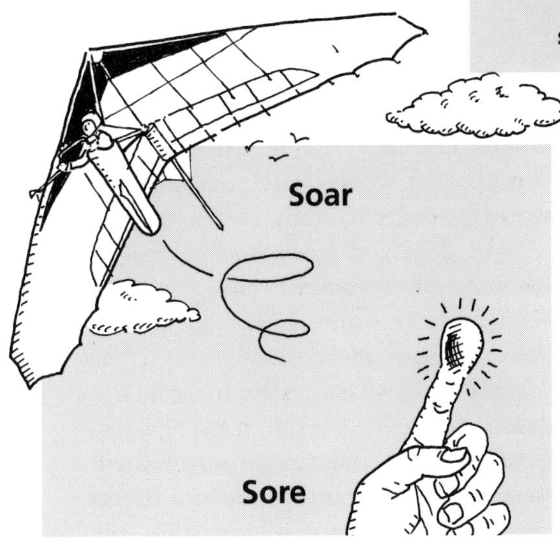

soon *adv.* presently, shortly, before long
soothe *v.* pacify, appease, mollify, ease, lull, comfort ★**irritate**
sordid *adj.* shabby, miserable, dirty, base, ▷*squalid*
sore [1] *adj.* tender, aching, painful, inflamed [2] annoyed, upset, grieved [3] *n.* ulcer, boil, carbuncle SOAR
sorrow [1] *n.* grief, woe, remorse, anguish ★**joy** [2] *v.* mourn, grieve, lament ★**rejoice**
sorrowful *adj.* sad, disconsolate, mournful, dejected ★**joyful**
sorry [1] *adj.* pained, grieved, hurt, dejected, doleful ★**glad** [2] wretched, mean, poor, shabby ★**delighted**
sort [1] *n.* kind, type, variety, group, class [2] *v.* sift, arrange, catalog, classify
soul *n.* spirit, substance, mind, vitality, fire, essence SOLE
sound [1] *n.* noise, din, tone ★**silence** [2] *v.* blare, blast *We were startled by a blast from the trumpets,* blow [3] *adj.* hearty, virile, whole, perfect, ▷*healthy* ★**unfit**
sour [1] *adj.* tart, rancid, bitter, acid ★**sweet** [2] morose, peevish, ▷*harsh* ★**genial**
source *n.* origin, spring, fount, cause, beginning
souvenir *n.* token, memento, keepsake, reminder, relic
sow [1] *n.* (as in *how*) female pig [2] *v.* (as in *mow*) *v.* plant, scatter, strew SEW SO
space [1] *n.* extent, expanse, capacity, room, accommodation [2] the universe, the heavens, firmament

spacious *adj.* roomy, extensive, commodious, broad, wide ★**restricted**
span [1] *n.* stretch, reach, extent, length [2] *v.* cross, bridge, link, connect
spare [1] *adj.* extra, reserve, surplus [2] bare, meager, poor, scanty, ▷*sparse* [3] *v.* afford, preserve, give, allow
sparkle *v.* glitter, glow, gleam, glint, twinkle
sparse *adj.* scanty, thin, ▷*meager* ★**dense**
spate *n.* flood, flow, deluge, rush, torrent
speak *v.* say, utter, talk, pronounce, lecture, express
spear *n.* pike, javelin, lance
special *adj.* distinct, different, unique, individual, ▷*particular* ★**common**
species *n.* breed, kind, sort, class, family
specific *adj.* definite, exact, precise, ▷*special*
specimen *n.* sample, example, type, model, pattern
speck *n.* dot, speckle, spot, particle
spectacle *n.* sight, scene, exhibition, presentation, ▷*display*
spectacles *n.* glasses, eyeglasses
spectacular *adj.* wonderful, fabulous, surprising, ▷*marvelous*
spectator *n.* onlooker, witness, observer
speech [1] *n.* talk, tongue *The people spoke a strange tongue related to Finnish*, language [2] address, lecture
speed *n.* velocity, rapidity, dispatch, pace, tempo *The tempo of life in the quiet seaside town was much too slow for us*
speedy *adj.* swift, rapid, fleet, quick, lively ▷*fast* ★**slow**
spell [1] *n.* charm, magic, witchcraft [2] period, term, space, time [3] *v.* form words, write out
spend [1] *v.* expend, lay out, lavish, pay, disburse [2] exhaust, use up
spendthrift *n.* wastrel, squanderer, prodigal ★**miser**
sphere [1] *n.* globe, ball, orb, planet [2] realm, orbit, domain, field
spice *n.* seasoning, flavoring, zest, relish, savor
spill *v.* pour, stream, run, overflow, spurt, upset
spin *v.* revolve, rotate, turn, whirl, make thread
spine *n.* backbone, needle, quill *The porcupine's body is covered in sharp quills*, ridge
spirit [1] *n.* essence, substance, nature, character [2] soul, air, breath [3] vigor, energy, courage [4] phantom, specter, ghost
spiritual [1] *adj.* religious, divine, unworldly, holy [2] pure, immaterial
spite [1] *n.* malice, rancor, hostility, hatred [2] *v.* grudge, annoy, offend, injure
spiteful *adj.* vicious, malicious, vindictive, ▷*hateful* ★**kind**
splash *v.* wet, spatter, shower, sprinkle
splendid *adj.* grand, brilliant, magnificent, showy, glorious, ▷*sumptuous* ★**ordinary**
splendor *n.* glory, pageantry, brilliance, ▷*pomp*
split *v.* cleave, sever *Our family quarreled with our cousins and severed relationships for years*, crack, snap, splinter
spoil [1] *v.* hurt, injure, harm [2] deface, disfigure, destroy [3] rot, decompose, putrefy, decay
spoiled *adj.* decayed, rotten, broken up, corroded
spontaneous *adj.* natural, impulsive, self-generated, voluntary

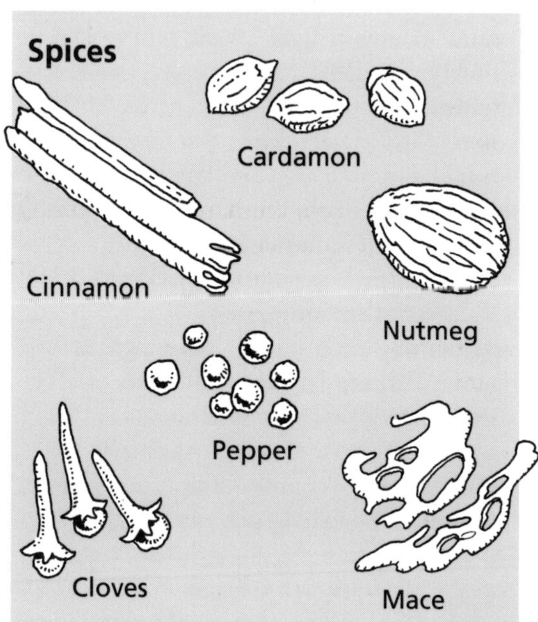

spoof 1 *n.* hoax, joke, bluff, prank, satire 2 quip, jest, wisecrack
sport 1 *n.* game, amusement, fun, athletics, recreation 2 *v.* play, frolic, gambol, romp
spot 1 *n.* dot, speck, mark, stain, blemish 2 *v.* espy, notice, recognize, distinguish
spotless *adj.* pure, clean, unstained, faultless, perfect
sprawl *v.* recline, stretch, extend, lie, ▷*lounge*
spray *v.* sprinkle, squirt, splash, shower
spread 1 *v.* scatter, strew, sow, circulate 2 extend, stretch, expand, open
sprightly *adj.* lively, vivacious, cheerful, agile, ▷*brisk* ★**sluggish**
spur *v.* arouse, drive, urge, incite
spurious *adj.* fake, counterfeit, false, ▷*bogus* ★**genuine**
spurn *v.* reject, scorn, disdain, disregard, ▷*snub* ★**respect**
spurt 1 *v.* stream, squirt, emerge, gush 2 hurry, hasten, rush
spy 1 *n.* agent, detective, observer, snooper, scout 2 *v.* see, glimpse, pry, peep, peek, spot
squabble 1 *n.* & *v.* quarrel, clash, fight, row, ▷*dispute*
squad *n.* group, company, troop, force, band, team
squalid *adj.* foul, dirty, untended, poverty-stricken, ▷*sordid* ★**clean**
squall 1 *n.* blast, gust, blow, tempest 2 *v.* blubber, cry, bawl, howl
squander *v.* misspend, waste, fritter *My brother won a big prize in a lottery, but frittered all the money away in a few years*, lavish
squash 1 *v.* mash, crush, squelch, pound 2 quell, suppress, humiliate
squat 1 *adj.* dumpy, stocky, tubby, plump 2 *v.* crouch, sit, roost, perch
squeal *v.* squawk, squeak, cheep, grunt, cry
squeamish *adj.* fastidious, delicate, finicky, nauseous
squeeze *v.* compress, press, constrict, force, pinch
squirm *v.* wriggle, fidget, flounder, twist, ▷*writhe*
squirt *v.* spray, splash, ▷*spurt*
stab *v.* & *n.* cut, jab, puncture, wound, thrust
stable 1 *adj.* firm, steady, solid, constant, durable, lasting ★**unstable** 2 *n.* barn, cowshed, shed, stall
stack 1 *n.* pile, pack, bundle, sheaf, heap 2 *v.* assemble, pile up, amass
staff 1 *n.* stick, cane, pole, rod 2 team, workers, force, personnel
stage 1 *n.* platform, dais, scaffold, podium *The famous conductor stood on the podium and raised his baton*, arena 2 step, degree, position 3 *v.* perform, produce, present, put on
stagger *v.* reel, totter, waver, lurch
stagnant *adj.* motionless, inactive, still, quiet, sluggish
staid *adj.* serious, steady, earnest, sober, demure, ▷*sedate* ★**frivolous** STAYED
stain 1 *n.* blemish, blur, spot, blot 2 disgrace, shame 3 *v.* tarnish, sully, blemish, defile
stair *n.* step, rung, spoke, footrest STARE
stake 1 *n.* stick, stave, paling, spike, pole, ▷*staff* 2 bet, claim, wager, involvement 3 *v.* prop, secure, support STEAK
stale 1 *adj.* musty, old, tasteless, faded 2 common, trite, banal, flat ★**fresh**
stalk 1 *v.* hunt, chase, follow, pursue, shadow 2 swagger, strut, stride, parade
stall 1 *v.* tarry, delay, hedge, obstruct ★**advance** 2 quibble, fence 3 *n.* compartment, booth, stand, bay
stalwart *adj.* rugged, sturdy, stout, lusty, ▷*valiant* ★**weak**
stamina *n.* endurance, vitality, strength, power, energy ★**weakness**
stammer *v.* stutter, falter, hesitate, stumble
stamp 1 *v.* print, imprint, mark, impress 2 *n.* impression, mark, print, brand 3 kind, make, genus, cast 4 seal, postal label, sticker
stand 1 *n.* board, counter, table, platform, ▷*stall* 2 *v.* rest, put, locate, place 3 tolerate, put up with, abide, endure ★**oppose** 4 arise, get up, be erect ★**sit**
standard 1 *adj.* normal, regular, uniform 2 *n.* pattern, criterion, norm 3 flag, banner, ensign
staple *adj.* main, principal, important, leading
stare *v.* gaze, gape, look, peer STAIR

stark *adj.* severe, plain, downright, bare, absolute
start [1] *v.* commence, begin, found, initiate [2] depart, set out, leave [3] startle, jump, wince [4] *n.* beginning, commencement [5] shock, scare, fit
startle *v.* frighten, alarm, scare, surprise, ▷*start*
starve *v.* be hungry, famish, want
state [1] *n.* condition, situation, position [2] country, nation, commonwealth [3] *v.* declare, say, express, utter, ▷*speak*
stately *adj.* imposing, grand, dignified, ▷*magnificent* ★**commonplace**
statement [1] *n.* declaration, utterance, remark, motto [2] bill, account, invoice
station [1] *n.* post, spot, site, position, terminal [2] *v.* park, place, put, establish *We got there early to establish our place in the line*
stationary *adj.* still, unmoving, standing, fixed ★**mobile** STATIONERY
stationery *n.* paper, envelopes, ink, pens, pencils STATIONARY
statue *n.* carving, bust, figure
staunch *adj.* constant, faithful, true, firm, ▷*loyal* ★**unfaithful**
stay [1] *v.* endure, last, remain, stand, linger [2] check, curb, prevent [3] *n.* halt, wait, ▷*stop*
steady [1] *adj.* firm, fixed, established, constant, ▷*staunch* ★**uncertain** [2] *v.* brace, stabilize, stiffen
steal [1] *v.* thieve, pilfer, filch, swipe, ▷*rob* [2] slink, flit, creep, ▷*prowl* STEEL
stealthy *adj.* furtive, sneaky, sly, secret, ▷*underhanded* ★**open**
steep [1] *adj.* sheer, sharp, hilly, precipitous [2] *v.* bathe, soak, souse, submerge
steer *v.* guide, direct, pilot, control
stem [1] *n.* stalk, shoot, stock, trunk [2] *v.* arise from, flow from [3] check, resist, restrain
step [1] *n.* pace, tread, stride, gait [2] action, method, deed [3] *v.* walk, skip, trip, pace STEPPE
sterile [1] *adj.* barren, unfertile, arid [2] sanitary, disinfected
stern [1] *adj.* strict, severe, harsh, grim, ▷*austere* ★**mild** [2] *n.* poop *The name of the ship was displayed in large letters on the poop*, aft end
stew [1] *v.* cook, simmer, boil [2] worry, fuss
stick [1] *n.* stave, pole, rod, cane, staff [2] *v.* adhere, cling, cleave, glue, paste, seal
sticky *adj.* gluey, gummy, adhesive
stick out *v.* project, bulge, extrude, ▷*jut* ★**recede**
stiff [1] *adj.* inflexible, firm, stable, unyielding, ▷*rigid* ★**flexible** [2] formal, stilted, prim, precise ★**yielding**
stifle *v.* suffocate, throttle, gag, muzzle, ▷*smother*
stigma [1] *n.* blot, blur, scar, ▷*blemish* [2] disgrace, dishonor, ▷*shame* ★**credit**

still [1] *adj.* fixed, stable, static [2] calm, quiet, serene, tranquil, noiseless, hushed, ▷*peaceful* ★**agitated** *v.* quiet, hush, muffle, ▷*calm* ★**agitate**
stimulate *v.* inspire, provoke, arouse, motivate, ▷*excite* ★**discourage**
sting [1] *v.* prick, wound, pain, hurt, injure
stingy (*stin*-jy) *adj.* miserly, tightfisted, selfish, niggardly, ▷*tight* ★**generous**
stink *v.* smell, whiff, reek
stint [1] *n.* job, task, chore [2] turn, spell, share, quota [3] *v.* limit, stop, scrimp, restrict ★**squander**
stir [1] *v.* move, excite, spur, agitate, ▷*stimulate* [2] whisk, mix, blend [3] waken, arouse ★**calm** [4] *n.* flurry, fuss, uproar
stock [1] *adj.* standard, regular, established, normal [2] *n.* reserve, hoard, supply [3] *v.* provide, supply, equip, hoard
stocky *adj.* thickset, chunky, sturdy, pudgy, ▷*squat* ★**willowy**
stodgy *adj.* dull, heavy, tedious, boring
stolid *adj.* stupid, dull, mindless, unintelligent, ▷*stodgy* ★**quick**
stoop *v.* bend, crouch, kneel, bow
stop [1] *v.* cease, desist, end, terminate, halt ★**start** [2] prevent, forestall, avoid [3] arrest, hold, fix [4] *n.* pause, end, cessation *A cessation of hostilities came into force after the peace agreement*
store [1] *v.* put by, reserve, hoard, save ★**use** [2] *n.* stock, supply, reserve [3] market, shop, emporium
story [1] *n.* yarn, tale, narrative, account, anecdote [2] untruth, lie, fib [3] floor, landing, level, flight, deck
storm [1] *n.* tempest, gale, cyclone, hurricane, tornado ★**calm** [2] turmoil, upheaval, attack [3] *v.* rage, rant, fume, attack
stout [1] *adj.* sturdy, tough, robust, ▷*strong* ★**weak** [2] fat, corpulent, ▷*plump* ★**thin**
stow *v.* deposit, store, ▷*pack*
straight [1] *adj.* right, undeviating, unswerving, ▷*direct* [2] frank, candid, truthful, ▷*honest* ★**crooked** STRAIT
straightforward *adj.* open, outspoken, reliable, trustworthy ★**devious**
strain [1] *n.* tension, fatigue, exertion, ▷*stress* ★**relaxation** [2] melody, tune, air [3] *v.* struggle, labor, ▷*toil* ★**relax** [4] wrench, injure [5] filter, sift, separate
strait *n.* channel, sound, narrows STRAIGHT
straitlaced *adj.* prim, prudish, strict, puritanical *My family was rather puritanical, and we were not allowed to play any games on Sundays* ★**broad-minded**
strand [1] *n.* coast, beach, shore [2] hair, fiber, tress, lock [3] *v.* desert, maroon, abandon
strange [1] *adj.* unusual, incredible, extraordinary, curious, ▷*odd* ★**commonplace** [2] foreign, alien, remote
stranger *n.* outsider, foreigner, visitor, newcomer, ▷*alien* ★**acquaintance**
strangle *v.* constrict, choke, garrote, throttle
strap *n.* belt, harness, thong, leash
stray [1] *v.* wander, deviate, depart, rove [2] sin, err, do wrong
streak *n.* stroke, stripe, band, line, bar, strip
stream [1] *n.* current, course, drift, brook, creek, run [2] *v.* flow, gush, spurt, pour
strength [1] *n.* power, force, might, ▷*energy* [2] boldness, nerve, intensity ★**weakness**
strenuous *adj.* laborious, resolute, determined, ▷*earnest* ★**weak**
stress [1] *n.* tension, force, effort, ▷*strain* [2] accent, emphasis [3] *v.* emphasize, accentuate
stretch *v.* expand, reach, ▷*extend* ★**shorten**
strict [1] *adj.* severe, rigorous, rigid, austere, ▷*stern* ★**lenient** [2] scrupulous, punctilious, accurate, ▷*precise* ★**inaccurate**
stride *n.* & *v.* walk, step, tread, parade, march
strife *n.* struggle, contest, quarrel, friction, ▷*conflict* ★**peace**
strike [1] *v.* beat, smite, collide, knock, ▷*thump* [2] discover, unearth [3] *n.* assault, thrust, attack [4] walkout, boycott
striking *adj.* eyecatching, wonderful, ▷*extraordinary* ★**commonplace**
strip [1] *v.* take off, peel, skin, shave, remove [2] *n.* ribbon, stroke, streak, line
stripe *n.* streak, band, bar, chevron *Soldiers in the army have chevrons on their sleeves to indicate their rank*, rule, ▷*strip*

strive *v.* endeavor, attempt, aim, compete, ▷*try* ★**yield**
stroke [1] *n.* shock, blow, knock, thump [2] seizure, fit, convulsion [3] *v.* pat, rub, caress, smooth, comfort
stroll *v.* & *n.* walk, promenade, saunter, tramp, ramble
strong [1] *adj.* powerful, vigorous, hardy, muscular, ▷*robust* [2] solid, secure, fortified ★**weak** [3] potent, hot, spicy, ▷*pungent*
structure [1] *n.* building, edifice, erection [2] construction, organization, composition
struggle [1] *v.* endeavor, labor, battle, wrestle ★**yield** [2] *n.* conflict, battle, ▷*fight* [3] distress, trouble, ▷*effort*
strut [1] *n.* support, mainstay, prop [2] *v.* parade, prance, swagger
stubborn [1] *adj.* dogged, persistent, tenacious [2] pig-headed, perverse, willful, ▷*obstinate* ★**docile**
stuck-up *adj.* vain, conceited, ▷*snobbish* ★**modest**

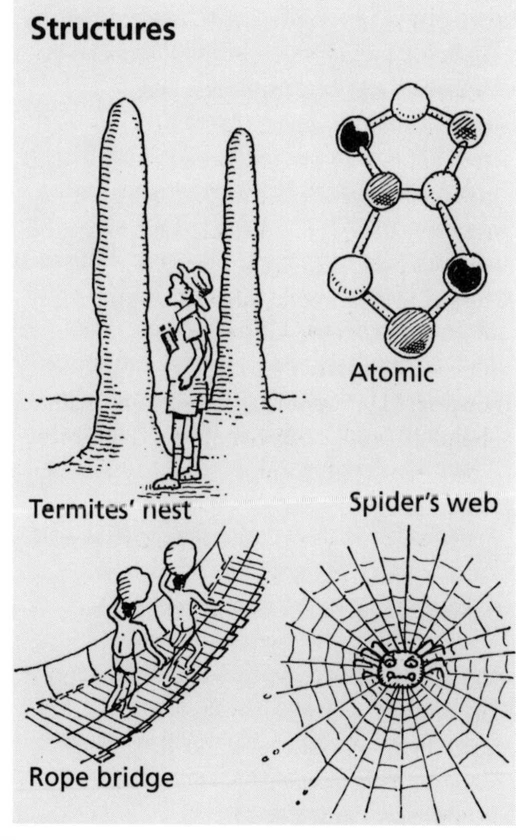

studious *adj.* scholarly, learned, thoughtful, ▷*diligent* ★**thoughtless**
study [1] *v.* read, peruse, examine, scrutinize, examine, train, ▷*learn* [2] *n.* learning, meditation, thought, contemplation, ▷*research*
stuff [1] *v.* fill, congest, pack, crowd [2] *n.* textile, fabric, material, goods
stumble [1] *v.* stagger, lurch, fall, ▷*trip* [2] stammer, falter, ▷*stutter*
stump [1] *v.* perplex, mystify, confuse, ▷*bewilder* [2] *n.* stub, tip, log, root
stun *v.* knock out, overpower, stupefy, dumbfound, ▷*confound*
stunt *n.* deed, feat, achievement, performance, ▷*exploit*
stupefy *v.* daze, muddle, bewilder, astonish, flabbergast, ▷*shock* ★**revive**
stupendous *adj.* astounding, amazing, overwhelming, ▷*wonderful* ★**ordinary**
stupid *adj.* simple, stolid, dull, senseless, ▷*foolish* ★**clever**
stupidity *n.* inanity, silliness, feebleness, foolishness ★**brilliance**
sturdy *adj.* rugged, stalwart, tough, strapping, ▷*hardy* ★**weak**
stutter *v.* stumble, falter, ▷*stammer*
style [1] *n.* mode, vogue, fashion, way, manner, form [2] *v.* name, call, christen STILE
suave (swahv) *adj.* agreeable, elegant, polite, pleasant, sophisticated *After living in the city for many years, my sister had developed very sophisticated tastes*
subdue *v.* suppress, soften, tame, tone down, ▷*repress*
subject [1] *n.* (*sub*-ject) matter, topic, theme [2] subordinate, dependant [3] *adj.* dependent, subordinate, liable [4] *v.* (sub-*ject*) *v.* rule over, subdue, subjugate
submerge *v.* plunge, immerse, sink ★**raise**
submissive *adj.* yielding, servile, meek, ▷*obedient* ★**obstinate**
submit [1] *v.* yield, give in, accede, surrender, hand over, [2] offer, tender, present
subordinate *adj.* junior, minor, subject, dependent, secondary ★**superior**
subscribe *v.* sign, enroll, register, agree, assent

subsequent *adj.* later, following, succeeding, after ***former**
subside *v.* decline, peter out, decrease, diminish, wane *I used to go mountaineering, but my interest waned after some years,* ▷*abate* ***rise**
substance [1] *n.* matter, object, stuff, material [2] essence, kernel, meaning, ▷*gist*
substantial [1] *adj.* steady, sturdy, firm, ▷*stable* [2] ample, large, real, solid ***imaginary**
substitute [1] *n.* alternative, makeshift, stopgap [2] *v.* swap, change, replace, duplicate
subtle (*sut*-l) [1] *adj.* shrewd, fine, delicate [2] clever, crafty, perceptive
subtract *v.* take away, withdraw, deduct, remove ***add**
succeed [1] *v.* flourish, prosper, thrive, triumph ***fail** [2] follow, inherit, replace ***precede**
success *n.* prosperity, triumph, victory, achievement ***failure**
successful *adj.* victorious, prosperous, fortunate, thriving ***unlucky**
suck *v.* inhale, take in, draw in, imbibe
sudden *adj.* unexpected, abrupt, impulsive, swift, prompt ***gradual**
suffer [1] *v.* bear, endure, put up with [2] encounter, undergo, ▷*sustain*
sufficient *adj.* adequate, ample, plenty, ▷*enough* ***deficient**
suffocate *v.* smother, choke, ▷*stifle*
suggest *v.* recommend, advise, submit, hint, intimate
suit [1] *v.* fulfill, gratify, please, suffice, accommodate, befit [2] *n.* ensemble, outfit, costume
suitable *adj.* fitting, appropriate, correct, proper, becoming ***unsuitable**
suite (sweet) [1] *n.* set, series, succession [2] apartment, rooms
sulk *v.* pout, grouch, brood, mope
sulky *adj.* glum, morose, churlish, moody, ▷*sullen* ***genial**
sullen *adj.* gloomy, heavy, dismal, cheerless, ▷*sulky* ***cheerful**
sum *n.* amount, total, whole, entirety SOME
summary *n.* synopsis, précis, abstract, summing-up, outline, analysis
summit *n.* peak, pinnacle, top, apex, zenith ***base**
summon *v.* call, beckon, command, invite, muster ***dismiss**
sumptuous *adj.* profuse, costly, gorgeous, splendid, ▷*lavish* ***frugal**
sundry *adj.* different, separate, several, ▷*various*
sunny *adj.* bright, cheerful, light, clear, ▷*radiant* ***gloomy**
superb *adj.* magnificent, stately, gorgeous, ▷*grand* ***commonplace**
supercilious *adj.* contemptuous, haughty, arrogant, ▷*snobbish* ***modest**
superficial *adj.* slight, imperfect, shallow, skin-deep, ▷*trivial* ***profound**
superfluous *adj.* in excess, inessential, spare, ▷*surplus* ***essential**
superior [1] *adj.* better, greater, higher, loftier, ▷*excellent* [2] eminent, conspicuous, principal ***inferior**
supersede *v.* succeed, replace, displace, suspend, usurp *The president's authority was usurped by her assistant* ***continue**
supervise *v.* superintend, control, manage, ▷*direct*
supple *adj.* lithe, pliable, flexible, bending
supplement [1] *n.* addition, complement, sequel, postscript [2] *v.* supply, add, fill
supply [1] *v.* provide, furnish, yield, contribute, purvey [2] *n.* hoard, reserve, ▷*stock* ***retain**
support [1] *v.* uphold, bear, sustain, maintain, help, ▷*favor* ***oppose** [2] hold up, prop, strut, brace [3] endure, tolerate, suffer [4] *n.* maintenance, upkeep
suppose *v.* assume, presume, believe, imagine, imply, ▷*consider*
suppress *v.* restrain, extinguish, destroy, stop, ▷*quell* ***incite**
supreme *adj.* dominant, highest, greatest, maximum ***lowly**
sure [1] *adj.* certain, positive, definite [2] secure, steady, safe [3] permanent, abiding, enduring ***uncertain**

surface [1] *n.* area, expanse, stretch [2] outside, exterior, covering **★interior**
surge [1] *v.* swell, rise, heave, rush [2] *n.* ripple, billow, wave SERGE
surly *adj.* morose, cross, testy, touchy, crusty, ▷*sullen* **★affable**
surmise *v.* guess, speculate, conjecture, suspect, ▷*presume* **★know**
surpass *v.* eclipse, outdo, outstrip, excel, exceed, ▷*beat*
surplus *n.* excess, remainder, balance, residue **★shortcoming**
surprise [1] *v.* startle, astonish, amaze, ▷*astound* [2] *n.* amazement, astonishment, ▷*wonder*
surrender *v.* quit, give up, yield, submit, ▷*relinquish*
surround *v.* enclose, encircle, encompass
survey [1] *v.* (sur-*vey*) look at, examine, scrutinize, ▷*study* [2] estimate, measure [3] *n.* (*sur*-vey) assessment, appraisal
survive *v.* live, exist, continue, outlast, abide **★surrender**
susceptible *adj.* sensitive, impressionable, inclined, capable **★insensitive**
suspect [1] *v.* (sus-*pect*) disbelieve, doubt, distrust [2] *adj.* (*sus*-pect) unbelievable, questionable
suspend [1] *v.* interrupt, delay, arrest, ▷*stop* **★continue** [2] swing, dangle, ▷*hang* **★drop**
suspense *n.* anticipation, waiting, abeyance *The club couldn't decide on a new president, so the matter was left in abeyance,* stoppage, uncertainty, ▷*tension* **★decision**
suspicious *adj.* incredulous, skeptical, doubtful, suspecting **★trustful**
sustain [1] *v.* uphold, keep, maintain, provide for [2] suffer, undergo, experience [3] nourish, nurture, feed
swagger [1] *v.* parade, prance, ▷*strut* [2] brag, bluster, ▷*boast*
swallow [1] *v.* absorb, consume, eat, digest, devour, ▷*gulp* [2] *n.* mouthful, gulp [3] bird
swamp [1] *n.* fen, bog, marsh, morass, quagmire [2] *v.* submerge, submerse, overflow, deluge, ▷*drench*
swap *v.* exchange, switch, trade, barter
swarm [1] *n.* throng, horde, shoal, flock, crowd [2] *v.* teem, abound, jam, mass, crowd, cluster
swarthy *adj.* dusky, dark, brown, tawny
sway [1] *v.* swing, rock, totter, lean, incline, ▷*waver* [2] *n.* rule, authority, control, ▷*influence*
swear [1] *v.* promise, warrant, affirm, attest [2] curse, damn, blaspheme
sweat *v.* perspire, ooze, leak, exude, swelter *During that time of the year it was very hot, and we sweltered all day*
sweep *v.* brush, scrub, clean, scour
sweet [1] *adj.* sugary, syrupy, luscious **★sour** [2] melodic, tuneful, musical, mellow **★discordant** [3] gentle, tender, mild, lovable **★unpleasant** [4] fragrant, pure, clean, fresh **★putrid**
swell *v.* expand, distend, inflate, bulge, ▷*enlarge* **★contract**
swerve *v.* veer, deviate, skid, skew, lurch, ▷*waver*
swift *adj.* speedy, rapid, quick, ▷*fast* **★slow**
swill [1] *v.* swig, consume, imbibe, tipple, ▷*gulp* [2] *n.* refuse, garbage, waste
swim *v.* bathe, wade, paddle, float, glide
swindle [1] *n.* trick, fraud, blackmail, racket [2] *v.* hoodwink, deceive, hoax, dupe, ▷*cheat*
swine *n.* pig, boar, sow, porker
swing [1] *v.* hang, suspend, dangle, lurch, reel [2] *n.* tempo, time
switch [1] *v.* change, exchange, alter, substitute, swap [2] *n.* lever, pedal, control, button
swivel *v.* pivot, spin, rotate, revolve, turn
swoop *v.* pounce, descend, stoop, plummet, plunge
sword *n.* rapier, blade, foil, épée, cutlass, saber, steel SOARED
symbol *n.* character, figure, numeral, letter, sign, token, emblem CYMBAL
sympathetic *adj.* thoughtful, understanding, kind, affectionate **★indifferent**
system [1] *n.* method, plan, order, scheme, arrangement, routine [2] network, organization: *a hierarchical system*

T t

table [1] *n.* board, stand, slab, tablet, counter, stall [2] list, catalog, schedule, index, statement
tablet [1] *n.* pill, capsule, lozenge [2] board, table, pad
tack [1] *n.* thumbtack, nail, pin, brad [2] aim, direction, set [3] *v.* affix, fasten, join, stitch
tackle [1] *n.* outfit, gear, rig, harness [2] *v.* grasp, halt, intercept, seize [3] deal with *I dealt with the problem of the school fund shortage,* undertake, set about
tact *n.* diplomacy, judgment, skill, discretion *If you want your secret to be kept, you had better not rely on his discretion* TACKED
tactful *adj.* diplomatic, wise, subtle, prudent, ▷*discreet* ★**tactless**
tactics *n.* strategy, campaign, method, procedure
tactless *adj.* inconsiderate, gauche, clumsy, boorish, ▷*inept* ★**tactful**
tag *n.* label, ticket, docket, slip, sticker
taint *v.* sully, tarnish, infect, stain, contaminate, ▷*defile* ★**purify**
take [1] *v.* grasp, grab, seize, procure [2] receive, accept, obtain [3] carry, convey, lead, conduct [4] interpret, understand
take place *v.* occur, happen, befall *Our parents were concerned about what might befall us when we left school*
tale *n.* story, fable, anecdote, yarn, narrative TAIL
talent *n.* knack, genius, gift, ability, aptitude ★**stupidity**
talk [1] *v.* speak, say, utter, gossip [2] describe, comment on, talk about [3] *n.* speech, chatter, conversation [4] lecture, speech, discourse
tall *adj.* lanky, lofty, big, high, towering ★**short**
tally [1] *v.* count, enumerate, compute [2] agree, conform, coincide ★**disagree**
tame [1] *adj.* domesticated, gentle, mild, docile ★**savage** [2] flat, dull, boring, tedious [3] *v.* train, discipline, domesticate *The tame house cat was first domesticated by the ancient Egyptians*

Tame

The tame European or American cat was first domesticated by the Egyptians.

tamper with *v.* meddle, interfere, damage, tinker
tang *n.* smell, scent, aroma, flavor, savor, taste
tangible *adj.* concrete, solid, substantial, real, material ★**spiritual**
tangle *n.* & *v.* twist, muddle, jumble, knot
tantalize *v.* tease, taunt, thwart, disappoint ▷*frustrate* ★**satisfy**
tantrum *n.* rage, fit, hysterics, storm
tap [1] *v.* pat, hit, knock, rap, strike [2] *n.* spout, cock, nozzle, faucet, bung
tape *n.* ribbon, filament, braid, strip, riband
taper *v.* dwindle, narrow, contract, decline, wane, narrow ★**widen** TAPIR
tardy *adj.* slow, sluggish, reluctant, slack, ▷*late* ★**prompt**
target *n.* goal, aim, ambition, purpose, butt, end
tariff *n.* tax, rate, toll, duty, payment, schedule of fees
tarnish *v.* stain, sully *Mark's reputation at school was sullied after he was accused of stealing,* spot, darken, blemish, rust ★**brighten**
tarry *v.* delay, stall, wait, loiter, ▷*linger* ★**hurry**

tart [1] *adj.* acid, sour, sharp, pungent [2] *n.* pie, quiche, pastry, flan

task *n.* job, stint, chore, assignment, undertaking

taste [1] *n.* bite, mouthful, flavor, savor, tang [2] *v.* try, sip, sample, relish

tasteful *adj.* artistic, graceful, elegant, smart, ▷*refined* ★**tasteless**

tasteless [1] *adj.* flavorless, insipid [2] gaudy, inelegant, ▷*vulgar* ★**tasteful**

tasty *adj.* appetizing, piquant, savory, ▷*delicious* ★**disgusting**

tattle *v.* gossip, tittle-tattle, blab, prattle

taunt *v.* jibe, reproach, rebuke, ridicule, scoff at, ▷*sneer* ★**compliment**

taut *adj.* tense, tight, stretched, ▷*rigid* ★**relaxed** TAUGHT

tawdry *adj.* flashy, loud, gaudy, showy, ▷*vulgar* ★**superior**

tax [1] *n.* levy, duty, impost, tithe, toll [2] *v.* load, oppress, overburden TACKS

teach *v.* instruct, educate, tutor, coach, guide, train, drill

teacher *n.* educator, professor, lecturer, schoolmaster, schoolmistress, coach, tutor

team *n.* party, group, gang, crew, company TEEM

tear (tare) [1] *v.* rip, rend, tatter, shred [2] dash, bolt, rush, sprint TARE

tearful (teerful) *adj.* weepy, moist, wet, sobbing, sad

tease *v.* annoy, harass, vex, irritate, torment, ▷*tantalize* ★**soothe** TEAS TEES

tedious *adj.* wearisome, tiresome, irksome, exhausting, ▷*boring* ★**fascinating**

teem *v.* abound, swarm, overflow, increase, be full ★**lack** TEAM

tell [1] *v.* disclose, speak, state, talk, utter [2] discern, discover, distinguish

temper [1] *n.* temperament, disposition, nature, humor [2] anger, annoyance, passion [3] *v.* moderate, soften, weaken, restrain

temporary *adj.* short, limited, impermanent, brief ★**permanent**

tempt *v.* entice, invite, attract, persuade, ▷*lure* ★**deter**

tenacious [1] *adj.* stubborn, firm, obstinate, unwavering ★**weak** [2] adhesive, glutinous

tenant *n.* occupant, householder, occupier

tend [1] *v.* take care of, manage, serve, guard ★**neglect** [2] affect, lean, incline, verge ★**diverge**

tendency *n.* disposition, leaning, inclination, bent ★**aversion**

tender [1] *adj.* delicate, soft, ▷*fragile* [2] mild, kind, sympathetic, ▷*gentle* [3] raw, painful, sore [4] *v.* proffer *Charlotte proffered her services as a babysitter,* present, volunteer, bid

tense *adj.* tight, strained, taut, nervous, edgy ★**relaxed** TENTS

tension *n.* strain, stress, rigidity, suspense, worry ★**relaxation**

term [1] *n.* expression, denomination, title, phrase [2] time, season, spell *We stayed in Hong Kong for a spell during our trip to the Far East,* duration [3] *v.* entitle, call, dub

terminate *v.* cease, stop, end, conclude, ▷*finish* ★**begin**

terrible *adj.* frightful, terrifying, fearful, dreadful, ▷*horrible* ★**superb**

terrify *v.* petrify, shock, appall, alarm, ▷*frighten* ★**reassure**

territory *n.* region, area, expanse, dominion, land, ▷*country*

terror *n.* alarm, panic, horror, dismay, ▷*fright* ★**confidence**

terse *adj.* brief, concise, short, pithy, abrupt, ▷*curt* ★**long-winded**

test [1] *n.* examination, trial, check, proof, experiment [2] *v.* examine, try out, check, quiz, analyze

testy *adj.* irritable, bad-tempered, touchy, peevish, ▷*cross* ★**genial**

tether *n.* rope, cord, lead, leash, chain

text *n.* contents, reading, passage, clause

thanks *n.* gratitude, credit, appreciation

thaw [1] *v.* melt, fuse, liquefy, soften ★**freeze** [2] unbend, relax

theft *n.* robbery, fraud, larceny, plundering

theme *n.* subject, text matter, topic

theory *n.* idea, supposition, concept, hypothesis

therefore *adv.* consequently, hence, accordingly, thus

thick [1] *adj.* dense, solid, bulky, compact [2] stiff, set, congealed [3] viscous, gummy, stodgy ★**thin**
thief *n.* crook, robber, burglar, bandit, pirate
thin [1] *adj.* slender, slim, slight, lean, skinny ★**fat** [2] waferlike, delicate, flimsy [3] watery, dilute, unsubstantial ★**thick**
thing *n.* article, object, something, being, substance
think [1] *v.* ponder, consider, ▷*reflect* [2] conceive, imagine, ▷*fancy* [3] surmise, conclude, ▷*reckon*
thirsty *adj.* parched, dry, craving, burning
thorn *n.* barb, prickle, bramble, thistle
thorough *adj.* outright, absolute, complete, utter, absolute ★**haphazard**
though *conj.* although, even though, notwithstanding, however, yet
thought *n.* reflection, consideration, study, concept, deduction
thoughtful [1] *adj.* pensive, studious, contemplative [2] considerate, kind, heedful, careful ★**thoughtless**
thoughtless *adj.* heedless, careless, rash, neglectful, ▷*indiscreet* ★**thoughtful**
thrash [1] *v.* whip, flog, hit [2] stir, pitch, toss *I couldn't sleep last night; I tossed and turned for hours*

Thrash

I couldn't sleep last night; I tossed and turned for hours.

thread *n.* filament, twist, yarn, fiber
threadbare [1] *adj.* shabby, ragged, worn [2] commonplace, hackneyed, stale ★**fresh**
threaten *v.* intimidate, bully, blackmail, ▷*menace* ★**reassure**
thrifty *adj.* frugal, careful, economical, saving, sparing ★**wasteful**
thrilling *adj.* exciting, gripping, stimulating
thrive *v.* prosper, flourish, succeed, grow, increase ★**decline**
throb [1] *n.* tick, beat, palpitation [2] *v.* beat, palpitate, vibrate
throng [1] *n.* crowd, horde, mob [2] *v.* pack, crowd, swarm, fill
throttle *v.* choke, smother, ▷*strangle*
through *prep.* by way of, by means of, as a result of
throw *v.* fling, cast, hurl, project, propel, thrust ★**keep** THROE
thrust *v.* & *n.* push, project, drive, force, prod
thug *n.* hoodlum, bandit, assassin, mugger, ruffian
thump *v.* & *n.* beat, hit, knock, bang, wallop
thunderstruck *adj.* open-mouthed, amazed, astounded, staggered
thus *adv.* accordingly, so, therefore, consequently
thwart *v.* frustrate, balk, baffle, hinder, obstruct ★**assist**
ticket *n.* pass, label, card, coupon, token
tickle [1] *v.* caress, stroke, pat, brush [2] titillate, convulse, amuse [3] delight, gratify
tidbit *n.* delicacy, morsel, dainty, snack, treat
tide *n.* stream, current, drift, ebb, flow TIED
tidings *n.* information, intelligence, report, advice, ▷*news*
tidy [1] *adj.* neat, well-kept, spruce, orderly [2] ample, large, substantial
tie [1] *v.* join, attach, secure, unite, ▷*fasten* [2] *n.* cravat *These days, a necktie is more commonly worn than a cravat*, necktie, bow tie [3] bond, connection
tight [1] *adj.* fast, close, compact, tense ★**loose** ▷*taut* [2] miserly, tightfisted, ▷*stingy* ★**generous**
tighten *v.* strain, tauten, constrict, cramp, crush, ▷*squeeze* ★**loosen**

till [1] *prep.* until, up to, as far as [2] *v.* plow, cultivate, tend [3] *n.* cash drawer, cash register

tilt *v.* & *n.* slant, slope, incline, lean, list, tip

time [1] *n.* period, duration, season, age, era, term, span [2] meter, measure, tempo, rhythm THYME

timid *adj.* fearful, afraid, timorous, diffident, modest, ▷*shy* ★**bold**

tinge *v.* & *n.* color, tincture, tint, stain, shade

tingle *v.* thrill, throb, tickle, vibrate

tinker *v.* meddle, fiddle *Bill fiddled with the old clock for ages, trying to make it work*, patch up, putter, trifle

tinkle *v.* jingle, jangle, ring, clink

tint *n.* dye, hue, tinge, shade, ▷*color*

tiny *adj.* small, diminutive, puny, wee, ▷*little* ★**huge**

tip [1] *n.* apex, peak, point, extremity, ▷*top* [2] gratuity, gift, donation, reward [3] information, hint, tip-off [4] *v.* list, lean, tilt, ▷*slope*

tipsy *adj.* inebriated, drunk, drunken

tire *v.* exhaust, bore, fatigue, harass, weaken

tiresome *adj.* wearisome, tedious, boring, ▷*humdrum* ★**interesting**

title [1] *n.* name, denomination, term, style, designation [2] claim, interest *When my father died, I was left an interest in his business*, ownership

toady *v.* fawn, crawl, grovel, crouch, cringe

toast [1] *n.* pledge, compliment, salutation [2] *v.* brown, roast, heat

together *adv.* collectively, jointly, simultaneously, at the same time ★**separately**

toil [1] *v.* & *n.* struggle, labor, travail, ▷*work* ★**relaxation**

token *n.* memento, keepsake, symbol, omen, ▷*souvenir*

tolerable *adj.* endurable, supportable, bearable, passable ★**unbearable**

tolerant *adj.* forbearing, indulgent *Sally's parents are very indulgent with her and buy her whatever she wants*, liberal, easygoing, ▷*lenient* ★**intolerant**

tolerate *v.* accept, bear with, put up with, endure, suffer, ▷*allow* ★**resist**

toll [1] *v.* ring, strike, chime, clang [2] *n.* charge, duty, tax, levy

tone [1] *n.* pitch, loudness, noise, note [2] emphasis, accent, inflection [3] temper, manner, attitude [4] color, cast, hue, shade

too [1] *adv.* also, as well, besides [2] extremely, very, unduly

tool [1] *n.* implement, utensil, machine, agent [2] pawn, puppet, catspaw, stooge TULLE

top [1] *n.* summit, pinnacle, peak [2] lid, cover, stopper, cap [3] upper surface ★**bottom** [4] spinning toy [5] *adj.* highest, best, uppermost *After climbing for four days, we reached the uppermost part of the range*

topic *n.* subject, motif, question, ▷*theme*

topical *adj.* contemporary, popular, up-to-date

topple *v.* collapse, founder, overturn, totter, ▷*fall*

topsy-turvy *adj.* upside-down, overturned, confused, chaotic

torment [1] *v.* & *n.* pain, distress, ▷*torture* ★**ease**

torrent *n.* flood, stream, cascade, cataract, waterfall ★**trickle**

torture *v.* agonize, rack, anguish, ▷*torment*

toss *v.* fling, hurl, pitch, cast, project, heave, ▷*throw*

total [1] *n.* aggregate, whole, sum, completion [2] *v.* add, tot up, reckon [3] *adj.* complete, entire

totally *adv.* completely, absolutely, entirely, utterly ★**partially**

touch [1] *v.* feel, finger, fondle, handle, stroke [2] move, affect, concern [3] beat, hit, collide with [4] adjoin *Our house is situated at a spot where three counties adjoin*, meet, border [5] *n.* tinge, hint, suspicion

touchy *adj.* peevish, petulant, snappish, ▷*moody* ★**genial**

tough [1] *adj.* hard, strong, vigorous, rugged, sturdy [2] arduous, difficult [3] *n.* hoodlum, hooligan, bruiser, bully

tour *n.* trip, journey, jaunt, excursion, voyage, ride, visit

tournament *n.* contest, championship, competition, ▷*match*

Empress

Thane

Professor

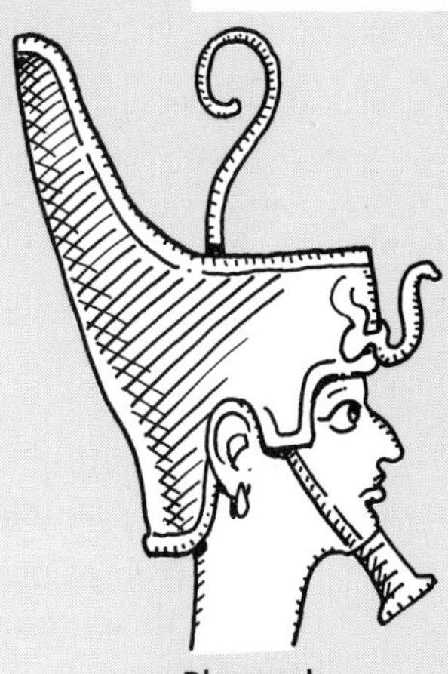
Pharaoh

Titles

admiral ambassador archbishop
baron baroness brigadier
cardinal chancellor colonel
commodore constable count
countess czar czarina
dame deacon dean don doña
duchess duke
earl emir emperor
general governor graf
infanta
kaiser khan king knight
lady laird lama lieutenant lord
madame maharajah maharini
major mandarin marchioness
margrave marshall mayor mikado
mogul monsieur monsignor ms
pasha pope priest prince
princess provost queen

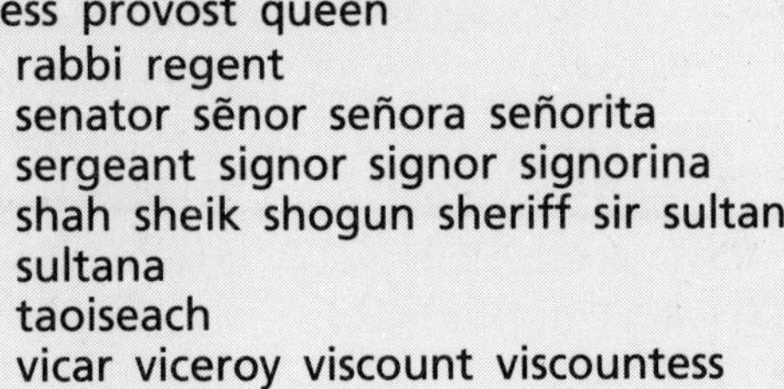

rabbi regent
senator sẽnor señora señorita
sergeant signor signor signorina
shah sheik shogun sheriff sir sultan
sultana
taoiseach
vicar viceroy viscount viscountess

Ayatollah

Rajah

Bishop

Sheriff

Captain

Mister

Samurai

tow *v.* haul, drag, tug, haul, heave, ▷*pull* TOE
tower 1 *v.* soar, dominate, surmount 2 *n.* turret, spire, belfry
toy 1 *n.* plaything, doll, game 2 *v.* play, tinker, fiddle, twiddle
trace 1 *v.* trail, track, follow, pursue, discover 2 sketch, draw, copy 3 *n.* trail, track, spoor 4 drop, speck, vestige
track *v.* search out, follow, ▷*trace*
tract 1 *n.* area, space, extent, plot 2 booklet, leaflet, pamphlet TRACKED
trade 1 *v.* barter, exchange, buy, sell, patronize 2 *n.* occupation, work, livelihood, business
tradition *n.* custom, convention, practice
traffic 1 *n.* business, barter, ▷*trade* 2 transportation, vehicles, movement
tragedy *n.* catastrophe, disaster, adversity, ▷*calamity* ★**comedy**
tragic *adj.* disastrous, catastrophic, miserable, wretched, ▷*deplorable* ★**comic**
trail *n.* spoor, track, ▷*trace*
train 1 *v.* teach, educate, instruct, drill, school 2 *n.* chain, procession, series
traitor *n.* rebel, mutineer, renegade, quisling, betrayer
tramp 1 *n.* vagabond, wanderer, vagrant, bum, hobo, ▷*beggar* 2 jaunt, stroll, ramble 3 *v.* roam, rove, range, walk, travel
trample *v.* tread on, walk on, flatten, ▷*crush*
tranquil *adj.* peaceful, placid, serene, restful, ▷*calm* ★**restless**
transaction *n.* business, performance, dealing, negotiation, proceeding
transfer *v.* move *My sister is being moved to head office after her promotion*, displace, change, ▷*exchange*
transmit *v.* dispatch, forward, relay, ▷*send* ★**receive**
transparent *adj.* clear, lucid, crystal, diaphanous
transport 1 *v.* carry, convey, conduct, transfer, ▷*move* 2 *n.* transportation
trap 1 *v.* ensnare, catch, net 2 *n.* snare, pitfall, noose, decoy, ▷*ambush*
trash *n.* junk, debris, rubble, ▷*rubbish* ★**treasure**
travel 1 *v.* & *n.* trek, voyage, cruise, ▷*journey*
treacherous *adj.* traitorous, unfaithful, false, deceptive *We mustn't swim on this beach; the tides and currents are deceptive*, ▷*disloyal* ★**faithful**
tread 1 *v.* step, walk, tramp, march, go 2 stride, gait, walk, step
treason *n.* treachery, betrayal, sedition
treasure 1 *n.* hoard, fortune, riches, wealth 2 *v.* appreciate, esteem, ▷*value*
treat 1 *v.* deal with, handle, manage, serve 2 regale, entertain 3 doctor, attend 4 *n.* banquet, entertainment, fun
treaty *n.* agreement, covenant, alliance
tremble *v.* quake, quaver, shudder, flutter, ▷*shake*
tremendous 1 *adj.* immense, enormous, ▷*huge* 2 terrible, dreadful, awful
tremor *n.* quiver, shake, flutter, ripple, ▷*vibration*
trench *n.* ditch, moat, trough, gully, gutter

trend *n.* tendency, inclination, direction
trespass [1] *v.* infringe, overstep, intrude [2] *n.* offense, sin, transgression
trial [1] *n.* endeavor, testing, experiment [2] ordeal, grief, suffering [3] essay, proof [4] hearing, lawsuit
tribe *n.* clan, family, race, group, set
tribute [1] *n.* ovation, compliment, praise [2] dues, toll, tithe, tax
trick [1] *n.* fraud, artifice, wile, cheat, deception [2] jape, prank, frolic [3] juggling, stage magic, conjuring [4] *v.* deceive, defraud
trickle *v.* leak, ooze, seep, drip, drop, dribble
trifle [1] *n.* bauble, plaything, foolishness, nonsense [2] *v.* dabble, idle, play with
trifling *adj.* paltry, petty, worthless, slight, ▷*trivial* ★**important**
trim [1] *v.* prune, clip, shorten, crop [2] ornament, smarten, decorate [3] *adj.* tidy, neat, orderly ★**scruffy**
trinket *n.* bauble, bead, jewel, ornament, toy
trip [1] *n.* journey, excursion, jaunt, ▷*tour* [2] *v.* stumble, fall, slip
tripe *n.* rubbish, trash, nonsense, twaddle *This is a silly story; I never read such twaddle* ★**sense**
trite *adj.* hackneyed, ordinary, corny, ▷*stale* ★**novel**
triumph *n.* victory, success, achievement *Being valedictorian is a major achievement* ▷*conquest* ★**defeat**
trivial *adj.* trifling, common, unimportant, ordinary, useless, ▷trite ★**important**
troop [1] *n.* band, gang, group, pack, team, unit [2] *v.* flock, crowd, swarm TROUPE
trophy *n.* prize, award, cup, souvenir
trot *v.* canter, jog, scamper, scurry
trouble [1] *n.* disturbance, annoyance, calamity, misfortune, ▷*misery* [2] *v.* disturb, annoy, harass, ▷*distress* ★**delight**
true [1] *adj.* accurate, precise, factual, correct ★**inaccurate** [2] faithful, loyal, constant [3] pure, real, ▷*genuine* ★**false**
trunk [1] *n.* body, torso, stem, stalk [2] chest, case, box [3] proboscis *The tapir's proboscis is not as large as the elephant's trunk*, nose, snout
truss *v.* fasten, secure, strap, tie, ▷*bind* ★**untie**
trust [1] *n.* faith, confidence, belief [2] *v.* believe in, credit, depend on ★**doubt** TRUSSED
trustful *adj.* trusting, innocent, naïve, ▷*gullible* ★**cautious**
trustworthy *adj.* dependable, credible, honorable, ▷*reliable* ★**unreliable**
truth [1] *n.* reality, fact, precision, ▷*accuracy* ★**falsehood** [2] integrity, faith, honor, ▷*fidelity* ★**deceit**
truthful *adj.* reliable, frank, open, ▷*honest* ★**false**
try [1] *v.* endeavor, attempt, ▷*strive* [2] examine, try out, ▷*test* ★**abandon** [3] *n.* trial, attempt, effort
trying *adj.* bothersome, annoying, troublesome, ▷*irksome*
tub *n.* basin, bowl, pot, barrel, keg, tun
tube *n.* pipe, spout, duct, hose, shaft
tuck *v.* stow, fold, pack, pleat, hem
tug *v.* drag, tow, haul, heave, ▷*pull* ★**push**
tumble *v.* drop, descend, trip, topple, stumble, ▷*fall*
tumult *n.* noise, rumpus, racket, uproar, disturbance, disorder ★**peace**
tune *n.* melody, harmony, air, strain, ▷*song*
tunnel *n.* subway, shaft, passage, gallery
turn [1] *v.* spin, revolve, whirl, ▷*rotate* [2] bend, curve, ▷*twist* [3] change, alter, ▷*convert* [4] spoil, ▷*sour* [5] *n.* stint, spell, chance [6] rotation, ▷*revolution* TERN
twaddle *n.* balderdash, nonsense, drivel, rigmarole, piffle, ▷*bunkum* ★**sense**
twinge *n.* pain, pang, spasm, gripe, ▷*ache*
twinkle *v.* glitter, gleam, glisten, glimmer, ▷*sparkle*
twist [1] *v.* bend, curve, turn [2] warp, contort, writhe [3] wind, intertwine *The octopus intertwined its legs around the little boat*, encircle
twitch *v.* jerk, jump, jiggle, blink, flutter
type [1] *n.* kind, sort, character, description [2] prototype, model, pattern [3] letter, symbol [4] *v.* typewrite
typical *adj.* characteristic, symbolic, regular, stock, representative ★**abnormal**
tyrant *n.* despot, autocrat, dictator, martinet

U u

ugly *adj.* unsightly, ungainly, frightful, ghastly, hideous, horrid, nasty ★**beautiful**
ultimate *adj.* furthest, farthest, most distant, extreme, eventual, ▷*final*
umpire *n.* referee, judge, mediator
unabashed *adj.* brazen, unconcerned, undaunted, ▷*composed* ★**sheepish**
unable *adj.* helpless, incapable, powerless ★**able**
unaccustomed *adj.* inexperienced, unfamiliar, ▷*strange* ★**familiar**
unaffected *adj.* natural, sincere, true, artless, ▷*naïve* ★**impressed**
unafraid *adj.* courageous, dauntless, intrepid, ▷*fearless* ★**afraid**
unanimous *adj.* harmonious, consenting, agreeing, ▷*united*
unassuming *adj.* diffident, reserved, quiet, simple, ▷*modest* ★**forward**
unattached *adj.* single, free, loose, ▷*separate* ★**committed**
unattended *adj.* alone, unwatched, ignored, ▷*abandoned* ★**escorted**
unavoidable *adj.* inevitable, irresistable, certain, ▷*necessary* ★**uncertain**
unaware *adj.* ignorant, unheeding, unknowing, forgetful, ▷*oblivious* ★**aware**
unbalanced [1] *adj.* top-heavy, lopsided, uneven [2] insane, unhinged *He seems to have become unhinged ever since he lost his job*, crazy, eccentric
unbearable *adj.* unacceptable, intolerable, ▷*outrageous* ★**acceptable**
unbiased *adj.* impartial, fair, just, ▷*neutral* ★**prejudiced**
uncanny *adj.* weird, ghostly, unearthly, creepy, ▷*eerie*
uncertain *adj.* doubtful, vague, chancy, indefinite, ▷*dubious* ★**certain**
uncivilized *adj.* primitive, barbaric, coarse, gross, ▷*vulgar* ★**civilized**
uncomfortable *adj.* awkward, embarrassed, cramped, self-conscious ★**comfortable**
uncommon *adj.* rare, scarce, infrequent, extraordinary, ▷*unusual* ★**common**
unconscious [1] *adj.* ignorant, unheeding, ▷*unaware* [2] insensible, senseless, stunned ★**conscious**
unconventional *adj.* unorthodox, peculiar *I have my own peculiar way of looking at things*, individualistic, ▷*eccentric* ★**conventional**
uncouth *adj.* crude, coarse, clumsy, vulgar, ▷*boorish* ★**polite**
uncover *v.* expose, discover, show, divulge, ▷*reveal* ★**conceal**
under [1] *adv.* underneath, below, beneath [2] *prep.* less than, lower than, subject to
undergo *v.* endure, tolerate, bear, suffer, ▷*sustain*
underground *adj.* secret, concealed, private, concealed
underhand *adj.* stealthy, undercover, deceitful, ▷*sneaky* ★**honest**
underneath *adj.* beneath, under, ▷*below* ★**above**
underrate *v.* undervalue, understate, disparage, belittle ★**exaggerate**
understand *v.* comprehend, appreciate, grasp, sympathize, ▷*realize* ★**misunderstand**
understudy *n.* stand-in, deputy, substitute, reserve
undertake *v.* attempt, commence, contract, embark on *We must choose our equipment carefully before we embark on the expedition*, ▷*tackle*
undesirable *adj.* objectionable, unpleasant, distasteful, ▷*unpleasant* ★**desirable**
undignified *adj.* improper, inelegant, ▷*unseemly* ★**graceful**
undo *v.* unfasten, disentangle, unravel, free, ▷*release* ★**fasten**
undress *v.* disrobe, strip, remove, take off, ▷*divest* ★**dress**
unearthly *adj.* eerie, uncanny, supernatural, ▷*ghostly*
uneasy *adj.* uncomfortable, restive, self-conscious, edgy ★**calm**
unemployed *adj.* unoccupied, redundant, workless

uneven *adj.* irregular, rough, bumpy, lop-sided, unequal ★**even**
unexpected *adj.* abrupt, impulsive, chance, surprising, ▷*sudden* ★**normal**
unfair *adj.* prejudiced, one-sided, partial, unjust ★**fair**
unfaithful *adj.* faithless, untrue, dishonest, ▷*false* ★**faithful**
unfamiliar *adj.* alien, obscure, fantastic, bizarre, ▷*strange* ★**familiar**
unfasten *v.* release, open, unlatch, untie, ▷*undo* ★**fasten**
unfinished *adj.* incomplete, imperfect, lacking, crude ★**finished**
unfit *adj.* unqualified, unsuitable, incapable, unsuited ★**suitable**
unfold *adj.* open, expand, develop, reveal, disclose, unwrap ★**withhold**
unforeseen *adj.* surprising, sudden, accidental, ▷*unexpected* ★**predictable**
unforgettable *adj.* memorable, impressive, noteworthy, exceptional
unfortunate *adj.* deplorable, lamentable, adverse, hapless, ▷*unlucky* ★**fortunate**
unfriendly *adj.* antagonistic, surly, cold, ▷*hostile* ★**friendly**
ungainly *adj.* gawky, awkward, graceless, unwieldly, ▷*clumsy* ★**graceful**
ungrateful *adj.* thankless, selfish, ungracious, ill-mannered ★**grateful**
unhappiness *n.* depression, misery, sadness
unhappy *adj.* miserable, dismal, luckless *Try as he might, the luckless Tom was almost last in the race,* melancholy, ▷*sad* ★**happy**
unhealthy [1] *adj.* unwholesome, harmful [2] sick, ill, diseased ★**healthy**
uniform [1] *n.* regalia, livery *It was a very grand affair, with the footmen in full livery,* costume, dress [2] *adj.* stable, steady, unchanging, level ★**varied**
unimportant *adj.* puny, trivial, insignificant, ▷*petty* ★**important**
unintentional *adj.* inadvertent, involuntary, unwitting, ▷*accidental* ★**deliberate**
union [1] *n.* alliance, association, league [2] agreement, accord, harmony [3] fusion, blend, compound
unique *adj.* original, exceptional, exclusive, single, sole ★**commonplace**
unit *n.* entity, single, one, individual
unite *v.* join, combine, connect, merge, blend, fuse ★**separate**
united *adj.* joined, combined, undivided, ▷*unanimous* ★**separated**
unity *n.* union, harmony, uniformity, agreement ★**disagreement**
universal *adj.* general, all-embracing, entire, worldwide *Our company has been very successful, with its products being sold worldwide*
unjust *adj.* partial, prejudiced, unfair, wrong, ▷*biased* ★**just**
unkempt *adj.* disheveled, shabby, sloppy, slovenly, ungroomed, ▷*scruffy* ★**neat**
unkind *adj.* inhuman, heartless, brutal, callous, ▷*cruel* ★**kind**
unknown *adj.* hidden, mysterious, undiscovered, dark ★**familiar**
unless *conj.* if not, except when
unlike *adj.* unrelated, dissimilar, distinct, ▷*different* ★**similar**
unlikely *adj.* rare, improbable, doubtful, incredible, unheard of, ▷*dubious* ★**likely**
unlucky *adj.* unfortunate, luckless, ill-fated, unhappy ★**lucky**

Uniform

It was a very grand affair with the footmen in full livery.

unnatural [1] *adj.* artificial, stilted, strained [2] inhuman, cruel, ▷*heartless* ★**natural**
unnecessary *adj.* nonessential, excess, superfluous, ▷*needless* ★**necessary**
unoccupied [1] *adj.* uninhabited, empty, deserted, ▷*vacant* [2] idle, spare, ▷*unemployed* ★**occupied**
unpleasant *adj.* disagreeable, displeasing, objectionable, ▷*offensive* ★**pleasant**
unpopular *adj.* obnoxious *I was glad to leave the party, for I had been forced to talk to some obnoxious people,* detested, shunned, rejected, ▷*disliked* ★**popular**
unqualified [1] *adj.* unable, incompetent, inadequate, ▷*unfit* [2] complete, thorough, absolute
unreal *adj.* imaginary, fictional, artificial, false, fanciful ★**real** UNREEL
unreasonable [1] *adj.* extravagant, excessive, extreme ★**moderate** [2] far-fetched, absurd, foolish ★**rational**
unreliable *adj.* untrustworthy, undependable, irresponsible, ▷*fickle* ★**reliable**
unrest [1] *n.* defiance, disquiet, protest, rebellion [2] anxiety, distress, worry ★**calm**
unrestricted *adj.* unrestrained, unlimited, open, free, unhindered ★**limited**
unripe *adj.* green, immature, callow *I was but a callow youth in those days, but I hope I have learned since then!,* unseasoned, unready ★**ripe**
unrivaled *adj.* inimitable, unequaled, matchless, peerless ★**inferior**
unruly *adj.* disorderly, troublesome, restive, ▷*rowdy* ★**orderly**
unseemly *adj.* incorrect, indecent, improper, unbecoming, shocking ★**seemly**
unselfish *adj.* generous, liberal, charitable, hospitable, ▷*kind* ★**selfish**
unstable *adj.* unsteady, shaky, inconstant, fickle, volatile ★**stable**
unsuitable *adj.* improper, unacceptable, unfitting, inconsistent ★**suitable**
untidy *adj.* bedraggled, disorderly, muddled, messy, ▷*slovenly* ★**tidy**
untie *v.* unfasten, unravel, free, release, ▷*undo* ★**tie**
until *prep.* till, as far as, up to
untimely *adj.* inopportune, ill-timed, premature ★**opportune**
unusual *adj.* strange, queer, exceptional, quaint, curious, ▷*odd* ★**normal**
unwilling *adj.* averse, disinclined, grudging, opposed, ▷*reluctant* ★**willing**
upheaval *n.* disturbance, disruption, overthrow, ▷**turmoil**
uphold *v.* sustain, keep up, endorse, ▷*support*
upkeep *n.* maintenance, care, conservation, support, expenses ★**neglect**
upper *adj.* higher, superior, elevated, uppermost ★**lower**
upright [1] *adj.* sheer, steep, perpendicular ★**horizontal** [2] honorable *Sister Mary Josephine was one of the most honorable people I ever met,* ethical, virtuous ★**dishonest**
uproar *n.* hubbub, noise, disorder, tumult, turmoil, ▷*clamor*
upset [1] *v.* bother, perturb, unsettle, annoy [2] overthrow, overturn, topple [3] *adj.* disturbed, confused, worried
upside down [1] *adj.* overturned, upturned [2] chaotic, muddled, jumbled
urge [1] *v.* goad, plead, spur, beseech ★**deter** [2] *n.* encouragement, compulsion, ▷*impulse*
urgent *adj.* important, earnest, intense, vital ★**trivial**
use [1] *v.* employ, practice, apply [2] consume, exhaust, deplete, expend [3] *n.* usage, wear
useful *adj.* valuable, favorable, practical, beneficial ★**useless**
useless *adj.* trashy, paltry, futile *Trying to train a cat to fetch is a futile activity,* inefficient, ▷*worthless* ★**useful**
usual *adj.* common, general, habitual, familiar, ▷*normal* ★**exceptional**
utensil *n.* tool, implement, instrument, apparatus, device
utilize *v.* employ, apply, exploit, ▷*use*
utmost *adj.* extreme, supreme, greatest, ultimate, last, distant
utter [1] *adj.* thorough, absolute, complete [2] *v.* declare, pronounce, speak, ▷*say*
utterly *adv.* extremely, completely, entirely, fully, wholly

V v

vacant [1] *adj.* empty, unoccupied, exhausted ★**occupied** [2] stupid, blank, expressionless, mindless
vacation *n.* holiday, rest, recess
vagabond *n.* vagrant, tramp, loafer, beggar, rover, bum, hobo
vague *adj.* indefinite, imprecise, inexact, uncertain, ▷*obscure* ★**certain**
vain [1] *adj.* conceited, arrogant, ▷*proud* ★**modest** [2] fruitless, useless, worthless, ▷*futile* VANE VEIN
valiant *adj.* stout, valorous, worthy, gallant, ▷*brave* ★**cowardly**
valid *adj.* genuine, authentic, official *No one is allowed into the meeting without an official pass*, proper
valley *n.* gorge, dale, dell, glen, vale
valor *n.* courage, fortitude, heroism, gallantry, ▷*bravery* ★**cowardice**
valuable [1] *adj.* costly, precious, priceless, expensive ★**worthless** [2] meritorious *She was awarded the medal for meritorious service during the war*, righteous, worthy
value [1] *n.* worth, benefit, merit, price [2] *v.* appreciate, esteem, prize, treasure [3] appraise, assess, rate, estimate
van *n.* truck, vehicle, wagon, cart
vandalize *v.* damage, sabotage, harm, ruin
vanish [1] *v.* disappear, fade, dissolve [2] exit, depart, go ★**appear**
vanity *n.* pride, conceit, pretension ★**modesty**
vanquish *v.* conquer, defeat, overpower, subdue, ▷*beat*
vapor *n.* steam, fog, mist, moisture, smoke
variable *adj.* changeable, fickle, unsteady, fitful, wavering ★**invariable**
varied *adj.* various, diverse *She was a woman of diverse interests*, miscellaneous, mixed, assorted ★**uniform**
variety [1] *n.* assortment, array, mixture, medley *The singers entertained us with a medley of popular songs* [2] sort, type, kind, class

Vehicles

Ambulance	Motorcycle	Trap
Automobile	Rickshaw	Trishaw
Bicycle	Roller skates	Trolley
Bulldozer	Saloon	Truck
Bus	Scooter	Skateboard
Cab	Sedan	Streetcar
Car	Stagecoach	Van
Cart	Surrey	Wagon
Charabanc	Tank	Wheelchair
Chariot	Taxi	
Fire engine	Tractor	
Go-cart	Tram	
Hearse		
Jeep		
Limousine		

various *adj.* mixed, different, many, ▷*varied*
vary *v.* differ, alter, change, diversify, diverge
vase *n.* jug, jar, beaker, ▷*pitcher*
vast *adj.* great, enormous, extensive, huge, wide, ▷*immense* ★**narrow**
vault [1] *n.* grave, mausoleum, cellar, crypt, dungeon [2] *v.* jump, clear, bound, leap, hurdle
veer *v.* swerve, skid, turn, tack, deviate, change
vehement *adj.* impassioned, fiery, passionate, ardent, eager, zealous, ▷*strong* ★**indifferent**
vehicle [1] *n.* automobile, car, conveyance, carriage, cart [2] agency, means, expedient
veil [1] *n.* cloak, cover, wimple, curtain [2] *v.* hide, conceal, shade, screen ★**expose** VALE
vein [1] *n.* seam, strain, streak, stripe, thread, course [2] disposition, mood, style, phrasing VAIN VEIN

velocity *n.* rate, pace, tempo, rapidity, impetus *After I won the school prize, I had greater impetus to follow my studies,* ▷*speed*
venerable *adj.* respectable, revered, august, dignified, honored, ▷*sage*
vengeance *n.* reprisal, retaliation, ▷*revenge* ★**pardon**
venomous [1] *adj.* poisonous, toxic, vitriolic [2] spiteful, malicious, hostile, ▷*vindictive*
vent [1] *v.* discharge, emit, express, let fly, release [2] *n.* aperture, duct, opening, outlet
ventilate [1] *v.* aerate, cool, fan, blow [2] express, debate, discuss, examine
venture [1] *n.* enterprise, undertaking, endeavor [2] *v.* risk, bet, hazard, ▷*chance*
verbal *adj.* stated, said, expressed, spoken, unwritten ★**written**
verdict *n.* decision, judgment, finding, conclusion, opinion
verge [1] *n.* border, brink, edge, boundary [2] *v.* incline, tend, border, come close to
verify *v.* confirm, declare, authenticate, corroborate *The witness corroborated the story told by the defendant* ★**discredit**
versatile *adj.* adaptable, variable, adjustable, handy ★**inflexible**
verse *n.* poem, rhyme, stave, canto, jingle, doggerel *Call this stuff poetry? It's just doggerel!*
version *n.* account, form, interpretation, adaptation, type
vertical *adj.* upright, erect, sheer, perpendicular, steep ★**horizontal**
very [1] *adv.* extremely, exceedingly, greatly, intensely, absolutely [2] *adj.* exact, real, true, actual, genuine
vessel [1] *n.* bowl, pot, canister, container, basin, jar [2] craft, ship, boat
vestige *n.* remains, remnant, hint, glimmer, residue, trace
veteran [1] *n.* old timer, master, old hand, expert ★**novice** [2] *adj.* experienced, practiced, adept ★**inexperienced**
veto [1] *v.* ban, reject, prohibit, stop, forbid ★**approve** [2] *n.* embargo *The United Nations placed an embargo on the selling of arms to the two countries*, prohibition, disapproval ★**assent**
vex *v.* annoy, provoke, trouble, irritate, harass, ▷*displease* ★**soothe**
vibrate *v.* shake, quiver, oscillate, fluctuate, ▷*tremble*
vice *n.* evil, failing, fault, ▷*sin* ★**virtue**
vicinity *n.* area, environs, neighborhood, ▷*surroundings*
vicious *adj.* evil, sinful, malignant, immoral, vile, ▷*wicked* ★**virtuous**
victim *n.* sufferer, scapegoat, martyr, prey, pawn, dupe
victor *n.* winner, conqueror, champion, prize-winner ★**loser**
victory *n.* success, triumph, achievement, ▷*conquest* ★**defeat**
view [1] *n.* landscape, sight, panorama, spectacle [2] estimation, belief, theory, opinion [3] *v.* watch, see, behold, witness
vigilant *adj.* attentive, wary, alert, guarded, ▷*watchful* ★**lax**
vigor *n.* energy, vim, stamina, might, power, ▷*strength* ★**weakness**
vigorous *adj.* forceful, energetic, powerful, dynamic, ▷*active* ★**weak**
vile *adj.* low, wretched, contemptible, miserable, nasty, evil, ▷*despicable* ★**noble**
villain *n.* blackguard, knave *You are but a knave who is out to steal my money!*, sinner, rascal, ▷*rogue* ★**hero**
vim *n.* stamina, zip, strength, ▷*vigor*
vindicate *v.* warrant, sustain, support, defend, establish, ▷*justify* ★**accuse**
vindictive *adj.* vengeful, unforgiving, grudging, spiteful, ▷*malicious* ★**merciful**
violate [1] *v.* disobey, oppose, defy, resist, infringe ★**obey** [2] abuse, defile, outrage, desecrate
violent *adj.* furious, rabid, rampant, forcible, tempestuous ★**calm**
virile *adj.* manly, masculine, vigorous, vibrant, ▷*strong* ★**weak**
virtually *adv.* almost, nearly, practically, substantially
virtue *n.* goodness, honesty, chastity, purity, ▷*quality* ★**vice**
virtuous *adj.* chaste, innocent, honorable, moral, ▷*righteous* ★**wicked**

visible *adj.* perceptible, discernible, apparent, exposed, obvious ★**invisible**
vision [1] *n.* apparition, specter, ghost, mirage [2] concept, revelation, foresight
visit [1] *n.* call, sojourn, stay, excursion [2] *v.* call on, drop in, tarry, stay
visitor *n.* guest, company, tourist, caller
visual *adj.* seeable, observable, visible
vital [1] *adj.* essential, indispensible, ▷*necessary* [2] alive, vibrant, virile, dynamic *Our team won a number of games after we had been trained by the new dynamic coach*
vitality *n.* stamina, virility, vigor, ▷*strength*
vivacious *adj.* lively, spirited, vital, animated, merry, ▷*sprightly* ★**languid**
vivid [1] *adj.* clear, bright, ▷*brilliant* [2] vigorous, strong, lucid ★**dull**
vocal *adj.* articulate, eloquent, spoken, strident, vociferous ★**quiet**
vocation *n.* occupation, calling, job, mission, career, pursuit
vogue *n.* style, fashion, mode, popularity
voice [1] *n.* speech, articulation, utterance [2] choice, preference, opinion [3] *v.* utter, express, proclaim, pronounce
void [1] *adj.* bare, barren, empty [2] invalid, canceled, useless [3] *n.* cavity, chasm, space, opening, nothingness
volatile [1] *adj.* lively, changeable, fickle, giddy [2] elusive, fleeting, evaporable
volley *n.* discharge, fusillade, barrage, shower
volume [1] *n.* bulk, capacity, mass, quantity, ▷*amount* [2] loudness, amplitude [3] book, edition, tome
voluntary *adj.* free-willed, optional, intended, gratuitous ★**compulsory**
vomit *v.* spew, disgorge, puke, throw up
vote [1] *n.* ballot, election, poll, referendum [2] *v.* ballot, poll, choose, elect
vow [1] *v.* promise, swear, assure, vouch, testify [2] *n.* oath, pledge, promise
voyage *n.* journey, cruise, passage, trip
vulgar [1] *adj.* common, coarse, crude, indelicate, rude ★**elegant** [2] native, ordinary, common
vulnerable *adj.* unprotected, unguarded, exposed, defenseless, tender ★**strong**

wad *n.* bundle, chunk, block, plug
waddle *v.* wobble, totter, shuffle, toddle
wag [1] *v.* waggle, shake, ▷*vibrate* [2] *n.* wit, humorist, joker
wage [1] *n.* fee, pay, salary, remuneration [2] *v.* carry out, fulfill, undertake
wager [1] *v.* gamble, bet, speculate, chance, hazard [2] *n.* pledge, stake, bet
wagon *n.* cart, truck, van, ▷*vehicle*
waif *n.* orphan, stray, foundling *In the old days, children were abandoned in the streets, but some people set up homes for such foundlings*
wail [1] *v.* deplore, weep, grieve, lament, ▷*cry* ★**rejoice** [2] *n.* lamentation, weeping, grief
wait [1] *v.* expect, await, bide, stay, stop, ▷*linger* [2] attend, serve WEIGHT
waive *v.* relinquish, disclaim, disown, forego, defer, ▷*renounce* WAVE
wake *v.* awaken, stimulate, excite, ▷*arouse*
wakeful [1] *adj.* restless, awake [2] alert, wary, watchful
walk [1] *v.* advance, march, step, progress, move [2] *n.* stroll, hike, ▷*ramble* ★**run** [3] lane, alley, way [4] sphere, field *I started my career in the field of journalism, but I later went into politics*, career, interest
wallow [1] *v.* flounder, stagger, tumble [2] delight, enjoy, revel
wan *adj.* pale, ashen, feeble, sickly, pallid, ▷*weak* ★**robust**
wand *n.* mace, baton, stick, scepter, rod
wander *v.* stray, meander, roam, stroll, deviate
wane *v.* droop, decline, decrease, lessen, ebb *As the little boat neared the rocks, Fred's courage ebbed away*, sink ★**wax** WAIN
wangle *v.* fiddle, contrive, fix, arrange
want [1] *v.* desire, covet, crave, need, require [2] *n.* need, necessity, demand [3] dearth, deficiency, ▷*scarcity* ★**plenty**
wanton [1] *adj.* unscrupulous, irresponsible [2] playful, frolicsome, wild [3] dissolute, immoral

war *n.* hostilities, fighting, bloodshed, enmity, strife ★**peace** WORE

ward [1] *n.* pupil, minor, charge [2] district, quarter WARRED

ward off *v.* prevent, forestall, avoid, stop, ▷*avert*

wardrobe [1] *n.* locker, cupboard, closet [2] outfit, clothes, apparel

warm [1] *adj.* tepid, hot, lukewarm [2] sympathetic, ▷*warmhearted* [3] eager, hot, zealous [4] *v.* heat, bake, cook, prepare

warn *v.* caution, admonish, advise, alert, apprise WORN

warning *n.* caution, admonition, forewarning, alarm, tip

warp *v.* contort, bend, twist, kink, deform ★**straighten**

warrant [1] *v.* guarantee, certify, justify, permit, allow [2] *n.* assurance, permit, license, authority *She produced documents which showed her authority on the board of directors*

wary *adj.* cautious, alert, careful, heedful, ▷*prudent* ★**rash**

wash [1] *v.* bathe, scrub, rinse, cleanse, wet [2] *n.* washing, cleaning

waste [1] *n.* garbage, debris, trash, rubbish [2] *v.* squander, spend, lavish, fritter [3] wither, decay, shrivel, perish WAIST

wasteful *adj.* lavish, prodigal, spendthrift, ▷*extravagant* ★**economical**

watch [1] *v.* note, observe, guard ★**ignore** [2] inspect, look at, oversee [3] *n.* timepiece [4] guard, sentry, watchman

watchful *adj.* attentive, observant, vigilant, ▷*wary* ★**inattentive**

water *v.* wet, bathe, wash, douse, drench, sprinkle, spray

wave [1] *v.* brandish, flourish, waft, swing [2] *n.* breaker, billow, undulation WAIVE

waver *v.* falter, hesitate, vacillate *There's no time to vacillate; make up your mind!* ★**decide**

wax *v.* increase, rise, grow, expand, enlarge ★**wane**

way [1] *n.* route, road, path, passage, track [2] technique *The company introduced a new technique for making glass*, procedure, method, style WEIGH

wayward *adj.* contrary, perverse, obstinate, ▷*stubborn* ★**docile**

weak [1] *adj.* feeble, frail, puny, helpless, delicate [2] foolish, soft, senseless, stupid [3] thin, watery, insipid [4] fragile, flimsy, tumbledown ★**strong** WEEK

weaken *v.* enfeeble, relax, sag, flag, ▷*languish* ★**strengthen**

weakness *n.* defect, fault, frailty, flaw ★**strength**

wealth *n.* riches, luxury, prosperity, money, opulence ★**poverty**

wealthy *adj.* rich, affluent, prosperous, opulent ★**poor**

wear [1] *v.* dress in, don [2] rub, scrape, waste, consume [3] last, endure, remain WARE

weary [1] *adj.* exhausted, tired, fatigued ★**fresh** [2] *v.* exhaust, tire, bore ★**refresh**

weather *n.* climate, clime, conditions

weave *v.* braid, plait, unite, blend

web *n.* net, tissue, webbing, textile, netting

wed *v.* marry, join, link, splice, tie the knot

wedge [1] *n.* block, chock, lump, chunk [2] *v.* crowd, force, jam, push, thrust, squeeze

wee *adj.* little, small, minute, ▷*tiny* ★**large**

weep *v.* blubber, snivel, sob, whimper *The lost puppy was found at last, whimpering in a corner,* ▷*cry* ★**rejoice**

weigh *v.* balance, estimate, ponder, examine, consider WAY

weight [1] *n.* load, pressure, burden, heaviness [2] importance, onus, significance, gravity WAIT

weighty *adj.* heavy, hefty, ponderous, onerous ★**trivial**

weird *adj.* eerie, supernatural, unearthly, mysterious, ▷*uncanny*

welcome [1] *adj.* pleasing, desirable, ▷*agreeable* [2] *v.* greet, accost, hail, salute [3] *n.* greeting, salutation, acceptance

welfare *n.* well-being, comfort, happiness, benefit, advantage ★**harm**

well [1] *adj.* robust, healthy, hearty, sound ★**ill** [2] *adv.* properly, suitable, adequately, accurately ★**badly** [3] *n.* fountain, spring

well-off *adj.* comfortable, prosperous, ▷*wealthy* ★**poor**

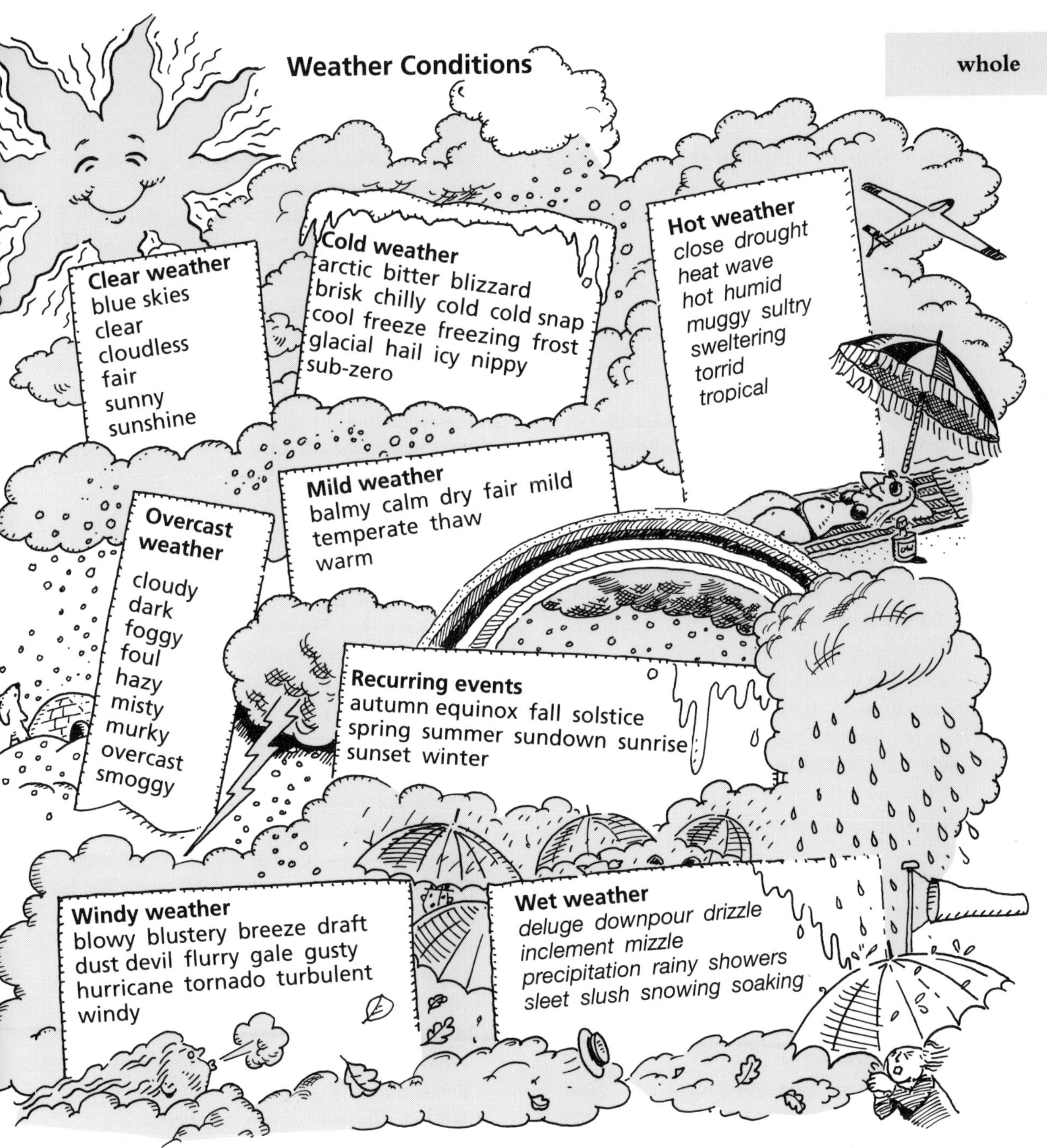

wet [1] *adj.* moist, damp, watery, drenched [2] drizzling, showery, raining [3] *v.* soak, moisten, dampen

wheedle *v.* coax, cajole, inveigle *We were inveigled into buying some of the local lace.* persuade ★**coerce**

whet [1] *v.* sharpen, hone, strop ★**blunt** [2] excite, stimulate, rouse ★**dampen**

whim *n.* fancy, humor, desire, urge, notion, impulse

whine [1] *v.* howl, wail, whimper, moan [2] complain, grouse, grumble

whip [1] *v.* flog, lash, thrash, chastise, spank [2] whisk, mix, blend

whirl *v.* twirl, spin, rotate, revolve, whir, ▷*twist*

whisk *v.* beat, brush, hasten, hurry, sweep, ▷*whip*

whisper [1] *n.* murmur, hint, suggestion, breath [2] *v.* breathe, murmur, divulge, buzz, intimate ★**shout**

whistle *n.* & *v.* cheep, chirp, warble, call

whole [1] *adj.* all, entire, total, intact [2] sound, complete, unbroken ★**part** HOLE

wholesome *adj.* healthful, nutritious, beneficial, sound, good ★**noxious**
wicked *adj.* infamous, corrupt, depraved, unrighteous, sinister, sinful, ▷*evil* ★**virtuous**
wickedness *n.* corruption, depravity, iniquity, sinfulness, villainy, ▷*evil*
wide *adj.* broad, ample, extended, spacious, roomy, extensive, vast ★**narrow**
widespread *adj.* prevalent, far-flung, extensive, sweeping, universal *The use of a universal language would be of great help in the United Nations* ★**limited**
wield [1] *v.* brandish, flourish, manipulate [2] control, command, exert, maintain
wild [1] *adj.* savage, ferocious, fierce, untamed ★**tame** [2] violent, unrestrained, boisterous ★**civilized** [3] careless, insane, reckless ★**sane**
wilderness *n.* desert, jungle, wasteland, wilds, outback
will [1] *n.* resolution, decision, zeal, accord [2] order, wish, command, request, demand [3] legacy, testament [4] *v.* choose, desire, elect
willful *adj.* temperamental, headstrong, deliberate, ▷*obstinate* ★**docile**
willing *adj.* disposed, zealous, ready, earnest, ▷*agreeable* ★**unwilling**
wilt *v.* wither, waste, sag, dwindle, ▷*ebb*
wily *adj.* cunning, sly, tricky, deceitful, ▷*crafty* ★**sincere**
win *v.* succeed, gain, get, acquire, procure, ▷*triumph* ★**lose**
wince *v.* shrink, quail, flinch *My little sister didn't flinch once when she had her vaccination*, start, ▷*cringe*
wind (as in *pinned*) *n.* breeze, blast, gust, gale
wind (as in *mind*) *v.* coil, turn, twist, bend WINED
wink *n.* & *v.* blink, flutter, flicker, glint
winner *n.* champion, master, ▷*victor*
wipe *v.* clean, brush, mop, remove, swab
wire [1] *n.* cable, telegraph, telegram [2] cable, cord
wisdom *n.* judgment, discretion, tact, thought, reason ★**folly**
wise *adj.* sensible, profound, astute, subtle, discreet, ▷*sage* ★**foolish**
wish [1] *v.* desire, crave, want, hanker for, long for [2] *n.* command, will, desire, liking
wistful [1] *adj.* pensive, musing, wishful [2] forlorn, melancholy, soulful
wit [1] *n.* fun, humor, levity, pleasantry [2] brains, sense, judgment, intelligence ★**stupidity**
witch *n.* enchantress, sorceress, crone, hag
withdraw [1] *v.* retire, retreat, depart, leave, ▷*flee* [2] extract, take out
withdrawn *adj.* unsociable, retiring, reclusive, aloof, solitary ★**sociable**
wither *v.* waste, fade, pine, languish, ▷*shrivel*
withhold *v.* retain, reserve, restrain, hold back, ▷*keep* ★**grant**
within *adj.* inside, interior, inner
withstand *v.* resist, oppose, confront, ▷*defy* ★**support**
witness [1] *n.* spectator, onlooker, bystander *One of the bystanders at the accident came forward to give evidence*, signatory [2] *v.* behold, observe, see, attest
witty *adj.* funny, jocular, waggish, amusing, ▷*comical* ★**dull**
wizard *n.* sorcerer, magician, conjurer
woe *n.* sorrow, sadness, grief, misery, trouble ★**joy**
woman *n.* lady, girl, female, wife
wonder [1] *n.* marvel, miracle, rarity, curiosity [2] bewilderment, surprise, amazement, ▷*awe* [3] *v.* speculate, question, marvel, muse
wonderful *adj.* marvelous, fabulous, spectacular, superb, ▷*splendid* ★ **commonplace**
woo *v.* make love, court, pursue
wood [1] *n.* lumber, timber, planks [2] forest, woods, copse, woodland, grove, thicket WOULD
word [1] *n.* expression, term, utterance [2] pledge, promise [3] tidings, news, information
work [1] *n.* toil, drudgery, labor, grind [2] task, job, stint, chore [3] *v.* operate, function, manipulate, run, drive
world *n.* globe, earth, sphere, planet

Borrowed Words

Modern French
police
rendezvous
liaison
menu

Dutch
boss
brandy
decoy
landscape

Scandinavia
fjord
geyser
lemming
ombudsman
ski

Italian
balcony
cameo
fiasco
influenza

German
blitz
delicatessen
dollar
kindergarten

Chinese
kowtow
sampan
typhoon
wok

Japanese
bonsai
futon
judo
karate
origami

Turkish
coffee
kiosk

Spanish
armada
fiesta
macho
patio
siesta
sombrero

Afrikaans
aardvark
apartheid
boer
trek
veldt

Inuit
anorak
igloo
kayak
parka

Gaelic
blarney
bog
brat
brogue
smithereens

Aztec
avocado
cocoa
tomato

Arabic
admiral
alcohol
algebra
alkali
sherbet
sofa
zero

Aboriginal languages
boomerang
dingo
budgerigar
kangaroo

Persian
bazaar
caravan
divan
paradise
tulip
turban

Hindi
bungalow
chintz
cot
pajamas
thug
veranda

Native American
chipmunk
moccasin
moose
papoose
wigwam

worry [1] *v.* bother, annoy, disturb, ▷*trouble* ★**soothe** [2] *n.* vexation, anxiety, concern, fear ★**delight**

worsen *v.* aggravate, decline, deteriorate, degenerate ★**improve**

worship [1] *v.* revere, adore, esteem, honor, praise ★**despise** [2] *n.* adoration, devotion, reverence

worth *n.* value, benefit, merit, caliber *This year's students were of a high caliber* dignity

worthless *adj.* valueless, paltry, trifling, useless, ▷*cheap* ★**valuable**

worthwhile *adj.* valuable, helpful, useful, beneficial ★**useless**

worthy *adj.* upright, admirable, excellent, honest, fine ★**vile**

wound [1] *v.* hurt, injure, gash, pain, distress, ▷*harm* ★**heal** [2] *n.* injury, bruise, harm

wrangle *v.* & *n.* squabble, fight, row, scrap, ▷*quarrel* ★**accord**

wrap *v.* fold, envelop, enclose, cover, clothe, conceal ★**unfold** RAP

wrath *n.* fury, ire, rage, passion, ▷*anger* ★**pleasure**

wreck [1] *v.* demolish, smash, ruin, destroy, spoil, ravage ★**repair** [2] *n.* derelict, hulk, shipwreck, ruin

wrench *v.* twist, wring, strain, sprain, pull

wrestle *v.* struggle, battle, combat, grapple, tussle, ▷*fight*

wretch *n.* vagabond, blackguard, villain, rogue, ▷*scoundrel*

wretched [1] *adj.* dejected, abject, miserable, ▷*despicable* [2] saddening, pathetic, ▷*pitiful* ★**joyful**

wriggle *v.* twist, writhe, squirm, worm, dodge

wring *v.* choke, squeeze, throttle, strangle, twist RING

wrinkle *n.* & *v.* crease, pucker, ruffle, rumple, crinkle, furrow

write *v.* inscribe, pen, sign, scrawl, scribble RIGHT RITE WRIGHT

writer [1] *n.* scribe, penman, clerk [2] author, essayist, narrator, playwright, poet, dramatist

writhe *v.* wind, twine, weave, twist, ▷*wriggle*

written *adj.* recorded, set down, documentary, transcribed

wrong [1] *adj.* unjust, unfair, immoral, wicked [2] false, mistaken, erroneous [3] *v.* injure, hurt, abuse [4] *n.* offense, atrocity, iniquity, sin, injustice ★**right**

wry *adj.* crooked, askew, awry, aslant, twisted, distorted ★**straight** RYE

Y y

yank *v.* draw, pull, snatch, ▷*jerk*

yap 1 *v.* bark, yelp 2 prattle, blather, gossip, jaw

yard 1 *n.* lawn, garden, courtyard, court, quadrangle 2 three feet

yarn 1 *n.* story, account, tale, narrative 2 thread, wool, linen, twist

yawn *v.* gape, open

yearly 1 *adj.* annual, perennial, per annum *We shall pay a salary of $50,000 per year* 2 *adv.* every year, annually

yearn *v.* ache, crave, desire, pine, hunger for ★**dislike**

yell *v.* shriek, squawk, whoop, screech, shout, ▷*bellow* ★**whisper**

yield 1 *v.* produce, provide, furnish, supply 2 surrender, give in, submit ★**withstand** 3 abdicate, resign, renounce 4 *n.* crop, harvest, product, output

yielding 1 *adj.* obedient, submissive, unresisting ★**stubborn** 2 plastic, malleable, flexible ★**solid**

yoke 1 *v.* join, couple, link, harness 2 *n.*chain, bondage *The children of Israel moved out of bondage in the land of Egypt*, enslavement YOLK

yokel *n.* bumpkin, rustic, boor, peasant

young *adj.* youthful, tender, juvenile, junior, little ★**old**

youngster *n.* child, youth, boy, girl, kid, lad, adolescent

youth 1 *n.* adolescence, prime, salad days ★**age** 2 lad, boy, ▷*youngster*

youthful *adj.* boyish, girlish, young, spry, juvenile, lively ★**aged**

Yule *n.* Christmas

Z z

zany *adj.* crazy, daft, droll, goofy, eccentric, ▷*funny* ★**serious**

zeal *n.* devotion, eagerness, enthusiasm, keenness, ardor ★**apathy**

zealous *adj.* devoted, fervent *Dave was a fervent supporter of the school's football team*, fanatical, earnest, ▷*eager* ★**apathetic**

zenith *n.* climax, height, apex, peak

zero *n.* nothing, nought, nil, nullity, zip, aught

zest 1 *n.* relish, gusto, appetite, keenness 2 flavor, piquancy, taste 3 rind, peel

zone *n.* area, district, region, tract, sector

zoom *v.* flash, fly, shoot, streak, hurtle, whizz